David
Jefferies

David
Jefferies

THE OFFICIAL BIOGRAPHY

Stuart
Barker

Haynes Publishing

Dedication: For Pauline

First published in April 2009

A catalogue record for this book is available from the British Library

ISBN 978 1 84425 663 1

Library of Congress catalog card no 2008943624

Published by Haynes Publishing,
Sparkford, Yeovil, Somerset BA22 7JJ, UK
Tel: 01963 442030 Fax: 01963 440001
Int. tel: +44 1963 442030 Int. fax: +44 1963 440001
E-mail: sales@haynes.co.uk
Website: www.haynes.co.uk

Haynes North America Inc.,
861 Lawrence Drive, Newbury Park, California 91320, USA

Designed and page built by Dominic Stickland
Printed and bound in the UK

CONTENTS

ACKNOWLEDGEMENTS

Thanks to the following (in alphabetical order) for agreeing to be interviewed for this book: Adrian Archibald, Geoff Duke OBE, Mark Forsyth, Dave Greenham, Stuart Hicken, Ian Hutchinson, Louise Jefferies, Nick Jefferies, Tony Jefferies, Ian Lougher, Niall Mackenzie, John McGuinness, Hector Neill, John Reynolds and Jack Valentine.

Thanks also to David's friends, Karl 'Carlos' Smith, Adam Evans, Martin 'Fergie' Ferguson and Alistair Smith for spilling the beans on their old mate. Also to David's sister, Louise, for guiding me through the family photo albums.

A mention must also go to all the staff at The Old White Lion in Haworth for making my research trips to Yorkshire so memorable.

A big debt of gratitude is owed to Chris 'Mossy' Moss for giving me permission to publish a lengthy interview he conducted with David Jefferies at Rockingham in 2002. It has never been published in any form before. A similar debt of gratitude is owed to film-maker David Wood for providing over two hours of never-before-seen interview footage of David Jefferies.

A huge thanks to my girlfriend, Ally Cubbon, for her work in transcribing interviews, compiling the results section, and patiently proof-reading the book. And to my parents, Jim and Josie Barker, for getting me hooked on bike racing in the first place. Thanks folks.

Finally, I must thank Tony Jefferies for trusting me with his private collection of newspaper cuttings, photos and results sheets without which this book would not have been possible. His courage, in the face of overwhelming adversity, is an inspiration.

FOREWORD

*by Tony Jefferies, three-times Isle of Man TT winner
and father of David Jefferies*

I was recently asked by someone who does not avidly follow motorcycle racing how I could justify following a sport which they perceived as being so full of tragedy. I thought for a moment before answering because it is so easy to say "Do you realise how many people are killed each year rock climbing? Hundreds. How many are seriously injured each year through horse riding accidents? Hundreds." When I was in hospital with a broken back, the single most common cause of paraplegia and quadriplegia was through diving accidents in shallow water. I did not mention any of those facts. I simply said "You have to have a passion for it. Without the passion you will never understand."

David had that passion for motorcycle racing. He had a passion for just about anything to do with wheels. At school he was outstanding on a bicycle. Riding sitting on the handlebars facing backwards was a standard mode of transport for DJ, and riding out of school down the steps on the back wheel was forever getting him into trouble. As he was surrounded by motorcycles through his family and friends, a career in motorcycle sport was on the cards. I knew he had a natural ability on two wheels but little did I know that from a family of sporting motorcyclists he would achieve far more than any of us had done before him.

I was, and still am, proud of having been able to help David through his racing career. He always had the full support of his family, none more so than from his mother Pauline and his sister Louise. We were very close as a family and enjoyed life to the full with David throughout his racing career, which was so dramatically and tragically brought to a premature end.

I spent hours discussing his racing career with him and especially the TT. We talked long into the night about the lines he took, the bikes he rode, the bike set-up, the sponsorship, the expenses, how to handle interviews, even the nights out he had. I saw the transition from me advising him how to take certain corners from when he first raced at the TT, and giving him advice about gear ratios etc., to the complete reverse when latterly he told me how it was now being done. How he had worked out new and better lines, how he managed to change some of the established ways of tackling the TT circuit to cope with the new high speeds that were being achieved on the modern Superbike – changes which have now been adopted by other top riders today. He became an outstanding TT rider. That is without doubt. I am of the opinion that he was the best of his generation and the best of recent times. He was able to capture the hearts of thousands of TT spectators and enthusiasts with his own dramatic style of riding which either drew a cheer or sometimes a complete hush from the crowd, as though they were in awe of what they had just witnessed.

He has been awarded many accolades from different sources, including his inclusion in the top ten all-time TT greats by the Isle of Man authorities themselves. He undoubtedly paved the way for a whole new set of records being broken with an aggressive but controlled style which caused so many, like TT legend Geoff Duke, after watching him go down Bray Hill to comment "I have just had a sharp intake of breath". DJ was spectacular.

Is that my everlasting memory of David? Is that why his family and friends were so proud of him? Well yes, of course it is, but there is more than that. Throughout his career he always had time for others and conducted his time in motorcycle sport with both compassion and dignity. He fought remorselessly against the odds of his size and not always being on the most competitive machinery. He never gave up and continued to show a wicked sense of humour until his dying day.

The circumstances surrounding David's death are regrettably far from straightforward and the facts that third party involvement may well have contributed to the accident will always be unsatisfactory. But what we can say is that David Jefferies lived life to the full and achieved more in his 30 years than all but a few achieve in a lifetime.

I hope this book will give you an insight into his life and his character, and will show what a down to earth guy he was. I, my late wife Pauline, and his sister Louise, are immensely proud of what he achieved and his friends have, without exception, had their lives enriched for knowing him.

Baildon, West Yorkshire
Spring 2009

Chapter 1

IN THE BLOOD

"Jack, there's an elephant in that field. We're just outside Daventry and there's a bloody elephant in that field!"
Allan Jefferies

When Joseph Jefferies threw open the doors of his second-hand car trading business for the first time in 1907, the motor industry was still in its infancy. Born on 5 June 1874, Joseph – or Joe as he was known – was a picture-framer by trade but was quick to spot the potential of a horseless carriage. With one eye set firmly on the future, he threw in his lot with a few like-minded friends and opened the Ross Motor and Cycle Company on what was then Gordon Terrace near Shipley's old steam tram shed, just a few miles from the centre of Bradford.

"My grandpa Joe was a bit of a motor car pioneer and entrepreneur," says Tony Jefferies. "He and a couple of mates went to France and bought a de Dion-Bouton (a French car manufactured between 1883–1932) and he went on to operate the first taxi service in Bradford in 1908. Later, during the First World War he used to ferry the wounded from the train station to the hospital, which was next door to Joe's business. It meant he could get as much petrol as he wanted.

"Joe couldn't fight in the war because of his peg leg. He had injured his foot playing football in 1881 and, after infection set in, had to have it amputated. But he reckoned that by the end of the war he had covered thousands of miles between Shipley and Bradford. When you think of the state of the roads back then – many of the local streets were cobbled – and the fact that cars had solid tyres, it was some going."

Even with just one good leg, Joe's contribution to the war effort earned him a citation, a fact the Jefferies family is still proud of.

With the mass production of cars still several years away, it's somewhat surprising that there were enough second-hand models on the market during the early years of the 20th Century – mostly little more than converted horse carriages with primitive combustion engines fitted – to justify this fledgling business. But stock could not have been a major problem as Joe soon split with his business partners because they couldn't agree on which makes of car to sell.

Joseph had a reputation for not suffering fools gladly. Tony relates one particular incident that clearly conveys his grandfather's attitude. "One day a customer came in demanding some wheel spokes 'just like this one'. He handed Joe a crumpled spoke from a wheel that must have been in a crash, though the customer refused to admit it. So Joe disappeared into the workshop where they kept a rack full of spokes and wheel-building gear, and returned a few moments later. He handed over a brand new spoke, identical in every twist and bend to the one he'd been given and asked the customer how many he wanted."

It was this attitude that earned Jefferies the unofficial title of 'sales prevention officer' within the firm and no doubt influenced his decision to strike out on his own. So with some experience in this all-new industry under his belt, Joe started up his own business, again selling cars, motorcycles and bicycles. From 1917, his new premises were located in Saltaire Road in Shipley where they remained open for business for more than half a century. Joe died in 1961 aged 86, having retained an active interest in the motor business right to the end. He passed on a legacy that remains to this day.

While the Jefferies family can thus lay claim to a direct link back to the very dawn of the motor industry, the connection with motorcycles only truly started with Joe's son Allan – Tony's father – who was born on 30 July 1905.

"It was my dad who was the first motorcyclist in the family," Tony says. "He could have followed his father into the car world but because he used to spend a lot of time down at the Scott motorcycle factory, he was more interested in bikes. My dad spent a lot of time hanging about there, running errands as a kid, and got to know the test riders and staff. The Scott factory was in Saltaire, just down the road from Joe's shop, and so the people from the factory used to hang around Joe's garage too because it was a good place to get bits and pieces. It was a garage in the old sense of the word, in that people used to garage their cars there overnight and have their accumulators charged. I lived in that building until I was eight or nine years old."

Allan Jefferies was mechanically proficient from a very early age thanks to the many years he had spent learning the ropes in his father's garage. His competitive career on two wheels started in 1923 when, at 18 years old, he borrowed a friend's side-valve BSA and entered the famous Scott Trial, though he was hardly prepared for such an event. "He rode the Scott Trial with ordinary shoes – no grip on them," says Tony. "That was a big mistake as he found out afterwards. You really needed to have studded boots to ride in trials. He used to ride with a tie and waistcoat and jacket too – that was the normal gear back then."

By 1928, Allan was considered good enough to earn a factory ride with Scott in the ISDT (International Six Days Trial) that was being held in Harrogate that year. One of the world's most famous and oldest trials events, the ISDT was first held in 1913 and it's still a major event to this day, having been known as the International Six Days Enduro since 1981. Allan Jefferies won a gold medal in the 1928 ISDT and would go on to take another five in the ensuing years, making him one of the country's biggest trials stars prior to World War Two.

Like most competition riders of his era, Jefferies practised a variety of disciplines. Unlike today's specialist competitors who focus almost exclusively on road racing, trials or motocross, Jefferies excelled in most disciplines including trials, hill climbs, scrambles, sand racing and, eventually, road racing. If it had two wheels and a set of handlebars, Allan Jefferies could ride it – and ride it well, as Tony remembers. "My father's forte was definitely trials," he says. "In those days they used to change the tyres and ride in a scramble – or motocross as we know it – and then they would ride in sand races, hill climbs, all sorts of things, and use the same bike for everything. As things developed of course, they eventually had to have different bikes but that's how the early days started."

In 1932, Jefferies earned the distinction of being the last man to win the Scott Trial on a Scott motorcycle. Adding another string to his bow, he also won the Lancashire Grand National Scramble in

1933. But even more importantly that year, he visited the Olympia Motorcycle Show in London where he signed a deal to ride for the factory Triumph team, ostensibly in trials events but with an option to go road racing. The deal led to Jefferies taking on the agency for the Coventry firm's machines and so started a long and glorious association between Triumph and the Jefferies family.

The Great Depression of the 1930s struck particularly hard in the industrial north of England and while Allan Jefferies just managed to keep his head afloat and his business ticking over, he, like so many others, was forced to find new ways to make money. If that could in some way be combined with motorcycle sport, then so much the better. One venture involved teaming up with Speedway star Frank Varey as a rider/mechanic in the one branch of bike sport that still seemed to be thriving in spite of the financial turmoil of the time. But the depression had not affected every country and Jefferies and Varey hatched a plan to contest the far-flung Argentine Grand Prix as a means of making some money in a country that was still largely solvent. It may have sounded grand and it may have attracted thousands of spectators, but the Argentine GP was held on dusty, bumpy back roads and was more akin to a modern Enduro event than a MotoGP race. The complete lack of any safety facilities soon became all too apparent when Varey crashed into a horse and cart and fractured his skull. Jefferies soon happened upon the scene and improvised as best he could. In the absence of any form of antiseptic, Jefferies reportedly used bleach to disinfect the wound, then bandaged Varey's head as well as possible. Varey survived the trip but would forever have a shock of grey hair where his skull had been fractured.

Allan won the British Experts Trial in 1938 and the prestigious Scottish Six Days Trial in 1939 before being involved in an escapade that wouldn't look out of place in a Hollywood movie. It was late August 1939 – just days before World War Two broke out – and that year's ISDT was being held in Austria at just the same time as that country's most infamous son decided to annex the land of his birth before invading Poland. Hearing of Hitler's seemingly unstoppable advances, and the likelihood of an all-out war in the not-too-distant future, the British teams were ordered home four days into the six-day event. Jefferies and his colleagues began an all-out dash for freedom back to France and, ultimately, Blighty, tipping the fuel from any bikes they spotted en route into their own in order to have enough to make it back to Calais.

At the time of World War Two breaking out, Allan Jefferies was 34 and deemed too old for active service. "My dad tried to get into the army but was told he was too old so he became a Dad's Army-type in the Home Guard," Tony says. "But as the war went on they needed more men, so he managed to sign up alongside a man called Jack Williams who was an International Six Days rider of some repute before the war. They both managed to get into OCTU (Officer Cadet Training Unit) and then joined the army as officers to train despatch riders.

"Most despatch riders at the time couldn't ride for toffee and kept falling off, especially because most of the time they were riding off-road, through shit and dirt and all sorts. They needed to learn how to ride like trials riders and that's where my dad and Jack Williams came in."

Allan Jefferies's sense of humour was legendary and he wasn't going to let a world war put an end to his pranks. In fact, as he rose through the ranks, he found the army offered no end of tempting situations for pranksters, as Tony relates. "My dad was an absolute lunatic – a real larger than life character. Coming back from an exercise on one occasion, he saw lots of pigs in a field and thought if he could grab one the men could all have a nice hog roast when they got back to barracks. So they caught a pig and took it back with them but decided it would be a good idea to put it in the sergeant major's bed first. That got my dad on a charge when the sergeant major found it. He was pulled up and told that he'd upset the sergeant major and that the pig would have to go. My dad argued that a few of the men had become fond of the pig and wanted to keep it as a mascot. So instead of ending up on the barbecue, Matilda the pig became the company mascot.

"The only problem was that it kept escaping. On one occasion the entire company was taking part in a big inspection in front of a lieutenant general who, after completion of the inspection, said to the commanding officer, 'I must say I was very impressed that even during inspection you kept up the men's training.' He had apparently seen two men running across the skyline in the background and thought they were training, but it was actually my dad and a mate trying to catch Matilda after she'd escaped again!

"Eventually the pig had to go and was taken back to the farm. They gave the farmer a ten bob note and Matilda was given an honourable discharge. She'd done her bit for Blighty.

"Not long after that, the unit was returning from another exercise just outside Daventry and dad turned to Jack Williams and said, 'Jack, there's an elephant in that field. We're just outside Daventry and there's a bloody elephant in that field!' They went closer and found it was a travelling circus and the elephant had been put out to graze. It was only about a mile from the army camp so my dad went and spoke to the man looking after the elephant and asked if he ever took it out for walks. When the man said he did, dad gave him 2s 6d and told him to walk the elephant down to the barracks. He instructed the man that when he got there, there would be a guard with a gun at the barrier who would ask what he wanted. The elephant keeper was to say 'I've brought this for Captain Jefferies – it's the new mascot.'

"Next thing, Captain Jefferies was hauled up in front of the Company Commander who was having a bloody fit, ranting about elephants. My dad was always up to stuff like that."

Tony remembers another occasion when his father undermined his superiors, this time in Germany during the liberation of Europe. "He was following the front line and repairing tanks and guns in the Royal Electrical and Mechanical Engineers (REME). One day he was tasked to drive some of the high-ranking officers over the Rhine to see what was going on. The bridge was crowded with vehicles so he turned off the road and drove straight into the Rhine. All the officers panicked and started trying to bail out. Only my dad knew that the captured German Volkswagen Schwimmwagen he was driving was an amphibious vehicle! But he hadn't reckoned on how strong the current was and they were halfway down the Rhine before they got to the other side!"

The Schwimmwagen wasn't the only German vehicle that Allan came across. His unit later took charge of one of the main Mercedes factories and Jefferies spotted a chance to greatly improve the British motor industry, as Tony explains. "He arranged for a lot of the supercharged Mercedes cars and bikes to be sent back to the UK because he thought it would be good for the British car and bike industries to learn their engineering secrets. Even then those cars were capable of doing 200mph during record runs on the autobahns. He managed to get them transported all the way to the docks in France but sadly the cars and bikes got nicked from the dockside. Not one of them made it back to England. He was a bit sick about that."

And cars weren't the only things the entrepreneurial Jefferies 'liberated' from the Germans. He once raided a whole winery in Germany, filled nine ten-ton trucks with bottles of expensive wine, took them back to the main depot and distributed them to the troops.

Jefferies was even photographed driving around in Hermann Goering's captured vehicle in Hanover but the larks soon stopped as the front line approached the concentration camps. The horror of what Jefferies witnessed on these occasions stayed with him for the remainder of his life. His company was the first to enter Belsen concentration camp – one of the most severe of all the camps. "He would never talk about it," says Tony, "except to say that the smell of the place alone was enough to make you really ill. I could tell how much it affected him because he'd start trying to tell me a bit about it and would then just clam up. I think an experience like that genuinely does scar people for life and that's where my dad, quite understandably, got his hatred for the Nazis.

"When I took over his bike shop in 1971 the opportunity came along to sell BMWs. I thought it would help because of the demise of the British motorcycle industry, but my dad was very much against it. It was the same with Japanese bikes – at first he said it would be over his dead body, but eventually it happened. He was smart enough to see that was the way things were going but he still didn't like it. When I came home from work one day and said I'd agreed to become a BMW agency, he walked out of the kitchen and didn't speak to me for a week."

Tony's brother, Nick Jefferies, disputes this version of events. A famous racer and TT winner in his own right, Nick says, "Dad hated the Nazis but he never hated the Germans. He had met a lot of Germans he really liked while competing in trials. I think he was upset simply because the family business had been dealing in Triumphs since 1934 and now they were being swept aside."

Even though he had witnessed such horrors during the war, and contracted typhoid in Belsen, Allan Jefferies remained a joker – something that one of his rivals after the war, six times World Champion and TT winner Geoff Duke, recalls. "He was a great man with a fantastic sense of humour," Duke says. "That was something that seemed to creep into a lot of motorcycle sport in those days. Allan was an immense practical joker. I think it was at the Scottish Six Days trial one year where he was reputed to have dropped his motorcycle from the top floor of his hotel – that created quite a do! [He had, in fact, dropped a car wheel from the top floor that then smashed through the roof of a Masonic chapel.] That sort of thing used to happen a lot in those days. It wasn't particularly my cup of tea though – I perhaps took my riding a bit too seriously for that."

Allan Jefferies delivered the results, however, when it came to two-wheeled competition. In 1948 he became something of a national hero when he captained a five-man team in the ISDT. He not only won an individual gold medal but also the manufacturer's award for Triumph. It was this victory that led to Triumph naming its new-for-1949 bike the Triumph Trophy – a legendary motorcycle to this day. It was this bike that really established Triumph as a major player in the motorcycling world.

There would be further success for Jefferies and Triumph in 1949 when, to help celebrate the launch of the Triumph Thunderbird, he formed part of a team that set off to Montlhéry in France with three of the 650cc machines in an attempt to average 90mph for 500 miles. All three bikes made it and the Yorkshireman had added the art of endurance record-breaking to his long list of two-wheeled achievements that also, from time to time, included the discipline that would make his two sons and future grandson so famous – road racing. "Just before the Second World War, he had started to ride for Triumph," says Tony Jefferies, "and that's really where road racing came in, at a circuit near Bradford called Esholt Park where he used to ride and win. He also rode at Scarborough and places like that and was very successful, but of course he also rode in the Clubman's TT. He finished second on two occasions to a young upstart called Geoffrey Duke. It was a bit unfortunate he was there or we might have had TT winners from three generations – but Geoff spoiled that for us!"

The Clubman's TT was a stepping stone to the TT proper and was held during the same fortnight, unlike the Manx Grand Prix, another amateur event held on the same circuit in August/September. Jefferies had tried his hand at the Manx in 1933 but his Scott's experimental gearbox stuck in fourth gear and ended his race. The following year he went to the TT proper as Triumph's factory reserve rider but, since none of the team suffered any mishaps, he never got to race. He did, however, manage a few laps in practice and promptly crashed at the Gooseneck while trying to impress his Triumph boss who he knew was spectating there.

It was only in the Clubman's TT after World War Two that Allan Jefferies would have any sort of success on the famous mountain course. He competed in the event on three occasions, the first being in 1947 when he finished in second place on a Triumph Tiger 100, prepared in his Shipley workshop, at an average speed of 75.23mph. He retired from the race with a split petrol tank at Ballaugh Bridge the following year and showed some remarkable ingenuity in order to buy the spectators a beer. "A big radio star of the time was watching at Ballaugh," says Nick Jefferies. "My dad tried to get him to buy everyone a beer but he was too tight to put his hand in his pocket. My dad, having no money on him because he was racing, went into the pub and auctioned off his racing spark plugs – which were seen as really special at the time – and managed to raise enough money to buy everyone a beer."

By 1949, at the age of 44, Allan Jefferies was favourite to win the Clubman's race after posting the fastest time in practice. The up-and-coming young rider who was to spoil Jefferies's party was Geoff Duke, who still remembers Jefferies as a giant amongst men in the world of motorcycle sport in those immediate post-war years. "I was surprised to beat him really because Allan Jefferies was a fantastic all-rounder.

He did so well at trials and that sort of thing, apart from riding over here in the Clubman's TT. He was also riding a Triumph in the 1949 event and one particular advantage was that, being a twin cylinder machine, it was very easy to start. I remember being very worried because I only weighed about ten stone in those days and I was concerned I wouldn't get enough weight behind the kick-start to get my bike going and that Allan would disappear off into the distance. So I had a two-inch extension welded on to the kick start, which gave me a longer stroke. It didn't work the first time, but it did the second and I got away cleanly and managed to win the race. I was quite chuffed about that win because I had a great respect for Allan Jefferies and his all-round abilities. He was extremely good at road racing so it was never going to be the easiest race in the world to win."

In the TT paddock that year for the first time was Tony Jefferies, though he naturally can't remember much about his first trip to the Island that would later play such a huge part in his own and his son David's lives. "I was born in 1948 and dad was riding against Geoff Duke in the 1948 and 1949 TTs, so my first visit to the Isle of Man was when I was one-and-a-half. I've been going there a long time really I suppose – even though I don't recall a lot of it."

As things turned out, that second place to Duke would prove to be Allan Jefferies's finest result as a road racer. He retired suddenly and unexpectedly after a meeting at Esholt Park later in that 1949 season, following an almighty tank-slapper – where a sudden bump or jolt causes the handlebars of a motorcycle to flap wildly, often causing the rider to lose control of his machine. "He broke the lap record that day but had obviously scared himself and decided to retire at the end of the meeting," Nick Jefferies says.

Tony adds, "He pulled up and said, 'Do you know, I've just frightened myself stupid.' So he parked his bike, went for a drink and never raced again."

At 44, Allan decided he was too old to laugh off such incidents in the way a younger rider might have done and, feeling that he had lost his competitive edge, decided to concentrate on the family business from thereon in. While Jefferies called a halt to his road racing activities, Geoff Duke went on to become the sport's first ever household name. He would later be awarded an OBE for his services to motorcycling and remains one of the all-time legends of the sport. But he never forgot the admiration he had for Allan Jefferies. "I wasn't a close friend of Allan's but we were quite friendly," he says. "I suppose in the early days I considered him out of my league. He was so good in trials that the thought of finishing ahead of him in a trial was an achievement in itself. You have to take your hat off to Allan Jefferies. He would always go to the TT Riders Association luncheons and make a speech – and his speeches were absolutely fantastic. They were full of humour and were so much appreciated that most people wanted him to go on talking forever."

* * *

Tony Jefferies started riding road bikes on 24 April 1964 – his 16th birthday – and set about pursuing a career in the motorcycle industry. In January of 1966 he began an indentured engineering apprenticeship with the BSA group, manufacturers of the famous British motorcycles based in Small Heath, Birmingham.

More accustomed to dealing with Triumphs through his father's shop, Tony reckoned the workmanship at the Small Heath plant to be shoddy at best and within a year had managed to get himself transferred to Triumph. Here, he got an education in every aspect of building a motorcycle in the firm's Meriden plant in the West Midlands. Again, he was shocked to find shoddy working practices and, when he rejected a batch of faulty clutch bodies, forcing the temporary shutdown of a production line, he created something of a furore at the plant. So much so that, the following evening, Tony found himself answering his door to three heavies who threatened him with loss of his union membership – and much worse besides – if he didn't toe the line. "There was a knock on the door and they warned me that I better behave myself because they knew where I lived and where my car was parked – they knew all about me," he says. "I was summoned to go to a meeting at a pub in Coventry and taken to an upstairs room, and there were three blokes sat under one of those great big union flags – I was shitting myself! They told me that, as an apprentice, I didn't have the right to make decisions like that. I said, 'who are you? You're not my employer.' They just said, 'we control everything. We control when you take a shit.' They warned me that if I didn't want my legs broken I better make sure work at the factory didn't come to a halt again.

"They didn't care about the quality of the parts; all they were concerned about was that the production line kept moving so people kept working and got paid at the end of the day. It didn't stop me though – I had the production line halted again at a later date because of more dodgy components. But that time I got away with it."

Somewhat inevitably, given his family heritage and line of work, Tony Jefferies decided in July 1964 that it was time to open his own account as a competitive motorcyclist. Following directly in his father's footsteps, it was to trials riding that he first turned his attentions and he began entering events on a Triumph Tiger Cub. Although he was instantly competitive, Jefferies found he had an uncanny ability for breaking the machine and soon switched mounts to an Ariel HT5 that had come into his father's showroom on part-exchange. Happily, and despite what could be classified as overuse, Tony found the 500cc Ariel practically indestructible. "I used it for trials, weekly commuting between Meriden and Shipley, and I even took it abroad. It was a tough old bike – it almost broke me!"

Despite the fact that it was Allan Jefferies who initially encouraged his son to try his hand at road racing, he would later become vehemently opposed to the notion. Tony explains, "It was very difficult to know where you stood with my father. We had a real funny bike come into the shop in the summer of 1967. It was a Triumph built by a local guy who had tried to copy a Featherbed Norton. He put leading link forks on it and sunk a tuned engine into it – did a lot of clever things on it. We'd taken the bike in part exchange and it had race numbers on so was ready to race. My dad said, 'Well, we're not going to sell it over the weekend so you might as well use it and go and have a race on it.' I went to Croft and that's how I started racing. It was the first ever bike race at Croft and my dad actually took me to the circuit, so for him to later chuck me out of the house for going road racing was a bit daft really.

"Anyway, the bike oiled a plug so I was late getting to the start line for my first race. The marshal put a rope across my path and said 'No more, that's it.' I thought 'Fuck that – I'm racing,' so I turned round, rode out of the paddock and across a field back to the start line from the other direction. I finally got on to the circuit just after the riders had left the grid, but I was travelling at about 80mph so I just set about chasing them. I was in the race and that's all that mattered. I think I finished about 12th or something like that and my dad was saying, 'You're bloody useless,' and I got a complete bollocking from the race officials, so it was all quite eventful. But I got away with it."

Realising the limitations of the T100 'bitsa', Tony soon replaced it with another Triumph, this time a T100 Daytona. Since he was still working in Triumph's Meriden plant, Jefferies was able to source many rejected parts free of charge and was soon coaxing 50bhp out of his new project. The bike may have been fast but it proved to be extremely unreliable (somewhat unsurprising since it was largely made up of rejected parts) and when a life assurance policy worth £220 matured in 1969, Jefferies ignored his father's advice to invest it wisely and instead bought a Metisse rolling chassis into which he slotted a 750cc Norton Commando twin-cylinder engine borrowed from Colin Appleyard. Appleyard – a family friend and a director of Allan Jefferies for 20 years – had raced the engine in his sidecar outfit but, after a crash at the Isle of Man TT had left him hospitalised, he donated his engine to Jefferies. He clearly had no idea of the trouble his charity would cause.

Perhaps because he was so fully aware of the dangers of road racing, Allan Jefferies had discouraged his son from pursuing the discipline, instead trying to persuade him to persist with trials riding. Tony refused to listen. "Dad told me 'Don't bother to come home.' He wanted me to concentrate on trials. So I had to go and live with my girlfriend – I had nowhere else to go. It didn't last for that long and it was more about me staying away on purpose to prove a point really. It was probably because of the expense of road racing rather than the danger or anything else.

"We never really thought about the danger aspect of racing any kind of bike. He wanted me to become a good trials rider before I turned to road racing and, at 19, he thought I was too young as well. It was a lot of things. He just didn't agree that I should be a road racer."

At least the Metisse led to an easier life on the racetrack and Jefferies soon started making a name for himself. After winning his first club race, he found himself racing in an international event and hunting down none other than motorcycle racing legend Giacomo Agostini. By the time he retired from racing in 1977, Ago would be the most successful racing motorcyclist of all time with 15 World Championships and 10 TT victories to his credit. His haul of world titles remains unbeaten. Yet Tony Jefferies, with his limited racing experience, would find himself in third place, standing on the same podium as the Italian legend at Cadwell Park, with Dave Croxford in second.

A few weeks later at Mallory Park he would be involved in a race-long dice with another legend – this time the American rider Gary Nixon. Nixon – who was one of Barry Sheene's best friends – was riding the works Daytona Trident but Jefferies gave him a good run for his money. "Nixon got me every time on the straights and I got him into the corners," he says. "It just went on and on. But it was getting harder and harder as he learned the circuit. Eventually this and his faster bike got him across the line first."

Jefferies's results continued to improve until, in 1971, he achieved something that his father had never managed – he won an Isle of Man TT race. It remains the proudest moment of his racing career. "The moment that's embedded in my mind without any doubt is winning the Formula 750 TT in 1971," he says. "To win such a prestigious event was fantastic – I'll never forget that as long as I live. I remember walking behind the grandstand to see my mum and dad. They had now changed their attitude and were totally with me on the racing front."

Not one to forget a slight in a hurry, Tony had the presence of mind amidst all the excitement to recall his father turfing him out of his home over the Metisse he had bought. As the Formula 750 TT winner accepted the accolades in the winner's enclosure, he asked his father, "What price the Metisse now dad?"

His father insisted he was now with his son "all the way" and any past arguments were forgotten. Tony now completely understands what Allan had tried to do by banishing him from the house. "My father's theory was that I had to make the decision that I really wanted to race, so he made it hard for me. I've nothing against that – I don't think it did me any harm."

After collecting another win in the Junior race, Tony found himself on the verge of making TT history. At just 23 years old, he looked like becoming only the second man to win three TTs in a week after Mike Hailwood's momentous achievement ten years previously. "Suddenly I was really hitting the headlines because I had won two TTs in a week and had the chance of another race win on the Wednesday – the Production. The big question was could I win that as well? I didn't – I finished second. I was really cross – and I'm still cross to this day. Ray Pickrell won. It was a close race and, I just don't know – I could make a few excuses but maybe I just didn't try hard enough."

Despite his huge success as a racer, Tony Jefferies had other serious commitments away from the racetrack. He had taken over the family business in 1971 when he was just 22 years old, after his father stepped down and handed over responsibility – a step he soon regretted. One of Tony's first moves was to start selling the BMW bikes his father objected to so much, but it proved to be a wise investment and Allan Jefferies Motorcycles has never been out of the top five BMW dealers in the UK since.

Tony's private life could not have been going any better either. In 1968 he had met WPC43, a Leeds City policewoman called Pauline Matthews, and fallen head over heels in love. "Pauline was the sister of my flat-mate when I worked in Coventry, so I met her through him," Tony says. "We got chatting and I said I'd take her out for a drink when I got back from racing at Silloth that weekend. I figured out that I'd have to win all my heats *and* the final in order to win enough prize money to pay for fuel for the return trip and to have enough left over for a few beers. I did it though, and we went to the 'Rose and Crown' in Ilkley where I managed to buy Pauline about four beers with my prize money. Things just built from there and we eventually got married in Ilkley Parish Church on 2 October 1971."

In September 1972 Pauline was heavily pregnant with their first child. He would grow up to be the greatest road racer of his generation.

Chapter 2

YORKSHIRE BORN AND BRED

"You can't have it here – we're in bloody Leicestershire. He won't be able to play cricket for Yorkshire!"
Tony Jefferies

Many motorcycle racers claim they have been 'born into the sport' but in David Jefferies's case, it was quite literally true as it was a racing incident that hastened his birth.

Tony Jefferies was competing in the Race of the Year at Mallory Park in September 1972 and was accompanied by his heavily pregnant wife. When he suffered a massive crash right in front of her, the trauma of witnessing the accident sent Pauline into labour. Tony explains: "As I went into Devil's elbow, Ray Pickrell's gearbox failed and down he went. John Cooper missed the oil but Percy Tait went down and I followed him in sympathy. I remember seeing the Armco and thinking 'Bloody hell, this is going to hurt.' But just before I slammed into it, a straw bale, which had been thrown up into the air by one of the crashing bikes, fell right back down neatly into place between me and the Armco and I didn't get injured at all. Pickrell was very poorly and that crash ended his career. It was a big crash.

"Pauline had been told not to go to the race meeting or do anything stressful because she was so close to giving birth, but she came along anyway. After the crash, an announcement came over the tannoy saying, 'Would Tony Jefferies please go back to his car immediately.' When I got there Pauline said her waters had broken. Knowing nothing about such things, I said 'Is that important?' Once she explained that the baby was on its way I said, 'You can't have it here – we're in bloody Leicestershire. He won't be able to play cricket for Yorkshire! And he won't be able to win the Eddy Flintoff trophy in the Scott trial! We've got to get back to Yorkshire for the birth.'

"The first problem was that you had to cross the circuit at Mallory to get out but the officials wouldn't let me. They told me to wait and said they'd phone for a police escort to get me home, but I told them I wasn't waiting and that the police escort would have to catch me up. They forbade me from driving across the circuit but I ignored them and drove the wrong way round the circuit to get out. The marshals closed the gate and tried to stop me but I drove on through and eventually got onto the motorway. I had to stop for fuel and there were huge queues so I drove over the kerbs and barged my way in to get to a pump. Someone started having a go at me so I held the pump up and said, 'I'm next or this fucking pump goes round your neck.'

"I got filled up and drove absolutely flat out all the way home and the baby was born at about 1am."

Next came the argument about a name for the Jefferies's first child. "I wanted to call him Steve," says Tony, "because I thought that sounded fast – 'Steve Jefferies'. But Pauline didn't like Steve; she liked the name David. We then thought there should also be an 'Allan' in his name for his grandpa but we couldn't call him Dave Allen because of the comedian, so we picked Allan David Jefferies. But it seems to be something of a Jefferies family tradition to use middle names as first names so everyone ended up calling him David. Pauline is a middle name – her first name was actually Jean; and when David's sister eventually came along she ended up getting called Louise, even though her first name is actually Helen. My middle name is Anthony, which is where I obviously got 'Tony' from."

For Tony Jefferies, happily married with a beautiful baby son, a successful business and a promising international racing career, life could not have been better. But that was all about to change. Tony would win another TT in 1973 when he took the honours in the Production race, but it would be his last. Tragedy was just around the corner. Somewhat ironically, the crash that changed his life forever would happen at a 'safe' short circuit meeting rather than at the notoriously dangerous TT. He takes up the story. "It was at the Mallory Park Race of the Year on 18 September 1973. Dave Croxford was in the lead and I got it all crossed up coming into the hairpin trying to overtake him. I locked the front wheel and half went down and half rescued it. Then it went completely sideways and flicked me over and slammed me into the ground and that's what did the damage – that's what broke my back. Then I got run over by about 30 other riders as I lay there. Because I was knocked out in the crash, I can't actually remember being thrown off the bike; my last memory was of just coming into the corner and getting a bit crossed up, then the next thing I knew I was in Leicester infirmary. The other details I've got from people telling me. But being knocked out meant I didn't feel any pain so it was a good thing.

"There wasn't a mark on my body – not even a bruise. It was a fairly slow crash but I was thrown onto the ground hard and landed awkwardly. With hindsight, I should have just let go of the bike instead of trying to wrestle it, then I might have been okay."

He didn't know it when he recovered consciousness, but Tony Jefferies would never walk again. "My wife knew straight away," he says, "but I didn't find out I was paralysed until six weeks later. When it eventually dawned on me that I wasn't going to walk out of hospital, I just thought, 'Right, let's get on with life. I've got a business to run.'

"I was never bitter about it. I didn't have to race. I fell off, it was my fault, and therefore I just wanted to get on with life to the best of my fortune."

If there was one thing guaranteed to help Tony Jefferies through the massive trauma of adapting to life in a wheelchair it was his responsibilities. Pauline Jefferies was pregnant with their second child and by the time Louise – or 'Loubie' as she would come to be known – was born on 22 April 1974, Tony had his hands full running a business and bringing up a young family.

Now the manager of the family bike shop, and with a change of surname following her marriage to James Jennings in 2006, Louise remembers that she got on with her older brother about as well as could be expected. "As kids we fought like cat and dog most of the time, like any other brother and sister that are close in age," she says. "I followed him around everywhere and that seemed to annoy him immensely."

The Jefferies family house was situated at the top of a steep lane in Baildon and before David Jefferies had access to powered vehicles, this provided the impetus for free-wheeling mischief, usually at the expense of his sister. "When I was two, David decided that he would try and dispose of me by strapping me to his Action Man tank and sending me down the lane at high speed, resulting in me crashing face first into a road sign at the bottom of the hill," says Louise. "I ended up with a black front tooth which the dentist we had at the time wouldn't remove, so I had it for another seven years."

The injuries, at David's hands, kept on coming and, if anything, got more severe. "When I was four I broke my elbow when he tripped me up by standing on the laces of my Paddington Bear wellington boots as we went through the school gates," says Louise. "Then, when we were five and six respectively, mum decided to have the bathroom window reglazed. It was raining and I was standing outside with my little brolly up watching the man glaze the windows when David came flying through the backyard on his Rally Boxer and ran into my brolly. He was really cross and shoved me out of the way. I landed on the box of broken glass the glazier had just removed and needed ten stitches in the back of my knee. I've still got the scar today."

It clearly wasn't easy being David's sister.

Most successful motorcycle racers took to two wheels at a very early age and David was no exception. "We got him a bike for his 4th birthday and we had a house with a garden just about big enough to be able to ride round in," Tony recalls. "He drove us nuts actually, going round and round the same patch."

David's uncle Nick remembers, "David's first bike was an NVT Junior Ranger. It was made by Norton Villiers Triumph and had a Dutch-made 75cc engine. It was a horrible, ugly thing with a two-speed engine."

When David was six, the man who kick-started the love of motorcycles in the Jefferies family passed away. Allan Jefferies died in late 1978, aged 73, but not before learning from Nick that Mike Hailwood had made a triumphant comeback at the Isle of Man TT after an 11-year retirement. "He was very ill," says Nick, "but I told him about Mike and the speed he'd lapped at and he was amazed. He maintained an interest in bikes right to the end."

David had been pictured on the Island that very year wearing Hailwood's helmet. It was a memory that would stay with him for the rest of his life.

For a while at least, it seemed that the novelty of riding bikes would be short lived for David. "I turned up for David's 7th birthday and gave him a bow and arrow set," says Nick. "The sort with suckers on the end of the arrows.

"He took it and went off to play with his mates. Tony gave him a brand new Yamaha TY80 bike with 'DA V1D' as the number plate. It was a lovely little bike but David just said, 'Thanks dad – can I go and play with my mates now please?' And off he went to play with his bow and arrow. He didn't even start the bike up. Luckily the enthusiasm for bow and arrows didn't last."

Nick Jefferies is four years younger than his brother Tony and is yet another exceptionally talented rider to have sprung from Joseph Jefferies's gene pool. Like his father Allan, his first love was trials riding and in the 1970s he made a big name for himself in the sport, most noticeably when he won the Manx Two Day Trial in 1976. He had started his competitive career by winning the 1968 Novice Award, Yorkshire Group, before going on to contest no fewer than 16 Scottish Six Day Trials, 12 Manx Two Day Trials and countless Welsh Two Day Enduros, and ISDTs and ISDEs, collecting a dazzling array of gold and silver awards along the way. But it was when he switched to road racing that he lined himself up for a unique distinction. As winner of the Manx Grand Prix Newcomers race in 1983 (when the other steps on the podium were filled by future legends Steve Hislop and Robert Dunlop) and the Formula 1 TT in 1993, he became the only man in history to have won those three pinnacles of Isle of Man sport (Manx Two Day Trial, Manx GP and TT). He has also amassed an astonishing 51 TT replicas (the much-coveted awards which are presented to riders who finish within a certain percentage of the winner's time in a TT race) and 12 Manx Grand Prix replicas. It is a collection that is second to none and qualifies Nick as one of the most experienced – if not *the* most experienced – living exponent of the TT circuit.

While David's father could pass on no end of advice to his son once he took an interest in two-wheeled competition, he sadly could not physically ride with him. Nick, on the other hand, could, so young David had the very best of tutors on hand from the moment he threw his leg over a motorcycle – although there were often a few scrapes to be got out of when uncle Nick was involved. "When David was 10, his mum and dad won a trip to Hong Kong so David was staying with me for a couple of weeks. At the time, I was the clerk of the course for a trial up on Ickorshaw Moor. It was proper *Wuthering Heights* stuff up there – really bleak.

"Anyway, I had to mark the sections out and I told David he could come on his little Italjet 100 trials bike because it would be good experience for him, riding over such rough countryside.

"It got dark really early so we decided to ride back along the road to get to where we'd left our van. Of course, we had no lights, no road tax, no insurance – because we were all on trials bikes – and David, being just 10, had no licence either. So, to guard him, I went first, David was in the middle, and a friend of mine, Steve, rode behind him. I don't know how he did it but at one point I looked back and he just wasn't there. There was hardly a bend on the whole road but he'd managed to crash. When I found him, he had all but swallowed his tongue – bitten chunks off it – when he'd hit the handlebars with his mouth as he'd gone over.

"He got back on the bike and made it back to base but the next day his lips were swollen up like balloons. His parents were coming back that night so I said to David, 'Look, you can't tell your dad we were riding on the public highway – you'll have to say you struck a ditch on the moor and dabbed your face into the handlebars.' If Tony had found out I'd let David ride on the road I'd have got a right bollocking."

He may have suffered the odd mishap, as anyone who rides a bike invariably does, but by the age of ten David already had several years of riding experience under his belt. "He competed at the age of about seven or eight in schoolboy trials," Tony says. "Like my father did with me, I made him ride trials because there wasn't really anything else you could do back then. Schoolboy motocross hadn't really got going and I didn't believe in motocross for kids because I thought it just ripped their joints apart and made them walk bad. Even though David waited until he was about 14 before he did motocross, he suffered with his knees all his life. I think a lot of that was because he was so tall and had such a massive amount of leverage on his legs. His joints weren't old enough as a kid to withstand the hammering that they got from motocross."

It wasn't just powered two-wheelers that David was interested in. Like all schoolboys of his era, he loved riding his BMX bike and his daredevil streak was apparent even then. "David was Baildon cyclist of the year – for cycling proficiency – two years on the trot at school," explains Tony. "But both times he got banned the following term for dangerous riding. Once was for overtaking the headmaster going down a hill on his BMX while the headmaster was actually driving his car! The other time was for riding down the stepped walls of someone's garden and flying off the end like Evel Knievel."

Louise Jefferies remembers her brother's first big injury on a two-wheeler and the first sign of the gritty determination and disdain for injury he would later display in his motorcycle racing career. "He was riding his bike home from school and, as usual, riding flat-out and doing tricks. One of the shortcuts he used to take was down the station steps on to the platform and out through the gate. This was normally performed by doing a big wheelie down the steps, but on this occasion it all went wrong.

"David had repaired a puncture the night before and he can't have replaced the front wheel properly because as he started to wheelie down the steps the front wheel fell out, resulting in a spectacular crash. He smashed his face to bits and broke his wrist. We have a picture of him later in the afternoon with a big pot on his arm and wearing a sling, but still riding round the garden on *my* bike, because his was broken! There was no stopping him where two wheels were concerned."

Louise would later turn David's two-wheeled prowess to her advantage by placing bets with other school kids over his riding abilities. "When we got to Salt Grammar School he used to cycle there every day and do tricks in the woods on his BMX at break times to impress anyone who might be standing around – which was generally all the smokers. Me being a smoker at the time, I used to bet cigarettes with the other kids that David would be able to do certain stunts. I usually won loads of fags but David would have gone ballistic if he knew – he hated smoking."

When Tony deemed he was old enough to withstand the physical rigours involved, David was permitted to take up schoolboy motocross, a sport which instantly seemed to suit him more than trials had. He would later recall, "I quickly found out that I used to enjoy doing the bits in between sections of the trials course rather than the actual sections themselves as I could get up a bit of speed. I suppose it was then I realised I needed to go quick. So all I had to do was convince dad to buy me a motocross bike! I was 14 years old then and, after giving up the trials, went motocrossing for about four years – which I loved."

One part he certainly didn't love: the huge jumps that were an unavoidable part of motocross racing. "He really didn't like the big fast jumps as a kid," says Tony. "He didn't mind the smaller ones but the 'tabletop' stuff he hated. But that soon changed when he got older."

But even scary jumps were better than going to school for the young Jefferies who, if he didn't have a natural interest in a subject, would apply only minimum effort. "He was pretty shite at school really," his father admits. "He did what he could get away with and nothing more. His school reports always said 'He has the ability, if only he would concentrate more.' A bit like mine actually. If I was interested in something I was good at it, but if I wasn't, forget it. David was just the same. He was good at making things – always practical – so he did well in those sort of classes, but his actual academic work was pretty shite. And it wasn't because he thought he would easily get a job at the shop. I always told him I *wouldn't* employ him, that he'd have to make his own way."

Somewhat surprisingly, DJ wasn't much drawn to school sports either. "He didn't like them. Wasn't interested in cricket, tennis, football, stuff like that. We tried to get him to play rugby at Bingley Rugby Club but he was quite pathetic to watch really – always running around after the ball but never actually catching it. He'd occasionally get caught out when someone threw the ball at him and he grabbed it but he'd look at me, like 'What the fuck do I do now?' And always, just before the last whistle blew, he'd throw himself on the floor and roll around just to get mucky so he'd at least *look* like a rugby player."

It was bikes and bikes alone that David Jefferies was interested in and much of his school time was spent daydreaming about the freedom he would enjoy when he turned 16 and could hit the open road for the first time. And when the magical day finally arrived, he didn't waste a minute of it. "I started riding on the road at one minute past midnight on my 16th birthday," he said, "and I did 12,500 miles in that first year on a Yamaha FS-1E."

Nick Jefferies remembers David being fast on tarmac from the very outset. "No one has ever ridden a Yamaha Fizzie (FS1-E) moped harder or farther than David, maybe a sign that he was going to be quite handy on a road race bike. In fact, you simply couldn't get the lad off the bloody thing. The family was left wondering, and sometimes shuddering, at how he managed to keep up with his mates on Yamaha DT125s, but he did."

"All my mates had 125cc machines and I used to be quicker than them," David once boasted. "Not in a straight line of course, but even then on a little 50cc bike I found I could brake crazily late into corners and drive out, typical racing style, so I knew I belonged on a race track."

As soon as he turned 17, David took his full bike test. Tony explains: "He took his bike test twice. The first time was on his Yamaha FS-1E. Everyone else called them 'Fizzy's' but David called it the 'fried sausage and one egg.' It was only 50cc, so that was all he could ride until he was 17, then he took his proper test. He was always getting pulled up for taking pillion passengers on his Fizzy because you weren't allowed to do that with 'L' plates."

He may have passed both bike tests easily but over-confidence saw him fail his car test at the first attempt. "They failed him for going through a gap that the examiner didn't think was there," says Tony. "There was one car parked up on the roadside and another car coming the other way, so David thought 'no problem' and squeezed through. But the examiner was breathing in and squeezing his cheeks together, trying to make himself as narrow as possible, thinking they were never going to make it. He was failed for putting them both in a 'dangerous situation.'"

Having obtained his full bike licence, David got his own Yamaha

DT125 and then there was really no stopping him. "He would tear all round Yorkshire and farther afield," says Nick Jefferies, "just the same as his grandfather, father and uncle before. No weather could stop him, not even the worst of winter, so his parents stood little chance."

With such a passion for riding on the road and given his family credentials, it was somewhat inevitable that David would want to try road racing, but at 17 he still wasn't quite sure how to go about it. "He wanted to race," Tony says. "I can remember him asking, 'Dad, what am I gonna do about going racing? How am I going to do it?' He was working as an apprentice and didn't have any money."

While Tony Jefferies's motorcycle shop seemed the obvious place for David to work after leaving school, dad clearly wasn't going to be a soft touch and insisted that his son find his own feet in the world. "When I left school my dad would never let me work in the shop," David said. "I had to go and find a job for myself."

Tony explains his thinking. "What was the point in me teaching him everything he needed to know? When I was an apprentice a bloke once said to me 'Once the apprentice, always the apprentice,' and it's so true. If David had started at the shop as an apprentice, then no matter how good he was or how high he later rose, he'd still be known as the apprentice. It's better to do your training and make your mistakes somewhere else. Then you're treated with more respect when you move into a new position of authority where no one knows you as an apprentice.

"I once went into a bike dealer's in Haworth and asked a question of the guy behind the counter. He said, 'Have a word with the lad over there, he'll know.' The 'lad' was about 82 but he was still referred to as the apprentice because he'd worked there for most of his life. That's why I wanted David to learn what he needed to know somewhere else."

David decided to train as a plant fitter so he could indulge his hobby of 'tinkering with big engines'. So after leaving Salt Grammar School in Baildon he started work as a trainee plant mechanic with the Brown Group at Pool in Wharfdale on 3 July 1989. His later CV gives some idea of the kind of work David carried out and why he maintained an enthusiasm for heavy machinery throughout his life:

During my time at Browns I worked on many types of vehicles, from small Thwaites dumpers to 35-ton Moxy dump trucks and Caterpillar 980cc loading shovels. I also worked on Hymac excavators, Fiat Allis dozers, Broyt face shovels and Akerman excavators. I have experience in a number of types of work which include changing engines from 980c, splitting dump trucks to change artic hinges, removing and changing rams, wheels, axles, drive shafts, buckets, cabs and many other jobs such as stripping down, ordering parts and rebuilding engines out of 980c, Moxy dump trucks and many other machines.

Here was a young man working on real life Tonka toys and clearly loving every minute of it. David's childhood friend, Karl 'Carlos' Smith, remembers DJ being obsessed with heavy plant machinery. After having known each other during their schoolboy motocross days, the two met again when both were sent by their respective employers on block release plant-fitting courses at Whitwood College in Castleford. Lunchtimes weren't spent chasing girls or sneaking quick pints, but ogling heavy plant machinery in the local open cast mine.

But while Smith shared DJ's enthusiasm for big machinery, he wasn't so keen on his friend's passion for riding at breakneck speed. "On our lunch breaks at college," he says, "we'd go to the open cast mines near Castleford. One time we took some sandwiches and I jumped onto the back of his Honda CBR600. Big mistake. He rode like an absolute nutter – I mean, I don't scare easily but I got off the bike shaking. I'd thought we were both dead men. It was the first time I'd had a proper argument with him. It was bloody crazy the way he rode that day.

"Anyway, when we got there, we used to climb through an embankment and just sit and eat our sandwiches and watch the heavy plant at work. There was one absolutely massive machine called 'Oddball' working there at the time because the mine had been flooded. David was fascinated by it. It was about the size of an office block. He always had a fascination with big stuff, but when I think back to us sitting in a quarry watching heavy plant, well, that was worse than train spotting really wasn't it?"

The trips to and from college were often packed with incident as David developed his skills on a succession of motorcycles. "He used to travel to college on bikes," says Smith. "He had a Yamaha DT125 at one point and would stand on the rear footpegs and wheelie it for miles. That was before I could drive so I'd be on the bus and he'd come speeding past with the thing stood up on the back wheel, looking in through the windows. Later, when I had a van and DJ had a XBR500 Honda, we'd often have a race on the way to or from college. I remember one time when he cut up inside of me on a roundabout and the next thing he was on his arse. Big crash. He'd hit a diesel spill. I stopped the van and we got the bike loaded into the back before the cops turned up. I remember the only thing he was worried about was that he'd ripped his Husky suit. It was a horrible bloody thing – like an Eskimo suit – but David loved it and he was quite upset that he'd damaged it."

Fine-tuning factory racing motorcycles would perhaps require a touch more finesse and sensitivity than working on heavy plant, but his engineering background would stand David in good stead when he eventually went racing. By December 1990 however – the year in which he finally did take part in his first race – Browns had gone into liquidation and he was made redundant. Only then did Tony Jefferies agree to employ his son in his own business as a motorcycle mechanic.

* * *

"I think it was in 1989 when I went on a track day at Cadwell Park with some of my dad's mates. I managed to blag a ride on a Honda CBR600. I didn't have any leathers, helmet – nothing! I really shouldn't have been there but I borrowed some gear, put it on and off I went. I knew there and then that this was for me."

The outing at Cadwell Park, coupled with the realisation that his knees were no longer up to the rigours of motocross, convinced David Jefferies to try his hand at road racing in 1990. "Even after a short career in motocross I'd knackered my knees," he said. "My dad quickly realised I had a bit of a talent for the road bikes so asked me if I fancied a real go at road racing. Of course I said yes!"

Tony provided a Yamaha FZR600 for his son's road race debut but added a typically straightforward proviso – that if his son was 'crap' at road racing, he'd sell the bike to try to get some of his money back. It was soon evident that David Jefferies was not crap.

Despite the Jefferies's family connections in the motorcycling world, that first year was far from a full factory effort. "All we did to the bike," said David, "was put on a carb kit, borrow a can from uncle Nick and off I'd go. I remember doing 35 meetings in my first year to get as much experience as I could."

According to a press release generated by his father at the end of the 1990 season, David had competed in no less than 160 individual heats and races during those 35 meetings.

His first race was in March and within a month he had ten races in the Superpsort 600 and Open classes under his belt. Successive third and second places were eventually capped with wins in the novice class and by the end of the month Jefferies had qualified for his restricted racing licence, meaning he could discard the orange novice jacket he started the season with. By 1 July – just four months into his racing career – David had gained his full national licence, an impressive feat, and decided he now needed a tuned engine if he was to go any faster. The engine was tuned by Russell Savory and Jefferies used it to compete in his first national race on 29 July. Although he continued to race in club events, DJ was keen to take in as many nationals as possible to gain more experience and to encourage him to raise his game further. On 27 August he scored his first ACU (Auto-Cycle Union) National Championship point by finishing 10th in the Supersport 600 class at Cadwell Park.

Towards the end of the season club racing was abandoned altogether. Jefferies felt there was more satisfaction and experience to be had from finishing mid-pack in a national race than there was to be easily winning club races.

Heeding the comments of more experienced riders is another sure-fire way to improve, but listening to his uncle's advice at Cadwell Park in late 1990 almost proved costly for David, as Nick explains. "Towards the end of the season, we were both entered at Cadwell Park on identical yellow and white Yamaha FZR600s. I noticed during practice that David had crashed at Charlie's Corner, so on the next lap I stopped and said 'Right, jump on my bike. I've still got a 750 to ride. You have this. Off you go.'

"Well, we got an almighty bollocking for that. We were hauled before the stewards and threatened with suspension and blah, blah, blah. I explained that, since I also had a 750 ride I was going to let David ride my 600. They said that wasn't allowed and I told them they would never have known if I'd given him the bike in the paddock – they were identical bikes. Some of the stewards were doing all they could not to laugh because they could see the funny side of it, so we ended up getting this half serious, half hilarious bollocking. But it was a bit worrying that Dave, at just 17, was being threatened with a racing suspension for listening to his 'experienced' uncle Nick!"

Of the 160 races DJ finished in that hectic first season, he scored an incredible 103 top ten finishes with 12 third places, 15 second places and 30 race wins. Alongside this, he crashed five times and suffered mechanical breakdowns three times – an impressive record by any standards, and even more so when considering that he prepared and maintained his own bike throughout the season.

Jefferies's results in his debut year had been impressive enough to attract some support from the motorcycle industry. For 1991, he would campaign a Honda CBR600 supplied by Honda UK and a Suzuki RGV250, with a basic race kit, supplied by John Crystal Racing of Redcar. Crystal had a long history of supporting the Jefferies family's racing efforts, first backing Tony in the 1970s and later Nick in the 1980s. Now it was David's turn to receive some support in the shape of an RGV250 which he would use in the Superpsort 400 class (despite the class title, 250cc two-strokes were eligible to compete against the larger capacity, but less-developed, 400cc four-stroke machines).

David also started getting some backing in the shape of free consumables from oil, brake pad and spark plug companies, as well as from helmet, glove and leather manufacturers – but racing was still an expensive business. A mid-season breakdown of costs for 1991 shows just how expensive:

Tyres (nine meetings)	£1,215
Honda CBR engine tuning from H&S	£1,250
Chains (Regina x 4)	£184
Rear shocks (Ohlins x 2)	£700
Fairings (replacement)	£450
Race entries	£1,105
Suzuki engine parts	£2,000
Honda parts (inc. accident damage)	£400
Fuel for race bikes	£375
Fuel for transporter	£750
Load lugger	£220
Year to date	£9,177

It may be a fraction of what top MotoGP teams spend today, but with a season of British racing at this level costing around £15,000 back in 1991 – excluding the cost of the bikes, the race transporter, food at race meetings etc – it's clear just how committed a young rider needed to be to pursue a career in racing. The same spread sheet reveals the items and luxuries still missing from the Jefferies set-up including testing time at circuits, dyno time to work on the bikes, spare engines for experimental work, mobile benches to make working on the bikes easier at race meetings, spare wheels, a generator...the list is almost endless. David Jefferies was by no means unique in lacking the funding to have an ideal set-up, but the figures vividly illustrate just how difficult it is for a young racer, no matter how talented, to fund a championship campaign without factory support.

DJ had no spare cash for squandering down at the local boozer at weekends – every penny he made went straight back into his racing. Tony Jefferies may have owned a successful motorcycle dealership but he did not spoil his son when it came to racing: if David wanted to pursue a career on two wheels, he was going to have to do it the hard way.

The prize money he had received by that mid-point of the season totalled £1,390 and that too was ploughed back into expenses like specialist equipment, including compressors and pillar drills, and other essentials such as garage hire at race circuits. Motorcycle road racing never has been, and never will be, cheap.

One of Jefferies's top priorities during the 1991 season was the new *Motor Cycle News* Superteen Championship. Backed by the weekly motorcycling newspaper, the series was designed to try to find Britain's racing stars of tomorrow. It was to be held alongside the prestigious *MCN* TT Superbike rounds and would take in Thruxton, Snetterton, Mallory Park, Donington Park (two rounds), Cadwell Park, Oulton Park, and Knockhill in Scotland. Former Grand Prix star Ron Haslam – father of current BSB and WSB star Leon – was signed up to coach the youngsters and advice would also be on hand from experienced riders like Steve Spray, Rob Orme and Mark Phillips. As well as being walked round each track and shown the correct lines and braking markers, the youngsters were taught how to present themselves to the increasingly important sponsors.

The prize fund was respectable at a time when British Championship racing had yet to benefit from full TV coverage at every round. A total of £1,600 was up for grabs at each round, with £500 going to the race winner and a bonus of £50 at each venue for the best turned-out team. The championship winner would be offered a ride in the 125cc European Championship which, back then, was the best feeder class for a career in Grand Prix racing. Although they were unfamiliar names at the time, there were some major stars of the future on the entry list for that first year of Superteens – names like Michael Rutter, James Haydon, John McGuinness, Jamie Robinson, Jason Vincent and David Jefferies himself – none of them older than 20 at the time (the series had an age limit of 21).

At 18 years of age, DJ was one of the top riders in the series battling for the overall title which, quite apart from the healthy amount of press coverage that came with being at the sharp end of the series, would see him gain valuable experience in all aspects of being a professional rider, from race craft to self-promotion.

By mid-season, he lay in fifth place in both the Superteen championship and the British Supersport 400 series, using his Suzuki RGV250 for both. Most bike racers are built like jockeys and, while size isn't as vital on today's ultra-powerful 1000cc Superbikes, it was of paramount importance on small 250cc machines as it affected both the power-to-weight ratio and the aerodynamic package of rider and machine. Jefferies, although still a growing lad, was giving away too much advantage to his smaller rivals, which makes his achievements that year even more impressive. Even so, he enjoyed the experience of riding a two-stroke. After a shakedown test at Mallory Park on 10 April, he said, "I had never raced a two-stroke before and it seemed so light and small. The RGV was delightful to ride. The steering was ever so quick and it felt so much easier to throw around than the CBR600 Honda."

When it came to the first race meeting on the Suzuki – at Pembrey in Wales on 14 April – Jefferies discovered the downside of riding seizure-prone two-strokes. "The CBR practice went okay, then came RGV practice – it flew for one lap and then seized." After borrowing a barrel and piston he had the bike ready just in time for its debut race but things didn't get any better. "I didn't even make the end of the front straight before the front cylinder seized again. I was getting fed up of walking back to the pits."

They located more barrels and pistons but the Suzuki seized once again after just four miles. Following extensive head-scratching and many, many phone calls to Mick Grant – a fellow Yorkshireman and seven-times TT winner turned Suzuki team manager – the problem was traced to a twisted crankshaft which was affecting the ignition timing on the front cylinder.

With the RGV still out of action, Jefferies only had his CBR to race at Castle Combe in Wiltshire on 20 April but he was well satisfied with his 7th place in a national event, first time out at the bumpy and difficult track.

With the Honda CBR600 being a new model for 1991, DJ was finding the going tough against the hordes of well-developed Yamaha FZR600s. But he learned a valuable lesson at Thruxton that would stay with him for the rest of his racing career – the harder you try, the slower you go. Of course, all road racers are trying hard but it remains a fact that the really fast lap times only come when a rider is relaxed, concentrated and riding smoothly. Ragged, edge-of-the-seat rides rarely deliver the best lap times. Take this example. "As I approached Church, a just off flat-out fifth gear corner at about 130mph, the bike alongside me forced me to the outside of the track and onto the grass. I then left the circuit for some serious high-speed grass tracking and motocross. Eventually I returned to the track but everyone else had gone and I was now half a lap behind the leaders.

"I rode as hard as I could, furious that I had missed a golden opportunity for a good place. I thought I was lapping really quickly and managed to get up to 16th place but my dad told me my times were in fact slower than my best qualifying time. I had been trying too hard and had been too wild."

After another four-and-a-half hour drive back home to Baildon, Jefferies found his dual life was beginning to take its toll. He was still attending Whitwood College in Casteford, a 70-mile round trip each day, on top of the long hauls to race circuits every weekend. And burning the midnight oil working on the bikes meant that it was a struggle to get up early for college and then not returning home until after 7pm.

But the results started coming and that was all the motivation needed. DJ finished 6th in the Supersport 400 British Championship race at Snetterton and 13th in the 600 class, despite suffering from a twisted knee. He was later diagnosed as having a tendon missing in the knee – the result of a previous motocross injury – and told this would need an operation to correct it. But that would have to wait until the winter. Right now, there were races to be run.

After taking 13th overall in the Supersport 600 races, which were run as part of the support programme for the Transatlantic Match Races at Mallory Park and Brands Hatch, Jefferies headed to the coast of his native Yorkshire to tackle Oliver's Mount for the first time. It may have been only his second season of racing but this trip was to prove a pivotal moment in David Jefferies's career.

Unlike the Isle of Man and Ireland, where the law allows for road closure acts to allow racing on public roads, the UK mainland has never permitted this kind of racing – which is why, even way back in 1907, the organisers of the first TT race were forced to approach the self-governing Isle of Man authorities about running their event.

There are two exceptions to this rule on the UK mainland – Aberdare Park in Wales and Oliver's Mount in Scarborough. Both are parkland circuits, which is how they managed to get around the road closures act, but they are, to all intents and purposes, pure road circuits, much like the Isle of Man TT course. They certainly share many of the associated dangers, such as the close proximity of trees and bankings to the circuit, but at least they don't run through villages and are not fenced in by stone walls. Even so, Jefferies was apprehensive enough about his first visit to a 'road' circuit and carefully heeded the advice of his father who had raced there back in the early 1970s. "He still knew his way around," said David at the time, "and told me just when and where to put the power on, which is important on blind corners. He also pointed out the braking points which were just the same as when he rode there 17 years ago."

The bikes may have become much faster in the intervening years but brakes had also improved. That levelled things out and meant that the braking points were still very much the same as they had been in the early '70s.

Jefferies qualified on the front row for the Supersport 600 race and took pole position for the 400cc event. He takes up the story of the races: "The 600 race was a great battle. I took the lead through the Esses but lost it by braking too late for the last hairpin. Geoff Baldock got in front and I never re-passed him. He only beat me by a bike's length and I suppose I should have won, but I didn't and, anyway, second was a super result for me – my best yet at a national event.

"But better still was to follow in the 400 race. After an indifferent start I took the lead from Andy Murphy on the first lap and led from then on to the end of the race. This was my first national win. I got a great cheer from the crowd and the team were jumping up and down on the motorhome roof so much I thought my mum would go through it!"

Having enjoyed the best results of his career to date on the tight, twisty and undulating seaside circuit, as well as setting a new lap record on his RGV250, Jefferies seemed instantly at home on 'real world' road circuits. It would be a long time before he would attempt to conquer the daddy of them all – the Isle of Man TT circuit – but when he did, he would astound everyone with his utter domination of the world's most difficult and dangerous race course.

David had been visiting the Isle of Man TT since he was a baby and he still hugely enjoyed the experience, especially now that he could assist his uncle Nick who was at the top of his racing game by this time. In fact, DJ was having such a good time at the 1991 TT that he didn't want to go home mid-week as planned, so he hatched a plan which would allow him to stay a little longer – though he didn't envisage spending some of that time at Her Majesty's pleasure! David explained: "Me and some mates were supposed to get the ferry home on the Sunday after watching the racing but we accidentally-on-purpose missed the ferry so I could signal for uncle Nick in the 400 race the next day.

"After explaining my unfortunate dilemma to dad [David said that an accident had blocked the road on the way to the ferry which meant he had missed it], I then promptly blasted down the full length of the seafront promenade on the back wheel, only to be dragged off the bike by the police who had watched me all the way. They actually threw me in jail! I dread to think what my dad said when the papers reported 'Jefferies told to keep his talents on the track!'"

The charge sheet from 2 June 1991 states that DJ 'did unlawfully ride so as to endanger the life or limb of any person in the said thoroughfare'. He was released on £100 bail and the following day had to attend the Douglas court house where he escaped with a hefty fine. Tony, who eventually got the full story out of David, remembers "Somebody spotted him at the traffic lights and shouted 'Go on then, give us a wheelie' and he set off from there and pulled a wheelie right along the length of Douglas Promenade. He then did a bit of a runner and hid in a pub, hoping no one had seen him, but an unmarked car had followed him all the way. The next thing they were pushing his head down into the back of the car and he was thrown in jail.

"They were going to hold him for another day for some reason but a friend of ours got onto the police and vouched for David and pulled a few strings to get him out. The Jefferies name came into it as well – the fact that his dad had won TTs and his uncle had won a TT – and that seemed to help. He just got a fine in the end. The magistrate said something like 'While we appreciate you are from a motorcycling background and may possess skills that people don't normally possess, this does not give you permission to show them off on public highways. And as your family enjoys such a good name on the Isle of Man, it would be much better if you behaved yourself in future.'"

Jefferies was required to sit on the other side of the court in July 1991 when he was called up for six weeks' jury service, something he wasn't best suited to as Tony recalls. "It was a fraud case and really complicated – all about accounts and what-not. David hadn't a bloody clue what was going on. They were locked in a hotel overnight while the jury was out, but David got bored so he climbed down the fire escape and went for a couple of beers, then sneaked back up and into the hotel with no one the wiser!"

When he wasn't falling foul of, or assisting, the law, Jefferies was starting to claim some class scalps in the Supersport 400 and 600 British championship races. At Brands Hatch in June he overtook British champion Jim Moodie before locking his front wheel under braking and dropping back slightly – though he still managed to finish ahead of championship leader Steve Ives. In the 600 race, DJ took third ahead of such luminaries as future four times World Superbike Champion Carl Fogarty and former British Superbike Champion Brian Morrison. His over-enthusiasm eventually caught up with him however and the race ended with a high-side as he was battling for the lead with Ives and Moodie. But he had made his point: David Jefferies was no longer an unknown student on the British racing scene and the paddock was starting to take notice of the third generation of racers from the Jefferies family.

One month after his debut national win at Scarborough, DJ took part in the inaugural race of the MCN Superteen Championship at Thruxton on June 23. Current TT lap record holder and 14-times winner, John McGuinness, who would later become a good friend of David's, remembers racing against him in the series. "Dave was on the RGV and I was on my Kawasaki KR1S. I think he was working in engineering or something and I was an apprentice brickie at the time. The money in Superteens used to be all right – about £500 for a win, which back in that time wasn't bad. And they used to have all these other little bonuses, like Frank Thomas awards, so you would get a pair of boots if you set the fastest lap."

Even at such an early age, Jefferies's large physical build was an issue. "He did look massive on that little RGV," McGuinness says. "You could always tell it was Dave on that bike. But he could ride it, you know? He could get tucked in for a big lad. He had a shit suit on though – it was like an orange and white thing with a horrible big DJ badge on the front of it."

Shit suit or not, Jefferies always seemed to get the better of McGuinness throughout his career in most of the many classes they raced in together. McGuinness is happy to admit it. "I didn't really have any close races with him that year – he'd always blow me off. He used to always beat me, did Dave. Yeah he did. He was better than me."

DJ returned to Oliver's Mount in July for the traditional Cock o' the North meeting and continued his winning ways at the track that he clearly excelled on. One notable achievement on this occasion was that he beat his vastly experienced uncle Nick for the first time – and not once, but twice, pushing Nick back into 2nd place in both Supersport 400 races. Nick had his revenge in the Battle of the Twins National Championship race when he led David over the line on his Ducati 888 after the younger Jefferies's bike had died on the opening lap. Once it fired up again, DJ set a new class lap record as he cut his way through the pack to take second place behind his uncle.

The other cause for celebration was that David's two wins were enough to finally gain him his international racing licence, meaning he could now race at any level of event anywhere in the world. It was a fitting 50th birthday present for David's mum Pauline, who had always been his biggest fan.

Now keen to gain some international racing experience, Jefferies applied to Suzuki GB, asking to be considered for a place in the Suzuki GSX-R750 World Cup event to be held at Hockenheim in Germany. His bid was accepted and Jefferies, still only 18 years old, would be representing his country in his first foreign race which was a support event for the increasingly popular World Superbike Championship. The standard GSX-Rs were all run-in in Japan before being crated over to Europe and allocated to riders from Europe, Canada, Australia and even the Far East, for what was to be a truly international event. Jefferies was teamed with up-and-coming star Jamie Whitham and motorcycle journalist Mark Forsyth.

"He was a bit green on that trip," says Forsyth. "It was his first race abroad and I think he was a bit awe-struck, but we still had a good laugh. Me and Whitham fell asleep on the bus on the way to the hotel and Mick Grant (team manager), DJ and the others got off without waking us up, presumably giggling like school girls. The first me and Whitham knew about it was when we woke up in the bus station. But we got our own back by charging a 200 deutschmark taxi to Mick Grant."

There was more comedy in store at the circuit as the international teams were given an official German welcome. "We had to march down the main straight waving little flags while German Oompah bands played our national anthems on big tubas."

After having squeezed his 6ft 2in frame onto a tiny Suzuki RGV250 all season, the much roomier 750 Suzuki provided some relief and Jefferies relished the chance to ride a Superbike for the first time. If Suzuki had taken a chance by offering David the ride ahead of many more experienced British applicants, the Japanese manufacturer was not to be disappointed. In his debut foreign race Jefferies turned in the best performance of his career so far by finishing as top Brit in 7th place overall. It was enough to make Jefferies realise that his future lay with Superbikes.

Forsyth remembers having close battles with Jefferies in both legs. "We were grabbing each other's seat humps along the straights. At Hockenheim they are so long that when you're watching the rev limiter in 6th, there's not much else you can do. I'd have my face pressed against the clocks, then notice I was losing a few hundred revs, then all of a sudden it would be 1,000 revs as DJ flashed past having grabbed onto my seat hump and hauled himself past me. It was so close that we did that to each other all the way round in both races."

Jefferies had proved he could ride smaller machinery by finishing his second year of racing in 3rd place in the Supersport 400 British championship, 5th in the inaugural Superteen series, and 6th in the Supersport 600 British championship, but he was always going to be at a disadvantage against smaller riders on such bikes. With their extra power and weight, Superbikes offered Jefferies a more level playing field and so he turned his attention to planning a Superbike campaign for 1992.

Chapter 3

CRASHING CARS

"He was a good driver but, fuck, he was fast!"
Karl Smith, David's friend

When he wasn't racing, David Jefferies's favourite pastime seemed to be crashing cars. Sometimes his own, but preferably his father's, his mother's, or even his sister's. "He wasn't a big drinker so he'd always drive when we went out on the piss," says childhood friend Karl Smith. "But that invariably meant he'd have a car full of drunk people egging him on on the way home. He could pile about eight people into his pick-up truck – sometimes making them lie down flat in the back – and he had more fun scaring us with his driving than he would have had getting pissed.

"Tony had a silver M Series BMW at one point and David used to borrow it. He was a good driver but, fuck, he was fast! One night he hit a jump absolutely flat out and there was an almighty bang and sparks everywhere. It turned out he'd cracked the sump of his dad's car. He had to pick his dad up later so I bailed out because I didn't want to get involved. Apparently he went to his dad looking all sheepish and said, 'I don't know what happened dad, I must have caught something.'"

"Another time he borrowed his mum's Land Rover and drove us to a nearby BMX track. He was convinced he could clear two big jumps in one go if he got a fast enough run-up. Unbeknown to us, Pauline had a typewriter in the back of the Land Rover and when we landed there was an almighty crash as it went flying out the back window, smashing it to pieces. My old man had a Land Rover at the house so we drove round there, took the whole tailgate off and fitted it to Pauline's car. My folks were away so we ordered a new one and had that fitted by the time they got back. But Tony and Pauline never knew that they were driving around with my dad's tailgate on for the whole time they had that Land Rover."

"He used to be obsessed with going off-road no matter what he was driving. And he would get cars in such a state that he was banned from the car wash in Baildon. So much mud and shit would come off any car he washed that it blocked all their drains!"

Once, after driving through a ploughed field in Germany, he went to a nearby car wash to clean his vehicle. There happened to be a local rally taking place at the time and a kid, seeing his car so utterly covered in mud, asked for his autograph, thinking he must have been a rally driver to get his car in such a state!

Jefferies's fondness for blazing new trails where none existed led to an embarrassing encounter for Smith. "I was up on Baildon Moor one night shagging a bird in my car in a lay-by. It was a full-on job – steamed-up windows, the car rocking, the lot. At one point I looked out the window and saw something bouncing up and down over the moors coming towards us. There was no road in that direction so I thought 'Fuckin' hell! What's that?' I tried not to let on to the girl because I didn't want to interrupt our fun, but eventually this car pulled up alongside us and I heard, 'Carlos, you dirty bastard!' It was David with his car rammed full of people, all staring in the windows and laughing at us. I was dying. He had just driven over the open moors, regardless of the fact that there wasn't any road."

In fact discomfort was not unusual when hanging about with DJ. "We used to do a rally on our bikes every year across the Pyrenees," says Smith. "We got steaming pissed in a bar one night, very late, and decided we didn't like the woman who was serving so we thought we'd frighten her by taking all our clothes off and streaking round the bar. It was all very funny until some of the other lads nicked all our clothes and we had to run all the way through this quiet little village bollock naked to get back to our tent. I'm not sure the locals had seen anything like it before."

David's sister, Louise, remembers the time when he smashed their dad's BMW 5 Series not once, but twice, in as many days. "He drove it to college and somehow smashed into the back of a skip. He tried to convince dad that he'd had his work boots on and his foot had slipped off the brake pedal. Dad went ballistic and Dave was banned from driving cars for a while – he was only allowed to drive vans from the shop. Dad told Dave to take the car to the BMW dealers and pay for it to be fixed with all the proper parts, no skimping. A friend drove dad's BMW to the dealers and Dave followed in a brand new Toyota van we had for the shop so he could give the guy a lift back once he'd dropped the car off. Now Dave was obsessed with big tits and when a 'big' girl walked past on the street, he was so busy staring at her that he crashed the van into the back of Dad's BMW."

Louise lays some of the blame at her dad's feet. "As kids, we had crashed number plates all the way round the hall in the house – only from the cars that dad had written off, not just crashed. It wasn't exactly setting a perfect example. I remember we always had to recover the number plates from the crashes so that dad could put them up on a pelmet round the hall. It was a fairly big hall but it was crammed full of written-off number plates."

Louise may laugh now but when David wrote off her own treasured car she was less than pleased. "I had a little Peugeot 205," she remembers. "A white 1.9 litre turbo diesel. I loved that little car. Dave didn't have any wheels at the time and he was banned from driving all the other cars because he crashed so much, so he asked if he could borrow mine one night. I agreed, as long as he drove me over to Harrogate where I was going to be staying with a friend. He was supposed to pick me up the next morning but never turned up, so I had to get a bus home. Just outside Otley, the bus got held up because there were all these police cordons on the road. I looked out of the window of the bus and there was my treasured little car lying upside down in a ditch on top of a tree stump. It had been DJ'd."

Considering how many cars David Jefferies got through, it was perhaps surprising that he hadn't become an expert wheeler-dealer, but Louise, now general manager of Allan Jefferies Motorcycles, still smiles at his lack of business sense. "He was going to buy a 4x4 at one time and dad told him to deal the salesman to the floor. Dave went to see the car and came back and said, 'I've done it dad – I've done it. I dealt the guy to the floor.' Dad said, 'Right, what's the deal then?' And Dave answered, 'My car and a grand!' He was dead chuffed with himself. So dad said, 'Okay, get £700 out of the bank and offer him the cash and if he doesn't take that, the worst that can happen is you write him a cheque for a grand.'

"You could see the light coming on in Dave's head. 'Oh yeah, right, right, good thinking.' Just then, the salesman called and we could hear Dave on the phone, all cocky saying, 'Look mate, it's like this – you can have my car and a cheque for a grand or my car and 700 quid cash.' Then the penny dropped and he looked across at dad as if to say 'I did that wrong didn't I?'"

Tony agrees. "He wasn't a businessman. He could work out exactly what it would cost him to do a job if he was interested in it but he didn't have the savvy to cut a deal."

Even when he did spot a business opportunity, David gave it up as soon as any questions were asked. "He had a Toyota Hilux truck in the early 1990s – like a big monster truck – and saw a woman stuck in the snow one night," remembers his friend, Alistair Smith. "He towed her home and she gave him a tenner so Dave saw the chance to make some cash. He spent the rest of the night driving round looking for people stuck in the snow and charged them ten quid to tow them out. I think he got about £80 that night but when one woman got awkward about having to pay he gave it up as a bad job."

There are enough crashed car stories to fill a book. Like the time he had a Renault Clio V6 Sport that ended up costing him a grand an hour to drive. It cost him £23,000 and he'd only had it for 23 hours before he wrote it off – bent it in half round a lamp post. Or the time he was driving a Bedford Midi van and nodded off in the outside lane of the motorway and peeled the side of the van off like a can opener on a tin.

His friend Martin 'Fergie' Ferguson remembers another. "He once tried to see how far he could get his mum's Land Rover down a footpath but it eventually narrowed so much he got stuck between two walls. Reversing it back out caused a hell of a lot of damage so we went round to a mate who had a bodywork shop and we were all working on it until five in the morning. It was perfect apart from a tiny scratch on the rear light. We ordered one but couldn't get it on the Sunday. We didn't worry because we were sure no one would notice anyway. But Tony did notice it, straight away, and DJ found himself once again having to concoct a story to pacify his dad."

John McGuinness also witnessed DJ's madcap driving. "I remember him driving *through* a fuckin' roundabout on the Heysham bypass in a Range Rover with massive tyres on it. Instead of driving round the roundabout he just drove straight through it – through the bushes, through everything – straight over the middle of the roundabout! That was Dave."

Even when he wasn't actually crashing cars, trucks or lorries, DJ wasn't the most conventional driver. Dave's family had given him HGV driving lessons for his 21st birthday present and once he passed his test he could not only drive the huge team trucks to races, he could also help his old friend Karl Smith in his line of work. "He used to help out driving big Scania articulated trucks and there was one journey that always took an hour, no matter which way you went," Smith remembers. "One morning Dave did it in about 38 minutes. We used to overload the trucks to 40 tonnes instead of 38 so I couldn't understand how he did it so fast. It turned out he'd ignored the signs on a little back road that said only trucks under seven tonnes could use it. No-one had ever dared do that before but DJ didn't think twice."

After passing his HGV test, Jefferies eventually bought himself a Volvo F12 Globetrotter articulated lorry cab that he sometimes drove to race meetings. John McGuinness remembers one occasion in 2002 when DJ unwittingly shut down all the power to the Oulton Park paddock after an alcohol-fuelled stunt demonstration in his truck. "It was one of our mad parties after the races," he says. "We were all pissed up. There was me, DJ, Glen Richards, Jim Moodie and all our girlfriends – and the crack was great. We were all parked on the grass and the next thing I knew Dave had got this flippin' big Volvo F12 Globetrotter on the grass doing big slides, burnouts, and big donuts. This was way over the top as usual – it had enough spotlights to light up White City, a big straight-through exhaust stack, side skirts, limited slip diff, enough bull bars to make a climbing frame – in fact, probably ready to take on Steve Parrish in a truck race.

"Anyway, he's doing these donuts and he's getting closer and closer to Casey Stoner's coach [2007 MotoGP World Champion who raced in the UK early in his career]. He had a bloody big coach at the time, and Dave's spinning was getting ever closer to smacking it. I'm like,

'Whooo – that was close' – then he burns off and he gets on the tarmac. Steve Brogan was sitting in the cab with him. Dave was going round and round until eventually he hit this massive electrics box, smashing it to pieces and lighting up the sky big style, shutting down the power. DJ made a hasty retreat out of the paddock, parked up and sat in his caravan while all the circuit people ran round asking which idiot was that. Of course, nobody had seen anything.

"This must have been about five in the morning so I left everyone to it and went to bed. Big mistake. When I came out in the morning I thought 'Where's my flippin' garden furniture? Where are all my tables and chairs?' All I could see was this load of ashes and a pile of burnt hinges and screws. I thought, 'Hmm, that'll be my garden furniture. They had fired the lot while I was asleep. Bastards!'"

* * *

After his experience of riding the GSX-R750 in the Suzuki World Cup, Jefferies knew his future lay in Superbikes. Not only was he physically more suited to the largest capacity class in motorcycle racing, but it represented the pinnacle of racing in the UK at the time, as it still does today. Grand Prix racing was the pinnacle of the sport but the World Superbike Championship – still only in its fifth year in 1992 – was growing in importance and popularity and if a rider proved themselves on a Superbike at British national level, he stood a good chance of earning a ride on the world scene in World Superbikes. This was David Jefferies's master plan.

Riding a near stock, ex-Brian Morrison 750cc OW01 Yamaha with sponsorship from Datatool, he aimed to contest the two major Superbike Championships in the UK. Before the single British Superbike Championship (BSB) format was created in 1996 there were always at least two different series held in Britain, even though, rather confusingly, most of the top riders were entered in each. It was a messy format for the fans, teams and riders alike, and why both series were not consolidated into one meaningful championship at a much earlier date remains a mystery. Whatever the case, the two main championships for 1992 were the British

Supercup Championship – which enjoyed occasional television coverage – and the MCN TT Superbike Championship. John Reynolds, riding for Team Green Kawasaki would win both, but David Jefferies would post some superb performances during his debut year on a Superbike and prove that this was the class in which he belonged.

Jefferies's season kicked off at an extremely wet Thruxton on 29 March with the opening round of the TT Superbike Championship. The grim conditions saw the racing being delayed, and when it did get underway at 3pm both Superbike legs were reduced to ten laps each. With many of the front runners crashing out in the tricky conditions, David kept his cool and took eighth and 11th place finishes, which earned him 13 championship points.

His results improved at Snetterton in April where he finished seventh and then fifth after getting the better of factory Norton rider and TT winner Trevor Nation.

The first round of the partially televised Supercup series took place at Donington Park on 24 May and sixth and seventh in the two legs meant Jefferies left the Leicestershire track in fourth place in the points standings. His results were the more impressive given that he'd had to start from the fourth row of the grid due to a chain snapping in qualifying.

Consistently the best privateer in both the leading domestic Superbike Championships, Jefferies took eighth and ninth at the Mallory Supercup round, ninth and seventh at the Knockhill round of the TT Superbikes and seventh and tenth at the Snetterton Supercup.

After a brilliant start at the second Mallory round, DJ was battling with the factory riders in second place and looked set to record the best result of his career. He had overtaken riders of the calibre of Rob McElnea, John Reynolds, Robert Dunlop and Brian Morrison to lie runner-up when, perhaps a little over-excited at being at the very sharp end of the field, he pushed that bit too hard, lost the front and crashed out.

After beating Sean Emmett for the position of best privateer in the opening Supercup leg at Cadwell, Jefferies suffered his first mechanical fault of the season on the way to the line for the second leg and had to sit out the race. Even so, he still comfortably led the privateers' championship.

Another mechanical DNF followed at the Silverstone TT Superbike round but once the carburettor problem was traced and solved, DJ romped through the rain to take 12th in the second leg.

Jefferies finished seventh and eighth at the televised Oulton Park Supercup round before heading back to Oliver's Mount – scene of his debut national victory one year earlier – to race in the circuit's most prestigious event, the Gold Cup meeting. There was a strong family history of success at this event, with David's father Tony having won in 1970 and uncle Nick taking the honours in 1990. The impressive Gold Cup, from which the meeting takes its name, had been claimed by some legendary names since the first meeting in 1950. That inaugural event was won by Geoff Duke who had been a sparring partner of Jefferies's grandfather, and the cup was also the last trophy Barry Sheene won shortly before retiring at the end of 1984.

Many of Jefferies's friends came from a motocross background and had never been to see a road race. They found themselves invited to Oliver's Mount and were gob-smacked at what their friend could do on a road race bike. "David invited us along to watch at Scarborough," says Adam Evans, who had met David through schoolboy motocross. "We were stood in the woods on the rollercoaster section down towards the finish line and he came flying along this bloody little narrow path at about 140mph, on the back wheel going over the jumps and still managed to wave at us in the woods. We were like 'Concentrate you stupid bastard! Look where you're going!'

"My sister asked him what the plastic things on his knees (his knee sliders) were for and if he used them. She didn't believe he would be touching the ground with his knee at those sort of speeds. So DJ got a marker pen and wrote 'Kim' on one slider and her boyfriend's name 'Dan' on the other. He came back after the race and handed them to her and there wasn't a name to be seen – the entire sliders were worn away."

Suitably impressed, DJ's friends watched him become the third Jefferies family member to win the prestigious Gold Cup trophy after he forced British Superbike star and close Yorkshire neighbour, Jamie

Whitham, into making a mistake and out-braking himself. A second place in the second leg was enough to give David the overall win and he also collected the Geoff Barry award for being top non-factory rider in the two International 750 races, both of which he finished in second place.

One week later, Jefferies temporarily relinquished the title of non-factory rider when he became an official JPS Norton team member. The team, running British-built rotary-engined machines, had set the British race scene alight with riders like Ron Haslam, Steve Spray, Trevor Nation and Robert Dunlop proving more than a match for the Japanese competition, and few who heard the evocative sound of the 588cc rotaries howling their way round British tracks will ever forget them. To cap it all, Steve Hislop had taken a Norton to victory in the Senior TT earlier that year in what was one of the TT's greatest fairy tale victories, and the first time a Norton had won the Senior TT since Mike Hailwood's victory way back in 1961.

While Hislop's effort had been run on a shoestring budget, the official JPS Norton squad had been one of the top teams in British racing for several years and for David to be offered a ride in the final Supercup meeting at Brands Hatch, just one day after turning 20, was a true measure of his talent. The ride came about after team regular Ron Haslam had failed a fitness test and was ruled out of the final round. JPS Norton team manager, Barry Symmons – who had spent many years as Honda Britain team boss, working with the likes of Wayne Gardner, Joey Dunlop and Roger Marshal – hand-picked David for the ride and was extremely complimentary about his first efforts on the Norton in practice. "I've been very impressed with David's riding. He has adapted to the bike very quickly. His riding style is very similar to Wayne Gardner when he was younger." Since Wayne Gardner had gone on to become 500cc Grand Prix World Champion in 1987 and is one of the sport's true legends, this was praise indeed.

Sadly, things didn't go smoothly for DJ in his first factory ride. The Norton was blindingly fast but unlike any other machine on the grid to ride, thanks to the unique characteristics of its rotary engine. With some private tests under his belt before the race weekend, Jefferies would no doubt have fared much better but, as it was, he was thrown in at the deep end and ended up twice taking the slow route back to pit lane. The first time was not his fault as the Norton seized in practice but, after starting from ninth spot on the grid, he overcooked it while running in eighth place and crashed out of the race. This time some stones were sucked into the motor and since it couldn't be fixed in time for the second leg, Jefferies was forced to finish his Supercup season on his trusty Datatool Yamaha.

Despite having to start from the back row of the grid – since he had qualified on the Norton and not the Yamaha – DJ rode superbly to cut through the field and take ninth place at the chequered flag and seventh place overall in the championship points standings at the end of the year.

Disappointingly, Jefferies would never get the chance to see what he could really have achieved, given some time on the fickle Norton – funds ran out and the team folded after the 1992 season.

There were also non-championship races to be contested throughout the 1992 season and DJ was, usually, the best-placed privateer. Two tenth places at Donington in August were backed up by a ninth and tenth in a round of the German Pro-Superbike Championship at the same meeting. An eighth and sixth in the two legs of the Mallory Park Race of the Year were followed by two fifths at the Stars of Darley meeting at Darley Moor, which gave Jefferies fourth overall in the annual event.

Jefferies's championship season culminated at the Brands Hatch International Power Bike meeting on 18 October. A 14th place in leg one and tenth in leg two gave him eighth position in the MCN TT Superbike Championship and once again he was the top privateer in the series. Throughout the year David had been mixing it with the factory riders in the upper echelons of the top ten and it was clear that to progress any further, he too would need factory support.

The final meeting of the season was the Donington Anglo/French Invitation event which saw a team of British riders, including future Grand Prix star Jeremy McWilliams, Jefferies and Andy Ward, take on a hand-picked team of French riders, none of whom were exactly household names in the UK, even amongst race fans. Nevertheless,

McWilliams, Ward and Jefferies finished first, second and third respectively to complete an all-British podium and raise some much-needed money for the Save the Children charity. It was a good end to what had been a promising debut season in Superbikes for Jefferies and, once again, as winter approached his thoughts turned to finding more competitive machinery for the season ahead.

By establishing himself as the best Superbike privateer in the UK, Jefferies had exceeded his expectations of the 1992 season. He had taken part in 47 races and scored 36 top ten places. Perhaps even more impressive was both David's – and the OW01's – consistency. He only suffered one mechanical breakdown on the bike he prepared and maintained himself all year, and only crashed twice – once on the Yamaha and once on the Norton. Given that crashing is an accepted part of the job for motorcycle racers and that most can expect to fall off up to ten times a year (for some, that figure is much higher), it was a remarkably consistent and mature season for a rider who had just turned 20 in the latter part of the year. His performance led Andy Smith from Yamaha UK to observe that, "David Jefferies is a name to watch. He rides with a maturity which belies his age, he is a credit to his team and his team is a credit to him."

In the extremely professional portfolio David and his father compiled each year in a bid to attract sponsorship, the pair made a bold prediction at the end of 1992. 'Give David a competitive machine' it read, 'and he will be the 1993 750cc British Road Racing Champion.'

As things turned out, he would never get the chance to be British champion in 1993. By the mid-point of the season, in just his fourth year of racing, Jefferies would find himself being whisked out of the UK to ride at the pinnacle of motorcycle sport in the 500cc Grand Prix World Championships, racing against the heroes he only knew from the posters on his bedroom wall. This racing lark was getting serious.

* * *

The costs of motorcycle racing spiral at an alarming rate as a rider moves up the classes. If 1991 would end up costing around £15,000, then the predicted budget for a season in British Superbike racing in 1993 was close to £100,000. A breakdown of those predicted costs makes interesting reading and emphasises the crucial need for sponsors:

Set-Up Costs

Yamaha YZF750 race bike	£7,000
Yamaha YZF750 (for engine only)	£7,000
Chassis preparation	£1,000
Engine race kit (x2)	£6,000
Engine specialist tuning	£3,000
Wheels, discs etc (x8)	£4,000
Exhaust systems	£800
Spares kit (engine)	£6,000
Spares kit (chassis)	£3,000
Paintwork	£1,000

Running Costs

Tyres	£6,000
Fuel	£1,200
Plugs, chains, oil, brake pads, consumables	£2,000

Riding Equipment

Leathers (x2), helmets (x3), boots & gloves	£2,300

Transport & Travel

Motorhome running costs	£1,500
Transporter (initial cost)	£15,000
Transporter fuel	£1,200
Shipping	£4,000

General

Mechanic's salary	£7,500
Entry fees/licences	£1,500
Team subsistence (days away)	£4,000
Administration	£5,000

TOTAL:	£96,000

It's sobering stuff, considering this is for a one-rider, private team and not a full-blown, two-rider factory effort. The plan for 1993 was once again to contest the Supercup and 750cc British championships on one of the new model Yamaha YZF750s, as well as selected European rounds of World Superbikes where these did not clash with British commitments.

With backing from leather manufacturer Akito, Jefferies headed to Brands Hatch for his first race of the year that also happened to be his first in the World Superbike Championship. Somewhat bizarrely, the race held at the Kent track was officially dubbed the Irish round of the championship. Ireland, although a nation of passionate and knowledgeable bike racing fans, did not boast any circuits deemed to be fit for World Championship racing (holding, as they do, most of their races on closed public roads). So Brands became a little slice of the Emerald Isle for the weekend. The other reason for a third round being held here, on top of the Donington round and another at Brands later in the season, was that Britain's Carl Fogarty stood a realistic chance of lifting his first WSB title after winning a race at Donington the year before and having now become a regular winner. Consequently, success-starved British race fans had gone WSB crazy and the series became more popular in this country than in any other. To this day, the Brands Hatch round remains the biggest event on the WSB calendar.

Jefferies's World Championship debut came on 2 May at a horrendously wet Brands Hatch. In fact, many riders said those were the worst conditions they had ever raced in and many fell victim to the waterlogged track. Again showing his maturity, DJ was the only British rider – Carl Fogarty included – to stay on board and finish both legs, taking a ninth place in race one and 14th in race two. It was a promising start and set DJ up nicely for the start of his British championship campaign that got underway at Knockhill in Scotland – once again in treacherous conditions.

It was fast becoming apparent that wet conditions suited David as they provided a more level playing field between his own and the plethora of factory bikes on the grid. Since factory bikes can't use their brutal power so much in the wet, smoothness and consistency become more important than highly tuned engines and DJ was able to show that, when his rivals' machinery advantage was largely removed, he was as fast as any of them. And he proved this beyond doubt when he won his first British Championship Superbike race at Knockhill.

After an incorrect tyre choice had left him floundering in 14th place in the first leg, Jefferies made a blinding start in the second to lead home the likes of Steve Hislop, Rob McElnea, Jamie Whitham and his former Superteen sparring partner, Michael Rutter. Even more impressive was the fact that DJ beat such experienced riders by a margin of over ten seconds. It was, without doubt, the best performance of his career so far. After the race, he explained, "In the first race we were looking at the weather and it just started to drizzle a bit. The track was still reasonably dry so we put some intermediate tyres on. But it was a bad choice as it just got wetter, so we tried to stay on and gain some points and thought we'd go for it in the second race."

DJ put his debut win down to a keen observation of the starting lights that enabled him to get the holeshot on his rivals. In MotoGP, Valentino Rossi famously watches the starts of 125cc Grand Prix races to gain some idea of how long the red light takes to turn to green. This time-interval varies from circuit to circuit, so wise campaigners like to get an idea of how long they will be held on the line so they can better gauge their start. It worked for DJ at Knockhill. "I'd been watching the starts of the races and they hadn't been very consistent," he said. "So I thought once I got on the line I'd just sit and concentrate on the green light and as soon as the green light goes, I'll go. There was a rider distracted on the line and I think some of the other riders were watching him. I just carried on staring at the lights and as soon as they changed I just went."

The miserable British weather continued to play havoc with the year's racing calendar at Oliver's Mount where, after a delayed start because of rain, Jefferies suffered a mystery misfire in both Superbike races and could only manage a brace of second places, although he did have the satisfaction of passing uncle Nick on the last corner of the last lap in the first race.

The team then headed for Mallory Park hoping they had cured the misfire and DJ had another two good British Championship rides to score fourth and fifth, once again getting the better of some of the factory teams. An oil leak caused a rare mechanical DNF in the first leg at Snetterton and the team packed up for the four-hour drive home to rebuild the seized engine in readiness for the opening H.E.A.T. Supercup round at Oulton Park. This was to be televised on *Sunday Grandstand* on BBC2.

Carl Fogarty had entered the race to give his home fans a chance to see him in action but he caused the first race to be stopped after crashing out on the second lap. In the re-run, Jefferies held second place behind Jamie Whitham until the dying stages of the race when former Grand Prix star Rob McElnea found a way past. Still, third place was another solid performance, although elation soon turned to despair when the mystery misfire reared its head again in leg two, forcing DJ out of the wet race. He wasn't alone. Of the 32 qualifiers, only 12 riders finished the race, such were the conditions.

There was more bad fortune in store at round four at Donington when David tangled with a backmarker in practice and badly injured his left hand. Derby hospital patched him up on Sunday, then he saw a specialist on Monday and went under the knife for corrective surgery. It meant he not only missed out on the chance of any points at Donington, but would also have to sit out the planned trip to Spain for the Albacete World Superbike round the following weekend.

Within a month however, DJ was back at Donington for the second round of the Supercup. Once again, the pace was hot, thanks largely to the presence of Fogarty, but DJ and the rest of the field upped their game in trying to follow him. Lap times were over a second faster than those set at the last British round held at the circuit. DJ came away with two eighth places to consolidate his seventh position overall in the championship. Once again he was the top privateer, but still no factory machinery was forthcoming. People were taking notice however, and one man in particular was keeping a keen eye on the progress of the burly lad from Shipley. And he held the keys to a much more glamorous and wealthy motorcycle championship…

The eternally unpredictable British weather sprang another surprise for round five of the British Superbike Championship as blazing sunshine bathed the Brands Hatch circuit all weekend. DJ had two tremendous battles with the hugely experienced Rob McElnea who had been team-mates to legendary riders including Kevin Schwantz and Eddie Lawson in 500cc Grands Prix in the 1980s. He may have been in the twilight of his career, but McElnea was still riding superbly and for David to challenge him throughout both races on a private Yamaha (as opposed to Rob Mac's factory-supported Fast Orange Yamaha) was further proof that he should have been given a factory ride himself.

Sixth and fifth place finishes moved DJ up to sixth overall in the points standings. He would not, however, get the opportunity to improve on that position as an offer had just come through that DJ simply couldn't refuse – would he like to ride in the remaining six rounds of the 500cc World Championship as a replacement for New Zealander Simon Crafar? Jefferies didn't need to be asked twice.

Chapter 4

THE BIG TIME

"I said we'd need to sleep on the seats in the grandstand – welcome to the big time David – welcome to Grands Prix!"
Dave Greenham, GP mechanic

First held in 1949, the Grand Prix World Championships were intended to be the very pinnacle of motorcycle road racing where the world's best riders, bikes and teams would compete for the ultimate prize – the 500cc championship of the world. The names that have claimed that prize are the definitive who's who of motorcycle racing. From the first winner, Les Graham, through the likes of Geoff Duke, John Surtees, Mike Hailwood, Giacomo Agostini, Phil Read, Barry Sheene, Kenny Roberts, Freddie Spencer and Mick Doohan to the Italian genius Valentino Rossi.

There have been several different support classes through the years including 50, 80, 125, 250 and 350cc, but the premier event was always the 500cc class, right up until 2002 when this switched from two-stroke 500cc machines to 990cc four-strokes. With that came a change in name to MotoGP, but the class remains the ultimate. So for a 20-year-old lad from Yorkshire to be given the chance to race against his own heroes was like manna from heaven and Jefferies jumped at it. With hindsight, he may have jumped too quickly.

Grand Prix racing is not judged as the pinnacle of the sport for nothing. The top teams have the direct support of the manufacturers, with hundreds of dedicated staff working behind the scenes to design, build and develop the fastest prototype motorcycles in the world. These thoroughbred racing machines bear no resemblance to the production bikes that the man or woman in the street can buy – and essentially what Jefferies had been racing for the last two seasons. Racing budgets are almost unlimited. It costs millions to fund a season of GP racing if a team is to be competitive, which by definition restricts the field. So much so that in 1993 grids needed to be boosted by lesser teams who would buy or lease bikes from the major manufacturers and go racing on a privateer level. They couldn't hope to compete with the big guns but the idea was that if a privateer rider proved his worth on a lesser machine, he would be given the chance in a works team.

Within this collection of private and semi-works teams there was a strict hierarchy. Some received help, support and funding from the factories or big-time sponsors while others really were privateers in the truest sense of the word. Peter Graves's team was privateer. It's no reflection on Graves's enthusiasm (he was an active racer himself at the time), but his YZR500 Yamahas were as standard as they came and the budget was simply not there to put in the amount of testing and development work necessary to make the machinery more competitive. Jefferies knew this, but he was also aware of another hard fact: rides in Grands Prix are like gold dust and may only come along once in a rider's lifetime. If he passed up the opportunity now, there might never be another chance. He accepted the challenge and, in doing so, became the youngest British rider in history to earn a GP ride.

In a roundabout way, Jefferies had the wayward American rider John Kocinski to thank for being given the biggest opportunity of his career. A brilliant rider, Kocinski also had the reputation for being difficult and wildly eccentric. He once blamed a fish for causing a crash during a practice session and was questioned by police for cleaning his sofa on his front lawn in the middle of the night "to avoid getting the house dirty".

When Kocinski parted company with Suzuki in the 250cc World Championship after a bust-up with his team, Peter Graves's rider, Simon Crafar, was offered the factory ride. "I got the ride when John Kocinski threw his usual wobbly when riding the Lucky Strike 250 Suzuki at the Assen round," DJ said. "Simon then went over to Suzuki and I got the Yamaha ride."

David would be forced to miss two Supercup championship rounds as well as the Dutch and British WSB rounds but both he and his father rightly realised that the experience he could gain by racing against the very best in the world, even if he was on an inferior mount, would more than make up for it. He would have to keep punching above his weight if he wanted to get to the top.

In the early 1990s, Grand Prix grids had dwindled to an alarming level. Sometimes just 14 riders started a race, and with points being allocated down to 15th position, it meant that even the slowest rider was guaranteed points. The organisers employed various tactics to attract more entries and one was the option of buying 'customer' bikes from Yamaha. These were nowhere near as competitive as the full-on factory versions but they would still give good riders a chance to show what they could do.

Several new privateer teams sprang up. Peter Graves's squad was one of these. "We were the lowest budget team in the GP paddock and that included the 125cc teams," remembers team mechanic Dave Greenham.

The team was also the smallest. "Peter Graves came to only one race – the British GP – because he was racing in Superbikes. So David never had a team manager to guide him. There was only me, a girl called Debbie, and DJ – that was the whole GP team."

Greenham insists that the bike itself would have been capable of decent finishes if the correct back-up had been in place and if the rider was experienced enough. "The Harris Yamahas were reasonably competitive – certainly capable of getting within a couple of seconds a lap of the slower factory riders," he says. "Sadly, our team didn't have the resources or the budget to be that competitive. At the Grand Prix before DJ came along we had Simon Crafar on board and he was the second privateer at Assen – I think he finished eighth behind Niall Mackenzie. So the bikes did have top ten potential, but of course David had to learn how to ride a 500cc two-stroke Grand Prix bike and he had to learn the circuits and the tyres, and all the rest. It was particularly difficult for him because he joined the team half way through the season when everybody else was up and running. It was a real baptism of fire for DJ."

In order to be able to race in GPs, David had to attend an IRTA (International Race Teams Association) test at Misano in Italy in the week leading up to what would be his debut Grand Prix at Mugello. He caught a flight from Manchester, and Greenham flew from London, the plan being to meet up at the circuit and sleep in the team's motorhome. The pair arrived at the track only to find the motorhome hadn't turned up – and nor had anyone else. "We arrived at Misano expecting to meet the team, but there was no one around – the paddock was completely empty," says Greenham. "There had obviously been a miscommunication. It was about 10 or 11pm and neither of us spoke any Italian. We didn't know how to get a B&B or anything, so I nodded towards the main grandstand and said to David, 'I guess that looks as good as anywhere.' He said, 'What do you mean?' I said we'd need to sleep on the seats in the grandstand – there was nothing else for it. I used a rucksack for a pillow and David had a little overnight bag that he used, but we didn't have any blankets or anything. As we put our heads down and tried to get to sleep, I remember saying, 'Welcome to the big time David – welcome to Grands Prix!'"

David spent two days getting used to the Yamaha at the test. He found that Crafar had established a good base setting and decided not to stray too far from that, given his limited knowledge of setting up a hugely complex thoroughbred racing motorcycle. With the handlebars, footrests and seat height all set to his liking, DJ then made the 100-mile drive to Mugello to compete in his maiden Grand Prix. It would also be the first time he had raced in such extreme conditions.

Being a Yorkshireman, Jefferies was not accustomed to riding in 90° heat and he soon found himself exhausted by the oppressive conditions, ending his first session in 27th place. He also struggled with the GP-spec carbon fibre brakes that were completely new to him. Accustomed to riding with steel brakes, Jefferies found the carbon models too vicious and reverted to his favoured system, but this lost him precious track time and he dropped to 29th place in final qualifying.

David approached the race itself cautiously and rode steadily throughout to work his way up to a respectable 17th place, just two places outside the points. Apart from being his first GP, it was his first time at the circuit, his first time on a 500cc machine, his first ride with the team, and his first time riding on GP-spec tyres. The aim had been to simply finish the race and so DJ and the team were happy to have done so when many others didn't – even if the incredible pace of the GP front-runners was proven by David being some six seconds a lap slower. But it was all that could be expected, given the package he had, and spirits were high as the squad packed up and prepared for the long drive back home for the British Grand Prix at Donington Park. At least there, DJ would know the circuit and be better suited to the weather conditions.

Before that, however, it was back to British championship duties on the 750 Yamaha at Cadwell Park. Jefferies was stunned to find how heavy and slow his Superbike felt after riding the GP bike, and a crash in practice hampered his qualifying and saw him start from 11th on the grid. Even worse was to follow in the race when he found himself last away from the start. Undeterred, Jefferies got his head down and started scything his way through the pack. By mid-race he was up to seventh behind his uncle Nick and, after passing him, he rode steadily to take fifth place at the flag. DJ made another poor start in the second leg and was held up in mid-pack traffic for most of the race, meaning he could only salvage 10th place. It was still good enough to leave him in eighth place in the championship as he now focused on his first ever British Grand Prix.

After finishing Friday practice in 27th place, Jefferies upped his pace for Saturday's final qualifying session. Unfortunately, his enthusiasm at passing World Champion Wayne Rainey led to him crashing at Goddards and, though there was little damage to man or machine, this meant that DJ could not improve on his qualifying time and he was once again bumped down to 29th place on the grid.

The first lap of the race saw the infamous crash involving Mick Doohan, Alex Barros and Kevin Schwantz and, while it provided a field day for photographers, it proved an unwelcome obstacle for Jefferies. He was forced to ride onto the grass to avoid hitting any of the stricken riders and lost precious time – something riders simply can't afford to do in the white hot competition of Grand Prix racing. DJ eventually finished in 20th place and was pleased enough to have scored two finishes from two GP starts, but he was now realising that GP racing was so fiercely competitive that one small mistake – which could be made up for in a British championship race – was enough to rule a rider out of the results at the top level. Jefferies was by no means the first British rider to realise the yawning chasm that exists between domestic and World Championship racing. The fact that the last Brit to win a championship in the premier Grand Prix class was Barry Sheene way back in 1977 proves just how tough it is. Since then many great names, including Carl Fogarty, Niall Mackenzie, Ron Haslam, Rob McElnea, Chris Walker and Neil Hodgson, tried and failed to win races at this premier level and DJ, disappointed not to have fared better at his home GP, was discovering why.

Jefferies competed in the remaining four rounds of the 500cc World Championship in 1993 but failed to score any points. Even so, his performances impressed the team. "I thought the lap times he was turning in were very, very respectable," says Dave Greenham. "I don't think he disappointed anybody. He had six starts and finished all six races and, while he wasn't at the front of the privateers' group, he was by no means at the back."

Jefferies learned a lot from the experience that would not be wasted in his later career. For one thing, he was struck by the level of professionalism that sets GP racing apart from any other championship. The paddock is laid out with military precision, each motor home having an allocated place in a perfectly neat line and all being required to be sparkling clean in order to lend the paddock a classier look. There was to be no rocking up in a travel-stained truck and parking wherever one fancied, as may have been the case back then at some British meetings. David also learned a vast amount about setting up bikes. As built-for-purpose thoroughbreds, GP machines are infinitely adjustable compared to the production-based Superbikes DJ was more accustomed to riding, and riders without the technical ability that David had always shown could easily have lost their way. Instead, DJ absorbed the technical tricks of the trade and benefited from the input of former GP star Ron Haslam who helped him in this direction.

A 19th place at Brno was followed by 22nd at Misano, but that weekend was momentous to DJ for another reason. Most bike racers, however famous, started out as bike racing fans and he was as starry-eyed as any other race fanatic would be to line up on a grid containing many of his racing heroes. Chief amongst those was the factory Honda rider Mick Doohan. The Australian would go on to win five back-to-back 500cc World Championships before a monumental crash ended his career in 1999. Never one to mince his words, Doohan's reputation off the track was almost as fearsome as that on it. So when he and Jefferies had a coming together during practice at Misano and both ended up running into the gravel trap, DJ expected to receive a bit of verbal, even though he felt the accident had been the Australian's fault. When he saw Doohan making straight for him in the paddock, his fears seemed to be confirmed. It was a huge surprise then, when Doohan patted Jefferies on the back and said, "Sorry about that mate. My fault. No harm done I hope?" David was thrilled that the most successful motorcycle racer of the Nineties, and one of the best of all time, had taken the trouble to hunt him out and apologise. He would always list that moment as one of the most cherished of his career.

David's next GP outing was at Laguna Seca in California and 16th place would prove to be the highest he would ever achieve in his short GP career. In a field of 29 it was a good result for a rider with only three years' experience and one who was on the least competitive package in the paddock. And with legs as stiff as DJ's were on race day, he was lucky to finish at all, as Dave Greenham explains. "He was a big guy and he could ride a motorbike, but he never had the best level of fitness as I found out when we went for a jog round Laguna Seca. I was 32 years old at the time and hadn't run for about a year. David was only about 20, but after 20 minutes of running he was asking if we could turn back – he was knackered. We kept going but he gradually dropped back until I couldn't see him any more.

"When I got back to the hotel, Neil Hodgson was there (the future WSB champion was riding in 125cc Grands Prix that year) and asked if I had been for a run on my own. I told him no – DJ had been with me, so Neil says 'Oh, is DJ in the shower then?' And I said 'No, he's not back yet.' Then DJ appeared, his face as red as a tomato and the veins in his neck ready to pop. Neil couldn't believe it. He said, 'No way would my mechanic beat me back from a jog – I'd burst my heart, but I wouldn't let him beat me back.' Next day, DJ was so stiff; he could hardly get his leg over the bike. His legs had seized up. It was so funny. He said, 'I'm never bloody doing that again before a race!'"

In what was to be the final GP of his career, the FIM Grand Prix in Spain, DJ would finish 18th, again frustratingly just outside the points, though he would later say of his six races in GPs, "I really enjoyed it and it was an amazing experience."

In between his GP commitments, Jefferies continued to race on home soil and he was given a master class by TT hero Steve Hislop at the sixth round of the British championship at Cadwell Park on 17 August. After leading the early stages of the race, Hislop ran wide, allowing most of the pack to overtake him. The Scot then set about regaining ground. When he passed Jefferies, the Yorkshireman was determined to follow him on his charge up the leaderboard. Jefferies buried himself in Hislop's slipstream and followed his every move as the more experienced rider carved his way through the pack. He managed to stick with Hizzy right to the end of the race and even followed his lead by diving up the inside of Michael Rutter on the last lap. Given enough time, Hislop could well have won the race – he often excelled when rattled and was clearly on a mission here – but there simply weren't enough laps and he had to settle for seventh, with Jefferies right behind him in eighth after his private riding lesson.

In the second leg, David was locked in a battle with his Grand Prix team boss Peter Graves for most of the race, eventually getting the better of him to take his second eighth place of the day. A sixth place and a DNF caused by the still persistent mystery misfire (eventually traced to spark plug breakdown and cured by fitting harder plugs) rounded out the British championships at Mallory Park to leave him in ninth place overall.

To finish the season, DJ headed to the Macau Grand Prix for the first time. Held on a 3.8-mile street circuit in the former Portuguese colony of Macau, on the coast of China, the race – a Grand Prix in name only and nothing to do with the official World Championship – has long been a traditional way to end the season, with a well-earned holiday in Thailand bolted on to the end of the race weekend. Jefferies's GP mechanic, Dave Greenham, had been invited along on the trip to work on David's Superbike for the first time. He remembers being shocked at how badly set up it was. "At the time, he wasn't the best rider for giving feedback," says Greenham. "When we went to Macau in 1993, Nick Jefferies followed Dave round in one session and came into the garage and asked me what the hell was wrong with Dave's bike. He said it looked terrible, that it was bouncing everywhere – the back end just wasn't working.

"When Dave came in, I asked him what he thought of the bike and he said, 'Oh, it's fantastic. Great.' That was the first time I'd worked on Dave's Superbike so I pushed the tailpiece down to check the rear suspension and it was absolutely solid. I asked Dave what the hell he'd done with the rear suspension and he said, 'That's the way I've raced it all year.' And he won on it in the wet at Knockhill! It was horrendous – I've no idea how he could have ridden a bike like that. I fiddled with the suspension for a few minutes and told him to go and try the bike again. When he came back in he said, 'Wow, that's incredible – there's nowhere near as many bumps out there now!'"

Jefferies didn't last long enough in the race to feel the benefits of a well set-up bike, as Tony remembers. "When he came round Lisboa corner, two riders had crashed in front of David leaving him nowhere to go. He crashed into them and his race was over."

His non-score didn't dampen DJ's spirits and Dave Greenham remembers one particular night when Jefferies got another master class from Steve Hislop – this time in a Mini Moke jeep on a lap of the Macau circuit. "Steve was driving and it's fair to say he'd been drinking a bit," says Greenham. "DJ was in the passenger seat, Simon Beck, Lee Pullan and me were in the back, and a cameraman from Greenlight Television was seated on the parcel shelf facing backwards with his feet on the bumper. This was at about 2.30am; Hizzy was giving us a running commentary while, to the best of his ability, he tried to keep on the racing line while revving the tits off this thing in every single gear, and trying to avoid parked cars and oncoming traffic. The tyres were absolutely screeching round every corner and the cameraman was often thrown forward into the front seat under braking. It was a fantastic experience – hideously funny – but it could have all gone so wrong."

It had been an eventful year and as DJ celebrated his 21st birthday in September by passing his HGV test, he could reflect on the fact that he had scored points in World Superbikes, the British Championship and the Supercup Championship, and had contested the final six Grands Prix of the season. He had finished each one of them to give him a 100% record – a feat matched by no other rider that season. He had earned his reputation as Britain's best rising star in the Superbike class and now had a wealth of experience under his belt. The only question was: what was he to do with it all in 1994?

* * *

By 1994 the World Superbike Championship was in its seventh year and rivalling Grands Prix as the most popular form of motorcycle sport – at least in the UK. The reason for that was down to one man: Carl Fogarty. With no British rider to shout for in GPs, and with the 500cc class becoming more and more dominated by Mick Doohan, British race fans turned their attention to WSB where they could not only cheer for one of their own (Fogarty had a very realistic chance of winning the title after getting so close in 1993), but could usually witness much closer racing than that seen in GPs. And as an added bonus, the racers would be mounted on bikes very much like those the fans rode themselves since the championship caters for production-based machinery rather than thoroughbred prototype race bikes built specially for Grands Prix.

Jefferies had acquitted himself well in GPs. Without doubt, he could have started breaking into the points had he been given another year on the YZR500, but his results were not good enough to secure him a top flight factory ride and without one of those there's little point in contesting the world's most elite bike racing series. Jefferies knew this and set about looking for more realistic alternatives, and it was in World Superbikes that he saw his future. "That's where racing is going," he predicted, "and large four-stroke bikes suit me really well."

The plan for 1994 had been to contest the WSB championship on the same Yamaha YZF750 he'd run in 1993 but with another bike as back-up and, for the first time, the luxury of a full-time paid mechanic. Tony and David calculated they could contest the full series for around £95,000 – a fraction of what the factory Ducati, Honda and Suzuki teams were spending but enough, perhaps, to allow David to get himself noticed by those very teams in the hope that they might sign him up in future years.

As things turned out, DJ would remain in the UK for the 1994 season as the money could not be raised to go World Championship racing. Instead, he would ride a Ducati 888 with backing from Akito in the British Superbike Championship. It may have been a disappointment to be staying at home after travelling round the world in Grands Prix, but 1994 would turn out to be an important stepping-stone back onto the world stage.

Perhaps the most significant moment in Jefferies's 1994 season came early on in the year when he travelled across the Irish Sea to take part in his first ever 'real' road race. While Oliver's Mount was a parkland circuit, the North West 200 was the real McCoy.

One of the best-attended sporting events in the British Isles, the North West 200 is held over 8.9 miles of closed public roads linking the Northern Irish towns of Portrush, Portstewart and Coleraine. The race enjoys a carnival atmosphere as upwards of 150,000 people flock to the picturesque Antrim coast to watch riders notching speeds of up to 200mph between houses, walls, lamp-posts and railway bridges.

Although this was once the fastest road race in the world, speeds have been tamed in recent years with the introduction of several chicanes, but 'the triangle' still remains one of the fastest courses, with average lap speeds of over 123mph. And unlike the TT, the North West is a massed-start race that means riders are clashing elbows, knees and fairings with rivals for the entire race distance rather than just racing against the clock in solitude as they do at the TT.

Like any pure roads course, the North West is dangerous. In 2008, road racing legend Robert Dunlop became the latest in a long line of stars to lose their lives on the circuit when his bike appeared to seize at the ultra-fast Mather's Cross corner. The same corner had claimed the life of Dunlop's brother-in-law, Mervyn Robinson, back in 1980.

Other famous names to have died at the North West include GP star and TT winner Tom Herron, and Frank Kennedy who, along with Joey Dunlop and Mervyn Robinson, formed the legendary 'Armoy Armada' in the late Seventies.

Pure road racing is a very different discipline from short circuit racing but, despite the dangers, it was obvious from Jefferies's very first attempt that he was going to be a force to be reckoned with.

Tony Jefferies remembers just how surprised he was to see David challenging the leaders. "He rode there on a Ducati and he couldn't really believe that first time there he was leading a race," he says. "Unfortunately the tread broke up on the tyre and he had to retire. But we'd gone to a road race meeting and he'd been leading it. We thought, 'Well, wait a minute, he's never done this before,' and, first time on it, he set a lap record as well I think. I'm not sure. But he was leading a race and there were a lot of top men there. We suddenly thought the TT was something he ought to have a go at."

Jefferies's TT debut was still two years away but the seeds were sown at the 1994 North West 200 and they would prove to be extremely fruitful.

DJ's only wins in 1994 came at Oliver's Mount in Scarborough where he cleaned up at both the Spring Cup meeting and the end-of-season Gold Cup event. He won all his heats and races in the Superbike class at both meetings to take the Gold Cup for the second time in his career and solidify his reputation as a growing force in road racing.

One of the highlights of 1994 for Tony Jefferies was taking part in the Darley Moor Past Masters Cavalcade. Such events, where former racing stars put on demonstration races for nostalgic race fans, are held quite frequently but this was one with a difference. Instead of riding round pillion behind David and waving to the crowds, father and son hatched an altogether more ambitious plan – Tony would ride the bike while David would sit on the pillion seat and change gear via a specially made gear linkage system which allowed him to change up or down using the rear footrests. It sounds crazy, and it was.

Tony takes up the story. "We thought we'd better have a practice so we jumped on the bike and rode out of the paddock at Darley Moor onto the main road. I was on the front of the bike – it was a Triumph 1200 Daytona – and Dave was on the back shifting gears. My feet were tied onto the front footrests to stop them flapping about. As we were leaving the circuit, an official tried to stop us to let another car out but I couldn't put my feet down so I just swerved round the car and past a caravan on the wrong side of the road and up over the grass – all over the place – with the marshal shouting after us.

"Anyway, we got out onto the road and DJ just started booting up through the gears, timing it perfectly. You wouldn't have known it was two riders at the controls. Without saying anything to each other, we just had it sussed. We were giggling under our helmets but how David anticipated every gear change so perfectly was amazing.

"On the way back I decided to give it some welly so we were doing about 120mph. This was in 1994 but I had my old 1973 racing helmet on. The lining and all sorts of shit were falling out. The visor was loose so it was rattling like crazy, but we had a great laugh.

"Back at the circuit it was only meant to be a demonstration race that we were doing but once a racer, always a racer, and everyone took off from the line like they meant it. I was the same, so we really gave it some and started passing all sorts of people. I remember passing John 'Mooneyes' Cooper and Dave grabbing hold of his elbow going down the main straight, laughing like a loon. Changing direction was difficult for me because I have no movement from the chest down, so when we approached the chicane a bit too fast I just rode straight over the kerbs! Then the bloody Heath Robinson gear linkage that we'd make broke so we just left the bike in third gear and carried on.

"We didn't get passed by many people and at the end the tyres were absolutely shagged. Totally destroyed. But it was brilliant fun. There used to be a woman we called the Sweetie Lady who went to all the races in the Seventies, handing out energy sweets to the riders. When we got back to the pits she was standing there with tears streaming down her face. When I asked her why, she just said she was so overjoyed to see me back on a bike again and enjoying myself after all those years. It was the first time I'd ridden a bike on a race track since I'd been paralysed in 1973."

There were some good results for DJ in the 1994 British Championship; he took fourth places at Donington, Pembrey, Cadwell Park and Oulton on his way to seventh overall in the championship, though he never quite made it onto the podium. But he *was* on a private bike and he *was* beating a host of factory-supported riders, so when a new team started looking for a second rider to take to the World Superbike Championship in 1995, David Jefferies's name cropped up. It was time to pack the suitcases again.

Chapter 5

CRAZY FROM THE HEAT

"When he got off the bike, his eyes were rolling round in their sockets and within three minutes we had him on a drip."
Stuart Hicken, team manager

For the 1995 season, David Jefferies had secured what – on paper at least – looked like a dream ride. He had signed to race with a new team called Revé Racing that had been formed over the winter of 1994/5 by sponsor Ben Atkins. The name Revé was a translation of the French word for 'dream' but, ironically for DJ, the season turned into something of a nightmare.

Double 1992 British champion John Reynolds had suffered a torrid time in 500cc Grands Prix in 1994, much as Jefferies had on a similar privateer bike the previous season. When pondering his 1995 options with his personal sponsor Atkins, the Revé idea was born. The plan was to enter the World Superbike Championship but only if factory machinery could be secured. After his tough season in GPs, Reynolds knew he needed to be on competitive machinery in 1995.

Thanks to his good relationship with Kawasaki after winning the British title for them, Reynolds's name was enough to get the nod from Japan who agreed to supply factory ZX-750RRs and in just nine weeks Atkins had assembled a fully functional team in time for the new season. Although the team was built around Reynolds it was decided that it would be more cost efficient to run a second rider, especially if that rider could bring some money to the team. Team manager Stuart Hicken explained at the time, "We quickly decided a two-man team would be more cost effective than just one, and interviewed several riders. I have to say David Jefferies was the most enthusiastic and to me that's very important."

Hicken admitted that Jefferies did bring money to the team. "We used JR's name to clinch the factory deal so we felt it was only fair that any second rider getting equipment that is not normally obtainable should pay for the privilege. It works that way in GPs and car racing. I must say, though, that both our riders will receive identical equipment."

In fact, Jefferies brought £50,000 to the team to secure the ride, says Tony. "Actually, it might have been more than that, I can't quite remember."

Although it was his first shot at running a race team, Ben Atkins was hugely optimistic – at least on Reynolds's part. "If we get the right kit, nothing short of the title will satisfy me," he said before the season started. "I realise it's our first season but we should finish in the top three or four."

By contrast, his expectations of Jefferies were considerably lower. "I don't want to put pressure on David, but I'd like him to qualify for all the races and get a few results."

While Stuart Hicken had equally high hopes for Reynolds, he also had more elevated expectations of his number two rider. "We hope to win the title with John Reynolds," he said. "Realistically he can finish top three, and I'd like to see David in the top ten."

Both Atkins and Hicken – let alone Reynolds and Jefferies – were to be disappointed. Rather than winning the title as seemed to be expected of him, Reynolds finished the season down in 10th place while Jefferies's best results were two 13th places, at Monza and Albacete. And, on worse days, he was finishing as low down the order as 26th – scoring only nine points during the entire season.

While Reynolds proved the pace of the bikes by taking two podiums (third places at both Brands Hatch and Assen), he too was finishing other races in 17th, 12th and 11th places, proving just how tough the World Superbike Championship was.

Reynolds says that learning new circuits was one of the hardest challenges DJ faced that year. "It was a whole new thing for David. His first year on the World Superbike stage and learning the circuits was probably one of his biggest problems. I knew most of the circuits from doing two years in Grands Prix but David didn't. He learned circuits as quick as anyone did, but to ride up against the best riders in the world you need to learn the circuits and then push that bit harder, so it's never easy the first time you go to a new circuit."

Another problem, according to Reynolds, was Jefferies's size. "The Kawasaki was a good bike," he says. "We had factory support so the bikes were as good as anything out there. But David was a big lad and I remember he had a problem at Salzburgring. He was saying the bike felt slow but at Salzburgring there's a big hill out the back that climbs for about a mile and I think David's weight went against him at places like that. There's no doubt about it, he would have been better off on a 1000cc bike than the Kawasaki, which was a 750. The 750 was a high-revving, peaky motor so weight was a big issue."

Stuart Hicken disagrees. "I don't think the 750 was too small for him. When we did a few races in the UK at the start of the season – his first time on the bike – he was ahead of people with a lot more experience and scoring third places. And 750s were not small bikes in those days – Superbikes have got smaller as the years have gone by. They're built for midgets now! So I don't think the size of the bike hampered him at all. It was just a huge, huge step forward for him. But to be fair, he coped well. He could probably have benefited from having a really good young mentor around him. We were all a bit older and maybe took things more serious than he did. I feel if he'd had someone around him that was equally as jovial, then some of his results would have been better. But he never disgraced himself – I mean there have been Brits in WSB who never even qualified and David always managed to qualify. And he was up against some real hard-chargers that season who had been around for a while."

Jefferies had put himself through an extensive fitness campaign over the winter and had shed a considerable amount of weight under Hicken's guidance. Hicken had enlisted the help of Loughborough University – who advised athlete Linford Christie at the time – to provide both Jefferies and Reynolds with dietary and fitness assessments. "We've got the technical backup to make the motorcycle go the distance," he said at the time, "so the last thing I would want to hear is that one of my riders lost places in the final five minutes of a race because they tired."

But despite the training regime, that's exactly what happened with Jefferies on a few occasions. "Maybe something David suffered a

RIGHT: *Pioneer. Joe Jefferies, David's great grandfather, was a motoring pioneer at the turn of the 20th Century.* (Nick Jefferies Archive)

BELOW: *David's grandfather, Allan Jefferies, pictured on his Triumph T100 in 1947.* (Nick Jefferies Archive)

LEFT: *Allan Jefferies jumping Ballaugh Bridge during the 1947 Clubman's TT.* (Nick Jefferies Archive)

BELOW: *Happy families. A nine-month old David, pictured with his mum and dad just after Tony had won the 1973 Production TT.* (FoTTofinders)

RIGHT: *Wearing Mike Hailwood's helmet at the 1978 TT – the year Hailwood made his legendary comeback.* (David Jefferies Family Archive)

BELOW RIGHT: *And they said he was too big to be a racer! DJ on his mini moto, aged nine.* (David Jefferies Family Archive)

LEFT: *First year at Ladderbanks Middle School, 1981.* (David Jefferies Family Archive)

BELOW: *Hold on tight. DJ treats his sister Louise to a ride round the garden in 1982. Note the personalised number plate.* (David Jefferies Family Archive)

RIGHT: *Does my bum look big in these? An 11-year-old David tries his dad's leathers and helmet for size.* (David Jefferies Family Archive)

ABOVE: *Bloodied but not bowed. DJ borrows his sister's bike because he's just wrecked his own!* (David Jefferies Family Archive)

LEFT: *DJ and fellow pupil show off their trophy for coming joint first in the cycling proficiency test.* (David Jefferies Family Archive)

RIGHT: *On the rocks. A 14-year-old DJ gets to grips with his Yamaha TY175 in 1986.* (David Jefferies Family Archive)

ABOVE: *Pride and joy. David with his beloved Yamaha TY175 in June 1986.* (David Jefferies Family Archive)

BELOW: *David and Honda CR125 take a breather during a schoolboy motocross event near York in 1987.* (David Jefferies Family Archive)

little bit from was fitness," Hicken says now. "I remember him coming out of the final corner at Laguna Seca with about five minutes of the race left to go. He was in about seventh spot but ended up in 16th place. He just got beat up towards the end."

Tony Jefferies disputes this version of events and claims his son's dropping off the pace was down to the fact that his bike suffered from over-heating problems in hot countries all season.

There are other factors to contend with when contesting a World Championship that UK-based riders don't experience, as Hicken explains. "Like the humidity when we went to Sugo in Japan. It was in the 80s, and after about 15 minutes of practice we noticed David wasn't paying any attention to the pit boards, so we hung out a huge 'IN' sign to get him to come back into the pits. It was a couple of laps before he saw it and came in.

"When he got off the bike, his eyes were rolling round in their sockets and within three minutes we had him on a drip. He was so dehydrated. We'd told him to drink as much as possible but I think he drank too much Coke instead of water. He was on a drip for about an hour. Then, I think that panicked John Reynolds so he started drinking bucket-loads of water. But he ended up drinking so much that it was sloshing around in his stomach and he finished up on the same drip! Going to so many different countries for the first time… there's a lot to cope with that most people don't appreciate."

Reynolds also noticed that Jefferies wasn't as fit as he perhaps could have been. In his autobiography, he described an event that season which seemed to imply that Jefferies hadn't done nearly enough training. He wrote 'At Monza, David Jefferies decided to join us [Reynolds and his mechanic Chris Anderson] for a run round the track. He got about a mile-and-a-half out and was completely knackered. He walked back and Chris and I kept on going.'

Jefferies's close friend, Adam Evans, admits that training – at least in the traditional manner – wasn't something DJ enjoyed. "He didn't do gym training – he hated it. Me and Dave got given free membership at a local gym and the intention was to start going regularly, but we never went. He much preferred mountain biking or motocrossing. That kept him 'bike fit' anyway."

But one thing everyone agreed on was that DJ was a great guy. Reynolds says, "We all loved having David around in the team – he was a great character. He was never down, he was always bouncing and jumping around having a laugh. He was good fun. If his results were getting him down he certainly didn't let it show. He always appeared to be full on and looking forward to the next weekend. A lot of riders would have been down, for sure, but David didn't let it get to him."

Hicken has similar memories. "I don't think anything was taken too seriously by David – he was great fun to be around. He was a comedian without knowing it. The first time we went to Italy David had come back from town and said he'd seen a really trick barrel and exhaust for his paddock scooter. I asked him if he really thought he needed them and he mumbled 'No, I suppose not.' But next day I heard this almighty racket coming through the paddock and there was DJ with his big bore kit and trick pipe on his scooter – he'd blown a whole month's wages on it!"

While Jefferies's results may not have set the WSB world on fire, Hicken insists he did all that could have been expected of him. "I wouldn't have said it was a bad year for David, results-wise. It was a huge step for him and probably came a little bit too early in his career. It was a lot to cope with and, apart from the two UK rounds at Donington and Brands Hatch, he didn't know any of the tracks. So there was a lot to learn and a lot to cope with.

"We thought if David could score points anywhere from 10th to 15th place then we were going to be happy. And he did score quite a few times around that area. But with a young buck in the team – as David was at the time – it's quite difficult to keep their heads up. It was his first time away from home; first time away from his friends and everything that was familiar to him – first time for everything really."

DJ's season in WSB was cut short when he broke his wrist before the Indonesian round. Australian Matt Mladin replaced him at that race but the team elected not to run a second rider in the final round of the championship in Australia.

All in all, it was a frustrating year for Jefferies, and not one that his father thinks he enjoyed. "The team was based around John

Reynolds," he says. "So much so that Dave even ended up having to run-in engines for John, which wasn't an ideal scenario. We were hoping that he was going to learn from John but he was too occupied with doing what he had to do to be competitive. The bikes were supposed to be identical but I don't think they really were – though I could never prove it.

"Dave broke his thumb at Assen, which ended his season prematurely, but it wasn't really an enjoyable year for him. I think he found Ben Atkins hard to get on with and always felt very much the number two rider. But I also think he just couldn't go quite quick enough for the team's expectations at that point. The whole thing just didn't quite gel."

Even if the atmosphere in the Revé team had been a bit too serious for Jefferies's liking, he still found time to have fun on the odd weekend off. Film-maker and long-time friend of the Jefferies family, David Wood, remembers one such occasion with fondness. "We went to Le Mans in 1995 to watch the 24 Hour car race. We went in Dave's huge motor home and I remember there was such a huge queue at Southampton that we decided to get out all the tables and chairs, food and beers, and have a party. The more people were gasping, the more we laid it on, getting the posh tablecloths and silver service out.

"Anyway, after we parked up at Le Mans we saw this guy trying to do wheelies in the camp site. We were pretty drunk – and he was bloody useless. Dave suddenly arrived on a scooter, saw what was going on and got talking to the guy, offering to show him how to do wheelies. The guy didn't know who David was so when he got on the guy's bike he decided to scare him a bit and started saying, 'Right, is this the throttle then? And this is the brake lever?' Then he stalled it on purpose, restarted it and wobbled along for a few yards like he was going to fall off. Then, just as the bloke's face was going white, DJ hoiked the bike up onto the back wheel and disappeared in a cloud of smoke.

"The bloke's jaw dropped and he just said 'Who is that guy?'

"Everyone in the camp site started cheering and shouting as David went back and forth on the back wheel, wearing just his tee-shirt and shorts. He put on a great show. When he came back he spent lots of time teaching the amazed bike owner how to do a wheelie. Then it clicked – he hadn't recognised him but knew who he was. He was so proud to have been taught how to wheelie by David Jefferies."

* * *

Not before time, British Championship racing received a major overhaul ready for the 1996 season and it still benefits from that pivotal year to this day. The old tradition of having two separate Superbike Championships was finally abandoned and all efforts were poured into a single, meaningful British Superbike Championship sponsored by *Motor Cycle News*. There would be more rounds than before, big name riders, more impressive teams, and major new sponsors were brought onboard to fund what would become the world's premier domestic championship.

A major coup for the series was the inclusion of Niall Mackenzie on a Boost Yamaha. Mackenzie had been on the Grand Prix trail for ten years and would provide a world class act for the other British riders to measure themselves against. A further boost came in the form of BBC TV coverage of every round of the championship in a highlights package screened the week after each race weekend. All the ingredients were in place for a superb British championship and happily the reality, for once, actually lived up to the hype.

David Jefferies's original plan for the 1996 season had been to lease a Ducati 916 direct from the factory in Bologna. But by late March this still hadn't materialised and it was clear that not only was Jefferies going to be robbed of any crucial pre-season testing, but he might have to sit out the opening races of the season too. As things turned out, however, neither of these concerns mattered as David managed to secure a last minute deal with the Medd Racing Team for the 1996 season. Team manager Stuart Medd explained at the time, "The opportunity to have Dave ride for us came out of the blue and we snapped him up. His World Superbike Championship experience and knowledge of the British circuits will hold him in good stead to continue our development of the Honda RC45. We will be putting the full backing of our team behind Dave as the number one rider."

It would be David's first time as a number one rider in a professional, well-established team. Medd Racing had been on the British and international racing scene for 12 years by 1996 and DJ was clearly relieved to finally have a bike to ride for the opening round of the new-look championship. "I was becoming very anxious about the factory ordered Ducati 916 which still shows no signs of arriving," he said after securing the deal. "I would have been without a bike for the opening rounds at Donington Park, and the opportunity to be involved with a top-level professional British team was just too good to miss."

Jefferies had contacted Stuart Medd to try and lease an RC45 for the opening BSB round but was told the team only had enough bikes and spares for one rider – Paul 'Marra' Brown. When Brown accepted a lucrative eleventh hour deal to ride in the 600cc class just before the start of the season, Medd did not hesitate in contacting Jefferies to offer him his place.

It may have looked like a good opportunity on paper but Honda's RC45 had attracted much criticism since it replaced the legendary but ageing RC30 in 1994. Jim Moodie had quit the Medd team following the 1995 season, saying the bike simply wasn't competitive – and he wasn't the only one. Other experienced riders including James Haydon had also tried to get the bike up to speed but failed. But Jefferies was undaunted by the task, saying, "Obviously I have heard all about the problems with the RC45 but I know I can get this bike into the points regularly this season."

After riding the bike for the first time in practice at Donington, he seemed even more enthused. "I think the Dunlop tyres have transformed the bike [it had suffered most of its problems on Michelins]," he said. "Tony Scott has built a brand new engine and it feels really good and clean all the way through the rev range – a good spread of power. Once we get that dialled in with the injection system and suspension the bike will be flying."

DJ's straightforward attitude towards racing, and life in general, was easy to perceive when he talked of the RC45 and its reputation.

"I don't listen to people who tell me it'll spit me off," he said. "I just get on with the job of riding the bike. At the end of the day, it's only a motorcycle. If there are any problems, we'll iron them out."

He seemed particularly happy with his new team right from the word go too, especially after an unhappy WSB 1995 season. "Stuart Medd is so enthusiastic and we've got a good team together," he said. "I'm looking forward to having a good laugh this year after last year with Revé, which was very serious. It's important to switch off and relax too."

It was a measure of how uncompetitive the RC45 was that Honda withdrew its official entry from BSB in 1996 leaving only the Medd team and the V&M team (with Mike Edwards on board) campaigning the bikes. This would be of huge significance to David Jefferies's later career as V&M boss Jack Valentine kept a close eye on the only other RC45 rider in the championship. He knew how outclassed the bikes were and would be stunned at some of DJ's performances on the Honda later in the year. Together, the pair would go on to make road racing history.

Jefferies suffered a misfire in the opening race at Donington but managed an eighth place in the second leg to open his points account for 1996. A 10th and 9th at Thruxton were relatively disappointing, but Jefferies was closer to the sharp end of the field at Oulton Park and delighted his Medd team by finishing 5th and 6th at a meeting that attracted a large crowd. There were still thousands queuing outside the circuit when the first race got underway.

Another outing in the World Superbike Championship at Donington saw DJ finishing just outside the points on both occasions, but his two 17th place finishes were more impressive than the results sheet suggested. Almost every bike in front of him enjoyed either full or partial factory support and his 750cc Honda was giving away 250ccs to the Ducatis at a time when the limit for four-cylinder bikes was 750cc and the limit for twins, like the Ducati, was 1000cc. Even Honda's top factory rider, Aaron Slight, protested that the Ducatis enjoyed an unfair advantage. The series organisers listened and an upper capacity limit of 1000cc for fours and twins was eventually introduced.

David finished just behind former GP star Niall Mackenzie in the opening leg and had some terrific scraps with his BSB rivals, including Michael Rutter and Ian Simpson. His riding seriously impressed factory Yamaha BSB rider and fellow Yorkshireman Jamie Whitham who told him after the race, "You were riding like a madman through Craner Curves. You're almost as mad as me!"

Team boss Stuart Medd was certainly pleased with DJ's riding. "David rode really well with some consistent lap times," he said. "A lot of people will be surprised at that result."

In May, Jefferies returned to Northern Ireland to contest the annual North West 200 road race meeting. He may have been in contention before dropping out with a shredded tyre in 1994, but he had yet to show his true potential on the roads by taking a win. Even so, Robert Dunlop, an acknowledged master of the circuit and with more wins than any other rider at the event, stated publicly that he rated Jefferies as his biggest threat for the 1996 event.

Dunlop had won the Superbike race on a Medd Honda RC45 in 1994, proving the machine had the pace on the ultra-fast circuit. That win was one of just two significant victories for the RC45 anywhere in the UK that season, the other coming in the hands of James Haydon at a very damp Snetterton. Even so, DJ was confident heading into the race. "I'm going there on the RC45 with the intention of winning it," he said before a snapped footpeg put paid to any ideas of a debut victory in the opening Superbike race. He came home in fifth place after riding the closing stages of the race with just one footpeg. "The peg dug in at the roundabout on the last lap and snapped off," he said. Still, he had been in good company, leading home road racing legend Joey Dunlop in a race that was won by another Ulsterman, Phillip McCallen, on the factory-supported Honda RC45. It had been the case since the bike's release in 1994 that the factory versions were reasonably competitive while the privateer machines were not. Yet in 1996, even Carl Fogarty failed to win the WSB title for Honda in his only season with the firm.

Jefferies finished seventh in the second Superbike event to prove he was a worthy rider on street circuits, but his performance still gave no indication of the dominant force he would soon come to be on such tracks.

In early July, Jefferies headed back to one of his most successful stomping grounds, Oliver's Mount in Scarborough, in a bid to add more wins to his rolling tally. He faced awesome opposition in the form of Phillip McCallen who had been dominating the pure road racing scene in 1996, taking an unprecedented four TT wins in one week on his factory Honda as well as a double win at the North West 200. Now in retirement, McCallen admits he was a fairly wild rider at times. But Jefferies was not afraid of him and, as things turned out, was the only man capable of matching – and on one occasion bettering – McCallen's pace at Oliver's Mount. While McCallen won the feature 'Cock o' the North' Superbike race, the 600 race and a further Superbike race, Jefferies won Saturday's 750 race to give the Medd team its first victory with the RC45 since 1994. And to make things even sweeter, he did it almost 50 years to the day since his grandfather won the first Scarborough meeting on a Triumph.

An eighth and seventh at the Knockhill BSB round were followed by a brilliant fourth place in the first leg at Cadwell Park behind Jamie Whitham, Niall Mackenzie and Steve Hislop. Sadly for Jefferies, he crashed out of the second leg and left the meeting lying ninth in the points rankings.

For the eighth round of the series at Mallory Park, the Medd team had a new V&M-tuned engine for Jefferies to try. He put it to good use, finishing fourth in leg one to equal his best result of the season so far. Jefferies was clearly pleased with his modified bike. "The bike handles as well as it did before," he said, "except now it's going like a train." The engine tune was reported to have boosted power by 10bhp up to 150bhp, and that race marked the first real collaboration between the V&M team and David Jefferies.

But there was even better to come as the BSB circus pitched its tents at Brands Hatch. After a solid seventh place in the first leg, in the second leg DJ beat the likes of Niall Mackenzie, Steve Hislop and Jamie Whitham to take second place behind Terry Rymer on the Old Spice Ducati. He had been challenging the Londoner for the lead at one stage before dropping back slightly but still grinned – "My Honda was going just great. The V&M-tuned motor was superb."

Had the team started the year with a V&M motor, who knows how much better their results might have been, but at least by this late stage in the season, Jefferies had kept his promise to make the RC45 competitive. His efforts in the second leg were enough to earn him the coveted 'Man of the Meeting' award, and it was well deserved. Virtually every rider who had raced the Honda RC45 throughout the 1995 season had said it was uncompetitive, yet in 1996 Jefferies never complained. He got on with the job of riding the bike and regularly mixed it with the factory riders – especially when he got hold of the V&M engine towards the end of the season. But if his efforts were not rewarded with any wins in the BSB championship, it was a very different matter in the two other championships DJ contested in 1996.

The International TT Production Challenge had been dreamed up on the back of the successful return of a Production class at the TT in June. As it was an eleventh hour idea, the first round was not held until August. And with it being so late in the season, there would only be a further two rounds at Oulton Park and Silverstone, but both of these were to be double-headers with two races at each meeting.

Still, interest in the series was strong, both from riders and manufacturers, and Jefferies found himself up against some top names including Jim Moodie on a Suzuki GSX-R750 and Michael Rutter and Phillip McCallen on Honda FireBlades.

The first problem for Jefferies was finding a bike to contest the championship. He had already sold the Honda FireBlade he'd ridden earlier in the year but after contacting the new owner, came to an arrangement. "I borrowed it back," Jefferies explained. "But I think I will have to sort out my own bike for Oulton Park in September."

Jefferies put his old mount to good use, finishing third behind Jim Moodie and Tom Cuddy on a machine he was careful not to damage. "I was lucky to be able to get it back. And the deal was if I bend it I mend it," he explained after returning the bike to its rightful owner intact.

The Medd team sorted DJ out with a FireBlade for the second and third rounds of the championship at Oulton Park and they proved to be scintillating races between Jefferies and Moodie. Jefferies managed to win by just half a second from Moodie in the first leg with Phileip McCallen taking third. But in the second race, the positions were reversed and it was Moodie's turn to take victory by the narrowest of margins after the pair swapped the lead four times on the last lap. The win left the Scotsman with a nine-point lead going into the final showdown at Silverstone on 22 September, but Moodie was to be disappointed at the Northants track. Mike Edwards, also riding a FireBlade, acted as a spoiler by taking the first race win, but DJ put in a superhuman effort in the final leg to win the race and draw level on points with Moodie. In such circumstances, the rider with the most race wins would normally be granted the title, but since Moodie and Jefferies had scored identical placings throughout the championship, they could not be split on wins, or even second and third placings. A decision was taken to award the title to Jefferies by virtue of the fact that he won the last race. Needless to say, Moodie was none too pleased with the decision.

Jefferies's other championship success in 1996 came in the Mobil 1 Triumph Speed Triple Challenge which was a one-make series featuring identical models of the unfaired, 900cc British-made machines.

The Challenge was one of the highest profile championships in the UK in 1996 with plenty of top BSB riders entering through dealer-supported teams. Many of Jefferies's BSB rivals like Michael Rutter, Paul Brown, Matt Llewellyn and Ray Stringer were entered in the series, which offered £2,000 prize money to the winner of each race and a brand new Triumph Speed Triple to the winner of the overall series.

After a disappointing eighth place in the opening round at Mallory Park, Jefferies went on to win the Cadwell round and proved that he was going to be a major contender for the title. Another disappointing ninth at the Donington Transatlantic meeting dropped him to second in the overall standings behind Mick Corrigan before Jefferies headed for Brands Hatch and controversy, as the majority of the Triumph Speed Triple field refused to race.

The uproar started when 125 riders went out on their warm-up lap only to discover that oil dropped from a 600cc bike in the previous race had made the track like an ice rink. Ex-British champion Robin Appleyard led calls for a race boycott as his fellow riders sat on the grid and confusion reigned until race direction abandoned the start and asked the Triumph riders – who were on treaded road tyres – to complete a sighting lap to assess whether it was possible for them to race. Rutter, Llewellyn and Stringer all said the track was too dangerous and refused to race while Jefferies, who was on pole position, found himself amongst the minority who were happy to continue.

In the end, the race was abandoned but the riders agreed to ride five demonstration laps in a bid to keep the fans happy. The abandoned race was to be rerun at Donington Park two weeks later as part of a support package for the British Grand Prix. Jefferies set pole and ran away with the rescheduled race that was held on the Saturday evening. It went some way to easing the disappointment of Brands as he explained. "I was bitterly disappointed that the Brands round was cancelled because of spilt oil as I had qualified on pole there and I don't regard Donington as my best track, so I'm delighted with this win."

For the second race on Sunday, in front of massive Grand Prix race day crowds, Jefferies found himself lining up against an unexpected challenger in the form of Grand Prix legend Randy Mamola. A four-times runner-up in the 500cc World Championship in the 1980s, Mamola is generally considered to be the best rider never to have won the 500cc crown. He was also instrumental in founding biking's favourite charity, Riders for Health, which raises money to buy bikes to carry much-needed medical aid to remote regions of Africa. It was in order to raise money for Riders that Mamola found himself lining up on the Speed Triple grid, four years after retiring from GP racing. The American was surprised at just how hard the Triumphs were to muscle round a race track. "I have never ridden a machine that's so hard to stop and turn," he said after qualifying 12th fastest for the race.

Mamola was not permitted to ride in the Saturday race as it was a replacement for the cancelled Brands Hatch round, but he enjoyed his debut Triumph race on the Sunday so much that he declared an interest in contesting the entire series. After finishing in a respectable ninth place, the American said, "With some time on the bike I could win these races. It felt just like racing used to be when I came here in the late Seventies, but I never had a race with so much pushing and shoving on the first lap."

Jefferies had to settle for third place after tyre problems led to some lurid slides at over 100mph. "I was more than halfway off the bike at Redgate," he said. "It went out from under me, and at Starkey's the sliding was causing even more problems. It wasn't good riding that kept me on, just a lot of luck. I decided that third place was better than dropping the Triumph."

But drop the Triumph Jefferies did during qualifying for the final round of the Speed Triple series. He suffered severe bruising in the spill at the super-fast Schwantz Curve at Donington on the morning of the title-deciding race, but braved the pain to take to the grid. Fortunately, DJ only needed a 14th place finish to lift the crown and he rode through the pain barrier to take tenth place and his second British title in one season. "I didn't break anything in the crash but I was so sore," he said afterwards. "On the warm-up lap I was in agony and thought I couldn't do it, but when the lights went green I put it out of my mind."

With a ninth place in the British Superbike Championship and the Triumph Speed Triple title under his belt to accompany his TT Production championship crown, 1996 had been a successful year for David Jefferies on the UK's short circuits. But what would prove to be most important of all for his long-term career was the fact that the season had also seen him make his debut in an event that he would eventually make his own and that would make his name famous the world over. For in May/June of 1996 Jefferies had become the fourth member of his illustrious family to tackle the most feared, most famous and most dangerous motorcycle race in the world – the Isle of Man TT.

Chapter 6

THE MOUNTAIN

"TT riders seem to have a mentality a little like people in the First World War trenches – whatever happens, it's not going to happen to them."
Tony Jefferies

"I always said I'd never come here – you had to be a nutter to race at this place," David Jefferies once said of the Isle of Man TT. "But my dad reckoned my style would suit the place and after a few good results at the North West and Scarborough I decided to give it a try."

It was understandable that Tony Jefferies had initially discouraged his son from racing on what was the world's most dangerous course, but both his and David's feelings changed once DJ had built up several years of experience and proved he was a safe and steady rider.

Tony says, "Inevitably the TT question came up with David and I really had to make sure it was his choice. We had discussed it before and I did stop him – well, put it out of his mind, shall we say – when he first started, because I think you do need some road racing experience before going there. It's not a place to learn to race. Pauline and I had discussed it – we knew that he was a good road bike rider and was good on the road circuits. He had ridden a couple of the dates in Ireland and had done very well there, as he also had in Scarborough. Although they're a million miles away from the 37.74-mile TT course, it does give you some idea of what it's like."

If DJ could lead an international road race event like the North West at the first attempt, it seemed logical to assume that he would go equally well on the Isle of Man's legendary course. But Tony insists that, even though he was David's manager, he never pushed his son into making his TT debut. "I think the TT is something you must choose to do and without anybody giving you any provocation – you've got to make your own mind up about it," he said in a 1997 interview with film-maker David Wood, much of which has never been heard before now.

"The thing that I suggested to him was that he's got to treat it like he's going to the shop for the Sunday paper – or that he's just on one of the ride-outs that he goes on with some of the lads from work. I said, 'Just jump on it and have a ride round. If you don't like it, we'll put the bike in the back of the van and go home or spend the rest of the week in the pub or whatever.' He was under absolutely no illusion that he had to do it."

David had all the advice he could have wanted on-hand from his father and uncle – both former TT winners in their own right. Tony explained to his son the huge difference in technique required to ride the TT course compared to any other circuit. "To ride the TT circuit there's a definite technique required. The first thing is you have got to know where you are going, which might sound a bit simple, but it takes some years to find that out and get to the point where you know every crest, and you know what's just beyond every crest, and you know what's round every corner. Once you've got that firmly implanted in your brain, then you can start practising – which is the quickest way to approach that particular crest, hill or corner, whatever it may be. So knowledge is probably the greatest asset.

"Then the next thing is overcoming the fear factor – knowing that you're going blind over hill-crests and into blind corners which sometimes look quite severe but actually aren't. You might come back into the pits saying, 'Perhaps I could have gone round that corner maybe 2–3mph faster', but it's always a lot better to come back and say that than to find out that you *couldn't* have gone around it any faster.

"So once you've got the confidence and you know where to go, then you can start putting the riding and practising ability into operation. I really think the way you ride in the TT is different than on short circuits. You can't afford to be doing the same sort of sliding and vicious type of riding that you do on short circuits. TT riding does require quite a lot of drifting and sliding, but it's in a much more controlled manner. Being smooth is the main thing; being really smooth and making sure that you maximise exit speeds on corners. The exit speed on the long fast corners is critical because that maintains or controls your speed for maybe the next mile, or even two miles, so it's really important you get that right."

Tony Jefferies didn't suffer any delusions about the dangerous nature of the TT course. He was fully aware of what he was letting his son in for. "The TT is a dangerous place and it has to be treated with respect, there's no doubt about that. But riders have a choice – they don't have to go there. Those that do go there, go there knowing full well what the risks are. The fact is, if you ride in a sensible manner – but still obviously trying to be competitive – the risks are minimised. The fear people have most of all is of machine failure, and there are certain parts of the circuit where that can happen. It's obviously very, very dangerous, so I don't know how anybody really overcomes that. I think they just tend to ignore it. TT riders certainly seem to have a mentality a little like people in the First World War trenches – whatever happens, it's not going to happen to them. They climb out of the trenches regardless. It's probably a philosophy that riders *have* to adopt. But we can't knock anyone for saying the TT is dangerous, because it is."

Shortly after making his debut, David reflected on his decision to compete in the TT and explained his method of preparation. "I went over with the mind that I was going to enjoy myself and just ride round. I do a lot of miles on the road on normal road bikes so I thought I could do reasonably well over there.

"I started learning the circuit through watching some of the videos my uncle Nick had done with a camera on his bike. I sat and watched those five or six times and then went through them with my dad, stopping the video in places and discussing certain parts of the circuit. Then when I got to the Isle of Man a couple of days before practice started, I did one lap on a road bike. I was hoping to do some more on the Sunday but it rained all day. Unfortunately I only managed that one lap and then I was straight out for practice early on Monday morning.

"With hindsight, not managing many laps on a road bike was a good thing because when you're on a road bike you're always conscious of other road users, traffic lights and other stuff, and you can only use one side of the road. Also, the speeds are nowhere near as great as what you're doing in the race. On the open roads you're maybe doing 70 or 80mph, whereas when you're racing and the roads are closed you could be reaching 180mph. So what could seem like an insignificant corner at road speeds can turn into quite a dramatic corner at racing speeds."

As things turned out, 1996 was not a good year to make an Isle of Man TT debut. Not only was practice week beset by the wettest May weather since records began in the 17th Century, it was also marred by a double tragedy when top riders Robert Holden and Mick Lofthouse lost their lives following separate crashes. If David Jefferies had needed any reminding of how dangerous the TT circuit was, he got it as he splashed round the unfamiliar 37.74-mile course trying to avoid the carnage all around him.

Yet Tony remembers the elation that David felt upon completing his first practice laps of the TT course. "The first morning he went out in practice and did a lap – two laps I think – and he came back in with such a smile across his face and saying, 'God, I've just had the biggest laugh I've had in my life. It's fantastic this!' He said there were wheelies and skids everywhere. His times were really respectable as well."

With typical understatement, David played down those early laps. "My first lap, wearing an orange bib on my first TT, I just went touring," he said. "Didn't even tuck in. Just enjoyed myself, and shut off anywhere I wasn't sure of."

Having an uncle who won the Formula 1 TT just three years previously would seem, to some, to be a distinct advantage when it came to learning the course, but Jefferies insisted it was of limited use in his first year. "I didn't follow him that much really," he said. "It's a big responsibility when you're doing that, and you're always looking behind. You have to learn your own way round really."

And one person's best way round may not be another's, as DJ explained. "People have different lines. I've spoken to Steve Hislop and, at Hillberry for example, he's got a completely different line to me. His line frightens the shit out of me. There's no way I would come out of there that wide, but that's his line and that's the way he goes. With the Isle of Man, my theory is that you have got to learn it yourself. Just take your time. I did follow my uncle Nick a few times to learn the quick bits, but apart from that I've learnt most of it myself."

Nick Jefferies did help David round part of his first ever lap but after that he left his nephew to his own devices. He says, "Before the first practice session on the Monday morning I said to David, 'Right, you set off about four bikes in front of me; I'll probably catch you at about Glen Helen, and then I'll sit behind you and make sure you look safe. Then I'll pass you and just set a steady pace to give you a clue of how much road to use, how early you brake and where you put the power on.'

"Once we got to the Gooseneck (about three-quarters of the way round the course), I looked round at him, we gave each other the thumbs up, then I left him to it. But he was flying – he was good right from the start."

Another rider making his debut at the 1996 TT would later become one of the event's all-time greatest winners. John McGuinness is now the TT's top man. A 14-times winner, he also became the first man in history to record an average lap speed of over 130mph when he clocked a lap at 130.35mph during the 2007 Senior race. Although he had known Jefferies since racing in the Superteen Championship in 1991, it was during the 1996 TT that the pair would form a close friendship that would last for the remainder of Jefferies's brief life.

McGuinness remembers that Jefferies was initially very much against racing at the TT. "We were both at Brands Hatch, chatting together with my mum and dad in DJ's motorhome, when the TT thing came up. I'm a massive TT fan – I've been across to the Island every year since 1982. In those days I used to go on my BMX bike. Anyway, I said to Dave 'How d'ya fancy the TT?' He said 'No way. I'm not doing that. No chance.' That was in 1991 and he was saying 'Never going to do that. Never going to do that.'

"Then he did Scarborough plus a few other bits and pieces and we also did the North West together – and here we were at the TT. What changed his mind, I don't know."

McGuinness still has fond memories of the learning experience he and Jefferies went through in their rookie year. "In '96 we just loved it," he later recalled. "We just loved the whole TT thing. Practice week was real hard work, because it was one of the worst years weather-wise, and after each practice we'd be in the beer tent or getting a cup of tea in the Hailwood Centre, chatting about things. He really did love it. And you could tell straight away that David had a natural ability at the Isle of Man."

No rider who enters a TT race does so ignorant of the inherent dangers. Rather, each has his – or her – own coping mechanisms. Jefferies was no exception. "People talk about the dangers of the TT and there's no two ways about it, the circuit is very dangerous. But you have to go with the attitude that you go to learn it in the first couple of years. There are quite a few occasions at the TT when I was thinking, 'is this corner flat-out or isn't it? I just can't remember.' Then you've just got to shut off. You've got to give the place the respect it deserves.

"As far as racing dangers go, my father is actually in a wheelchair, but that was a fluke accident. I mean, that was on a short circuit with safety barriers, hay bales, everything. He raced at the TT and was very successful but his accident was actually on a short circuit."

Another rider making his TT debut in 1996 was Chris Moss, a road tester with *Motor Cycle News* who was finally achieving a lifelong ambition. Moss had less racing experience than Jefferies but remembers the two trying to learn the daunting course together.

"I remember sitting on the 'newcomers' bus being shown round the course and being surprised to see David Jefferies on it," says Moss. "He'd done Grands Prix and World Superbikes so I thought, 'What the hell's he doing on this bus?' Because of his name and because I knew he would have done his homework with his uncle Nick, I was surprised to see him there. He could probably have told the guide more about the TT course than the guide could tell him."

Moss also remembers Jefferies being fast from the outset and a good man to learn from, even though he was just learning himself. "DJ passed me in practice a couple of times and I found that if I got stuck onto the back of him I could follow him for quite a long way before he dropped me," he says. "The only reason I could stay with him at all was because he was showing me the best way round – I had the best tutor I could wish for. One time I followed him for about half a lap and years later he pulled me up about it during an interview saying, 'Every time I looked back and saw you following me I went crackers.' Apparently it made him feel very uncomfortable because he was learning the course and just wanted to go out and do his own thing. I asked him why he hadn't said anything to me at the time, but he just laughed."

The lengthy interview Moss is referring to was conducted at Rockingham in 2002 and has never been heard before now. During it, Jefferies laughed at the memory of Moss doggedly hanging onto him as he tried to learn the TT course. "Every time I looked round I thought 'Fuck it – he's behind me again.' I just wanted to go and learn it on my own.

"The problem is, you think, 'Am I learning it quicker than he is? Am I going to go into somewhere quicker than he is?' And when I was learning it I just wanted to go out there and ride round on my own. But I loved it. It was just like going up to Devil's Bridge on a Sunday morning with my mates – but with no cars coming the other way."

After a week of practice marred by the deaths of Holden and Lofthouse, David Jefferies lined up for his first ever TT race, the Junior, for 600cc four-stroke machines. Never one to worry much before a race, even Jefferies admitted to a bit of pre-race nerves as he prepared to tackle the daunting Mountain circuit. "I'd actually managed to get in 20 or 21 laps in practice, which is quite a high number," he said. "That set me in quite good stead for the race. Fortunately I'm the sort of person who doesn't get too nervous but, even so, as I stood on the line while they sent us off one at a time, I was a little bit like 'Hmm, God, here we go. This is actually it.' But in the back of my mind I was thinking, 'Well, just do what you've done in practice – go out and enjoy yourself and have a nice, pleasant ride round.'"

For someone enjoying a 'pleasant ride round', Jefferies would soon get his eyes opened as to what it took to win a TT. Recalling his first race some years after the event, he said, "The first time over the

Mountain racing I remember coming out of the Gooseneck into lots of fog. I remember my dad had said to me, 'When you're in the fog just sit on the white line and take it steady.' So I was sat there, orange jacket on, pootling along and next thing I know Phillip McCallen came flying past me, feet down and all, trying to get round the corner. I thought, 'Oh my God! So this is the Mountain is it?' But once the fog cleared I really enjoyed it. It's a good section because of the speeds you can keep – you can keep flowing, and if you get it right you can make quite a bit of time up.

"I used to hate the bit from Ginger Hall to Ramsey. But because I don't really like it, I think I get more satisfaction when I get it right. I think, 'I've done it – I got it right at last.' But my favourite bit is the Mountain. As soon as I get through the Waterworks and up to the Gooseneck I think, 'Right, let's just get some nice, flowing lines.'"

Riding a Honda CBR600, Jefferies ended his first TT race in 16th place out of a total of 68 finishers – a very creditable result for a rookie on a course which most agree takes three years to learn well enough to challenge for a victory. Uncle Nick finished in eighth place in the same race, which was won by Phillip McCallen – the Irishman who had shocked DJ with his determined all-action style as he passed him over the Mountain section of the course.

McCallen's lesson seemed to pay dividends as Jefferies finished a brilliant tenth in the Production race. The race was back on the calendar for the first time since 1989 when another tragedy had forced it to be dropped from the programme. Two hugely popular and experienced riders, Phil Mellor and Steve Henshaw, had lost their lives in that 1989 race and many argued that near-standard street bikes were not up to the rigours of racing at such sustained high speeds round the Mountain course and therefore were an accident waiting to happen. Chassis and tyre technology in particular were nowhere near as sophisticated as they are today and many argued they were not capable of coping with the powerful engines of bikes like Suzuki's brutal GSX-R1100.

Whatever the case, the event was dropped and only reappeared in 1996 when it was decided that the new breed of road bikes like Honda's FireBlade (which accounted for more than half of the entire field, including Jefferies's entry), Kawasaki's ZX-9R, Yamaha's Thunderace and Suzuki's GSX-R750 were more than capable of lapping the TT course at racing speeds straight out of the box. It was a decision that seemed to be vindicated as the tragedies of '89 were not repeated and the race seemed to be as popular with the manufacturers as it was with the thousands of spectators who had ridden to the Island on the very same kinds of bikes.

The return of the Production TT played straight into David Jefferies's hands. Over the next seven years, he would enjoy tremendous success on production-based machinery both at the TT and on the UK mainland short circuits. For once, his size and weight did not matter so much; the bikes were larger, more powerful and more roomy for his considerable frame, and the softer suspension settings, inherent in a road bike compared to a race bike, meant the machines were perfectly suited to a larger, heavier rider. In fact, they provided one of the few scenarios in racing when it was actually a disadvantage to be built like a jockey as smaller riders sometimes struggled to muscle these bigger, heavier machines around a course as demanding and bumpy as the Isle of Man.

Jefferies's tenth place in what was only his second TT race proved from the outset that he was going to be a force to be reckoned with on 'Proddie' machinery in the future. Uncle Nick was only three places higher up the leader board in seventh and there were some hugely experienced TT stars behind DJ including Ian Lougher, Jim Moodie and Ian Simpson. His performance did not go unnoticed. One man in particular who was keeping a close eye on DJ both at that year's TT and on the UK short circuits, was Jack Valentine, who would later play a central role in the Jefferies legend.

Valentine was one half of the new-look V&M racing team that was running Honda RC45s in BSB. While Valentine took care of managerial duties, the engine work was left to tuning guru Steve Mellor. The pair had founded V&M Racing back in 1982 when Valentine was still competing in drag races. He claimed ten national and three European drag racing championship titles over a seven year period before the team turned its attentions towards road racing in 1990, supplying engines for various factory teams including Suzuki

GB and Yamaha UK. Riders of the calibre of Carl Fogarty, Rob McElnea and Jamie Whitham all benefited from the increased power of V&M-prepared engines in the early Nineties.

After V&M engines took the first four places in the 1994 British Supersport championship, Valentine and Mellor were appointed by Honda to run its official British Superbike and Supersport efforts. In 1996, Valentine and Mellor were campaigning the troublesome Honda RC45 in BSB. David Jefferies was campaigning a similar machine and it was this commonality which led to one of the most fateful meetings in modern road racing history. "In 1996 we started with Honda and were working on the RC45" Valentine recalled in an interview with Greenlight Television in 2003. "And although we only raced it at the Isle of Man that year, Steve Mellor was doing a lot of engine development and we had a really good, strong engine package. David was in Stuart Medd's team riding like a demon – like he always did. I was really impressed. But he was down on power compared to the other bikes. We got chatting because we had similar interests, having similar machines, and we ended up lending them an engine. David promptly got on the rostrum at Brands Hatch. So that's how we started it."

Jefferies's third and final race of TT96 was the Senior, which had been a blue riband event ever since the TT started in 1907. To this day, the winner of the Senior race is presented with the same spectacular silver trophy depicting Mercury – the Roman messenger of the Gods – that was donated by the Marquis de Mouzilly de St Mars for the inaugural TT meeting. The Senior also had the distinction of being the first ever 500cc Grand Prix in 1949. Before the TT lost its World Championship status in 1977, the Senior TT was effectively the British Grand Prix and therefore the most prestigious race anywhere in the British Isles.

Today, the trophy is engraved with every winner of the Senior since 1907 and it reads like a who's who of motorcycle racing. It is so precious that the winner no longer gets to take it home and it even has its own personal carer/security guard who never lets it out of his sight on the rare occasions when it's put on public display. This is a trophy that anyone who has ever ridden a motorcycle would want to win, and David Jefferies was no exception.

It was never going to happen in his first year at the TT, but another strong finish in 16th place – this time riding his uncle Nick's Honda CBR600 – clearly proved that Jefferies had a natural ability on the TT circuit. His three consistent finishes, all comfortably inside the top 20, earned him the 'Best Newcomer' award and fired a warning shot at his rivals: once that natural ability was coupled with experience, they were going to have a fight on their hands.

Chapter 7

ON ANY SUNDAY

*"The exhaust had been squashed flat from cornering so hard, and the back
light fell out because he'd been scraping it on the road doing wheelies."*
Adam Evans, David's friend

Davaid Jefferies was rare among professional motorcycle racers in
that he still rode normal bikes on public roads on a daily basis
throughout his career. "I still ride all the time, I just enjoy bikes, full
stop," he said. "I still enjoy Sunday morning runs with my mates up
to Devil's Bridge in the Yorkshire Dales and I'll still do a long journey
if it's pissing down with rain, because you get where you're going
quicker than you would in a car."

This may sound quite normal but most racers, accustomed as they
are to circuits closed to everyday traffic, ample run-off areas, safety
fencing and having top class medical facilities just minutes away,
deem normal road riding to be too dangerous. Jefferies was not
among them; he loved nothing better than taking a demonstrator
from his father's shop and heading out for a Sunday run with a
bunch of mates, just like every other biker in the country. It was this
attitude that endeared him to so many fans who saw Jefferies as one
of them, albeit a much, much faster version.

Even on public roads with all their associated dangers, Jefferies
was blindingly fast – and he didn't always pay too much attention to
the letter of the law either – as his friend Adam Evans testifies. "We
were going on a ride-out to a biker's meeting place one night and
there were no demonstrator bikes in the shop for Dave to take. So he
just grabbed the closest bike to him. It was brand new – not a mile
on the clock – so wasn't registered, didn't have a number plate, no
tax, insurance, nothing.

"We fixed up a plate and set off. I don't ride on the road much and
I was going faster than I was comfortable with, just trying to stay
with the pack – maybe about 120mph. Dave came past me pulling a

monster wheelie, then slammed it down and left a huge long line of rubber on the road. I thought something had broken on the bike and he was going to crash big time, but he was just messing about like he did, locking the back wheel. When he got the bike back to the shop, the exhaust had been squashed flat from cornering so hard and the backlight fell out because he'd been scraping it on the road doing wheelies. And this was a brand new bike that was supposed to be for sale! His sister gave him hell for that."

Keeping up with DJ's antics on the road wasn't easy, and if you got it wrong, you could expect no mercy from the man himself as another close friend, Karl Smith, remembers. "Me and David were on XR400 Hondas and had stopped at some traffic lights. When they went green we both pulled huge wheelies away from the lights, but I over-cooked it and flipped right over backwards. I hit a car as I slid along the road and was aware of a family standing on the pavement watching the whole thing. My dad had always taught me from my motocross days to get straight back on a bike when I fell off, so I did, even though my arm was agony, because I didn't want the family to call the police.

"I thought I had shattered my arm, but I'd just hit it hard on the road and it was all pins and needles. David was giggling his tits off. I got some stick over that."

TT winner Ian Hutchinson – a former employee of Allan Jefferies's shop and friend of David's – was more capable of keeping up with DJ but he remembers one occasion that almost ended in tragedy. "A big group of us went for a ride-out from Bradford to Ripon one Sunday morning.

"DJ was out on a BMW and he set off like a lunatic, flying round everywhere in just a pair of jeans and a leather jacket. One of my friends actually fell off his Triumph trying to follow him. He went through a wall and hurt himself quite badly. We all pulled up and I think Dave was pretty worried – he thought it was me in the wall.

"We hung around until my mate got air-lifted to hospital, then we carried on with the ride. I remember we ended up at a biker meeting place somewhere, and, after some breakfast, Dave fell asleep on the steps of a monument in the middle of the square. It was quite funny because here was the fastest man ever round the

TT course [the ride-out was in 2002] surrounded by bikers and no-one knew who he was."

And it wasn't just short Sunday blasts that Jefferies enjoyed: as a man who clocked up more than 8,000 miles a year on the roads, he was just as happy racking up big miles on any kind of bike, and in all weathers too. "He thought nothing of riding big miles," says Tony Jefferies. "He once rode to Eindhoven in Holland to get measured for a set of leathers. He then had a cup of coffee and rode back because he had something on that night. Didn't think anything of it."

Jefferies himself always felt he was a safe road rider – by his own standards at least. "I never stick my knee out on the road – never ever stick my knee out on the road," he said, before adding, "but I've never had anyone pass me yet. I think I ride fast but I also think I ride well within my limits on the road. I'm very conscious of other vehicles, towns, villages and farms – all the usual hazards."

In 2000, Jefferies joined *MCN* on a road test and discussed his fondness for road-riding and its relative dangers. "I reckon I've been pretty lucky on the road," he said, "no big crashes, just the usual 'Sorry mate – I didn't see you' car-pulling-out routine, and a couple of get-offs from digging in the pegs, going too fast."

Of his road-riding style Jefferies insisted, "I ride fast but I'm not a nutter. It's just loads of experience and knowing your limits."

Even when riding off-road, Jefferies was faster than his friends, many of whom were competition level motocrossers. Adam Evans recalls one of their annual trips to the Rally des Cimes in France."The week before, you're allowed to ride the stages, so we used to take dirt bikes down and have great fun. One year, David had a broken arm but we needed his truck to transport the bikes – and that's where we slept too – so there was no option of him not coming.

"Dave had a girl in tow and took a quad bike so she could go on the back with him. It was also easier for him to ride a quad with his arm in plaster than it would have been on a normal bike.

"So there he was with a broken arm, a pillion on the back, piled high with Jerry cans of fuel, tyres and other spares we'd made him carry, yet he was on a quad while we were on proper motocross bikes and he was *still* coming past us on every stage. We were really trying hard, to the point where it was getting dangerous, but Dave's 'dangerous' was obviously 20mph faster than ours.

"I like to think I'm pretty handy off-road but there were times when I was riding flat-out, as fast as I thought was possible, and Dave would come past me on the back wheel. Everything he did was fast; bikes, cars, mountain bikes – everything!"

*　*　*

By 1997, Honda's embarrassment at the RC45's lack of success was made clear when the firm took the unprecedented step of announcing it would supply ex-factory engines to private teams for the '97 British Superbike Championship in a bid to secure better results. Both David Jefferies's Medd Racing team and Michael Rutter's V&M squad were set to take delivery of the money-can't-buy, World Superbike-spec engines in the hope that they could improve upon the RC45's record of just one win at British championship level since the bike was introduced in 1994.

Former V&M rider, Mike Edwards – who quit the team in 1996 after just one meeting aboard the RC45 after being thrown from the bike – had his own ideas on why the Honda had failed to achieve results. "The bike is so unpredictable," he said. "One minute it's working fine at a track and the next it's evil. The problem is mainly with weight distribution. The bike felt like the front wheel was under me and the rear was all over the place."

The ex-factory engines were identical to those used by Carl Fogarty and Aaron Slight in the 1996 World Superbike Championship and they would come complete with special four-into-two exhaust systems, factory electrics, and sophisticated fuel management systems. Speaking in January 1997, David Jefferies was extremely upbeat about the forthcoming season, saying, "I think the advantage of the factory engine will not just be the extra horsepower but also the management system, which will allow us to maximise the power. I reckon the bike will have better power throughout the rev range and I should be able to pull out of the corners much better – more like the Ducatis. I'm really confident about 1997. I can't wait for the new engine."

By the end of the month however, it became clear that Jefferies would *have* to wait for his engine. Honda announced that, while the V&M team would receive engines in time for the start of the BSB season, Jefferies's Medd team would not be allocated theirs until after the TT – effectively half way through the season. It was believed that the engines were being kept in prime condition for Phillip McCallen to use at that year's TT before being handed over to Jefferies. Stuart Medd was furious. "We deserve the engines," he said. "I am not happy with us not getting the kit until after the TT."

Medd was also concerned that without the more competitive engines Jefferies would leave the team and look for another ride. In the end, the perceived lack of support from Honda, after Medd had spent three years developing the RC45, proved to be the final straw and he disbanded the Medd Racing Team. It was not only a loss to the British championship as a whole but to David Jefferies in particular, as he suddenly found himself without a BSB ride just weeks before the season got underway. It was a situation that would repeat itself with alarming regularity in the years to come.

With the Medd ride having fallen through, Jefferies started looking at other options. He came close to securing a ride with Russell Savory's RS Performance team on a Honda VTR1000 Firestorm, but when it became evident that the machine needed a lot more development to be competitive on short circuits the plan fell apart.

At least Jefferies had other rides to help him remain race sharp while he desperately tried to sort a BSB mount, though the first round of the Production Powerbike Championship (essentially the International TT Production Challenge which DJ had won the previous year but with a different name) was a disaster for the defending champion. After finishing way down in 16th and 15th places on his Honda FireBlade at the Thruxton double-header in March he said, "I didn't get the bike until last Thursday and there has been no time to practise with it. I've had a problem with the front suspension too – the bike just doesn't want to turn in."

Things didn't get much better for the remainder of the Production season for Jefferies and a string of poor results saw him lose his title by the end of the year.

April brought another opportunity for Jefferies to extend his racing experience as he took part in his first 24 Hour race at Le Mans in France. Riding for the British Phase One team alongside Andrew Stroud and Dave Goodley, Jefferies was about to discover the gruelling reality of endurance racing at the very highest level. Taking it in turns, the riders did stints of one hour each, all day and all night at an alarming pace, sometimes with only the light from their headlights pointing the way at 180mph. Endurance racing, as its name suggests, is recognised as one of the toughest forms of motorcycle sport and it was not an experience that Jefferies particularly enjoyed.

The team qualified in a respectable 12th position against the full World Championship grid with its seven works squads. After five hours of racing, things were looking even better when they moved up to 10th place but then their luck ran out. On the ninth lap of DJ's second stint – seven hours into the race – he was forced to take avoiding action to miss a rider who had crashed in front of him. As he returned to the track, Jefferies heard an engine problem and pitted to discover it was due to an inlet valve/valve head weld failure. Rather than retire from the race, the team decided to remove the engine and replace the damaged parts. According to the Phase One press release from the race, Jefferies, Stroud and Goodley were all keen to help, so two working groups were formed – one to strip the spare engine and the other to strip the engine from the race bike. After replacing a set of pistons, the cylinder block, cylinder head and camshafts, the engine was refitted and Goodley resumed the race.

Tony Jefferies claims there was another reason why David turned midnight mechanic – frustration. "David could have bikes in bits in minutes," he says. "He was very fast and very competent when it came to that. At Le Mans, when the bike blew up, he got very frustrated watching how slow the guy was stripping the engine. He just said, 'Oh, for fuck's sake, get out of the way' and got stuck in himself. He ended up pulling the engine apart and putting it all together again. You had to keep the same crank cases so they couldn't simply change engines – they had to get a crank out of another engine. They'd have been another two hours if David hadn't helped out."

As it was, the team had lost almost one-and-a-half hours (and 47 laps) in making the repairs. The time lost dropped them down to 54th position but each rider gritted his teeth and got his head down to eventually claw their way back up to 27th – scant reward for such a tiring 12 hours of work.

Back at home, Jefferies continued his search for competitive rides both in BSB and for his second attempt at the TT. The fact that he didn't consider Honda's Firestorm to be competitive enough for the short-circuit-based BSB championship didn't stop him from thinking the bike would prove to be an ideal tool for the TT, where stability and torque are more important than razor-sharp handling and outright power.

Without any firm offers of machinery for the TT, David hatched a plan to modify an ex-demonstrator Firestorm from his father's shop and race it under his own steam. The idea was to turn the used road bike into a proper race bike with the addition of new pistons, carbs, Ohlins suspension, and a racing exhaust system. Although it was going back to his privateer roots, Jefferies was clearly looking forward to the prospect. "I'm not going out to try and win because I'm still learning the course," he said. "But the Firestorm should be really good there. It has loads of torque and handles really well."

Despite the fact that he had only ridden a standard Firestorm on a short blast down a dual carriageway near his home, Jefferies felt the bike was ideally suited to the TT and he was hopeful of getting into the top ten. "I was in the top 16 on a 600 last year so I don't think a top ten is out of reach," he said. "I hope I can do better this year but I won't be going like a bat out of hell – you can't do that there."

It would have been fascinating to see how well Jefferies would have faired in his second year on the Mountain course riding a V-twin. Sadly, neither he nor his fans got the chance to find out as, just two weeks before practice started for the event, DJ broke his left collarbone after crashing a BMW K1200RS road bike on a track day at Donington Park. "That were a big one," Tony Jefferies says. "He destroyed that bike. Absolutely destroyed it. It was a demonstrator from the shop and the back wheel, with the swinging arm, was 100 yards away from the bike when it finally came to rest."

Tony believes that pride may have proved to be his son's downfall on that occasion. "Everyone was at the track day on fancy sports bikes and were saying to David, 'You'll never get round Donington fast on a BMW'. It was like a red rag to a bull. He was going for it and was absolutely blitzing everybody until he got to Starkey's Bridge and changed down gears instead of up because he was so used to riding race bikes all the time (whose gears work in the opposite direction to road bikes). It was a big bike but it was absolute mince once he'd finished with it."

Jefferies underwent intensive laser treatment in a bid to be fit for the TT but muscling a Superbike round the Island's punishing and horrendously bumpy course is hard enough for any man, even at full fitness, and Jefferies eventually had to face the fact that he wouldn't be racing at the 1997 TT.

It's tempting to wonder how much sooner Jefferies could have racked up his first win at the TT had he not been forced to miss a year so soon after making his Mountain course debut. But motorcycle racing has always been littered with 'ifs' and 'buts' and speculation is futile. Suffice to say that when Jefferies eventually returned to the Isle of Man in 1998, it would be two full years since he last rode the course and he would effectually have to set about learning it all over again, if not from scratch, then at least from very near it.

Still, his enforced lay-off allowed him to ponder how best to make use of the second half of the racing season and Jefferies's thoughts returned to the original plan from the start of the year – campaigning the ex-factory Honda RC45 engine that was frustratingly kept in mothballs for Phillip McCallen – and on which he won the F1 TT. With the TT now over, Jefferies rationalised, the engine and race kit should now be available again. Calls were made to Honda UK who in turn put David's request to their Japanese bosses.

In what turned out to be his third major disappointment of the year, as far as securing a competitive and reliable ride went, this deal also fell through and DJ found himself more than halfway through the UK racing season without a BSB ride.

The season went from bad to worse when Jefferies suffered a 140mph crash at the Spa 24 Hour race in Belgium in July and broke his collarbone again, putting him out of action for a further spell. It would prove to be DJ's last 24 Hour race. It wasn't the broken collarbone that had put him off, it was more the very nature of 24-Hour racing as Tony Jefferies explains. "He just didn't enjoy it. He said it was just cold, wet and boring."

David was back in action at Oulton Park on 23 July where he won the Triumph Speed Triple Challenge race (it would prove to be his only win in the Triumph series all year and he was forced to relinquish his crown by the season's end) but it wasn't until August that he finally returned to the British Superbike Championship, and when he did, it wasn't on McCallen's Honda but on a Ducati 916. After Honda bosses had denied Jefferies the chance to ride its precious factory machine, DJ took up the offer to ride a Ducati for the DeWalt Baxi team and made his long-awaited return at Knockhill in the eighth round of the series. Despite having been away for so long, DJ was competitive straight away and *MCN* reported that he 'scorched to a stunning seventh place in race one.'

Jefferies was delighted to be back. "I've been desperate to get out and ride in the BSB championship this year," he said. "I've not ridden all season and when you're not racing regularly people forget who you are."

His first leg result saw him being the highest placed privateer apart from Steve Hislop, who had enjoyed a superb ride to second place on a private Kawasaki after being sacked from his Red Bull Ducati team for under-performing. It was the highest position a privateer had ever achieved in BSB, so it was no shame for Jefferies to finish five places behind him. DJ had even beaten the privateer cup championship leader Ray Stringer – no mean achievement after such a lengthy lay-off from this level of competition.

He backed up his race one performance with a solid 10th in race two to prove that he belonged in BSB and deserved a chance on a factory machine. There was even better to come at Cadwell where Jefferies took sixth place to win the privateers' race (effectively a race within a race where privateer riders are awarded separate points from the factory teams), his team-mate, Andy Ward, having taken the privateers' win in the first race of the day.

But it was too little too late as far as the championship went and, having missed so many rounds through injury and not having a ride, Jefferies didn't feature in the overall standings at the end of the year.

There were more wins to come during the Gold Cup races at Oliver's Mount in September however. Not only did he win the feature Gold Cup race, he was also victorious in the second national Superbike leg and the TT Production race. It was DJ's third Gold Cup win and in taking it, he had denied circuit specialist Dean Ashton the chance to join racing legends Geoff Duke and Barry Sheene as four-time winners of the prestigious trophy – a feat Jefferies himself hoped to emulate. "It feels great to win after I won here in 1992 and 1994," he said. "And hopefully I'll be back next year to try and equal Duke and Sheene's record."

Jefferies wouldn't equal the record in 1998 – a broken pelvis saw to that. But before his season was cut short, he made his mark on a bike which would transform his career – the Yamaha R1.

When Yamaha launched its new YZF1000 R1 at the beginning of 1998, it set new standards for sports bike performance. Honda's CBR900RR FireBlade had been the benchmark for performance and agility since its introduction in 1992 but the new R1 outclassed it in every way. Weighing just 177 kg and producing a claimed 150bhp, the £9,199 bike had the tiny dimensions of a 250cc Grand Prix racer and looked fast even at a standstill. And that was just the standard road version. It was clear that when race tuners got their hands on this machine, it was going to be one hell of a potent missile.

David Jefferies took delivery of the first R1 to be shipped to the UK in January 1998. His excitement at getting his hands on the bike is made vividly clear in the following extract from his occasional newsletter, *DJ Racing News*. "It was amazing. The more we looked into the R1, the more we found in terms of real technology for the next century. We took it apart and within no time I had the whole bike spread across the garage floor. All the basics for a proper racing bike were there. Now it was time to study how I could modify and improve the bike to racing standards; but first things first, engine to Tony Scott – let the engine boffins do the engine work, this is not my speciality.

"I went to work on the chassis. Making a race bike means getting rid of all the unnecessary road parts, modifying the suspension, and disposing of as much weight as the rules would allow. Making a modified wiring harness, new lightweight footrests, racing gear linkages and a mass of bracketry modifications meant burning the midnight oil. I had a spare bike at Micron who were developing a brand new race exhaust system for the R1.

The engine was 'A joy to work on,' said Tony Scott, who had a race-prepared version ready in super quick time. I ran the new engine in and took it to the dyno at Micron. The first test showed 150bhp at the rear wheel. This bike had potential.

"Back to Shipley and put it all together. New Marvic wheels, PFM discs, Elliot clocks, Goodridge hoses, fuel lines, filler-caps, sprockets and chain just to mention a few of the race mods required. From sports bike to racer with a vengeance!"

Jefferies had entered the bike in the new-look British Powerbike Championship but only had the chance of one test day before the first round at Donington Park. In fact, on the Friday before Saturday qualifying, he was still to be found in the paddock fitting the fairings that were fresh out of the moulds that morning.

It hardly mattered. He utterly dominated the race on the bike he had prepared himself. Jefferies finished more than 10 seconds ahead of Paul Brown and Steve Plater and set the fastest lap of the race that also happened to be a new lap record. A delighted Jefferies told the *Yorkshire Evening Post*, "It was my first race of the year and I'd only had about 20 laps testing at Oulton Park the previous Wednesday. It's a brand new bike and no-one really knows its capabilities but we've a few things to do on it yet so I'm sure there's more to come."

Despite his three-time success in the Gold Cup meeting at Scarborough, Jefferies had never managed to win the Ken Redfern trophy at the circuit's traditional spring meeting. Armed with his new R1, it was time to make amends. Jefferies won the feature Ken Redfern Trophy race from Jason Griffiths and Dean Ashton but getting his hands on the famous trophy itself proved a touch more difficult.

Tradition has it that the winner of the trophy takes it home until the following year when he either wins the right to keep it for another year or presents it to the new winner. In 1997, the winner had been none other than David's uncle Nick Jefferies. When Nick announced his retirement from racing at the end of that year, he was careful to hand back the trophy to the Auto 66 Club officials who organise the Scarborough races. Nick eventually reversed his decision over winter and started racing again in 1998 – in fact he had taken part in the race that his nephew had just won – but the ornate silver trophy had remained in the club's hands. When officials tried to find the trophy to present it to David on the podium they drew a blank and had to send the race winner home empty-handed. Further investigation proved that the official who was looking after the trophy had it under lock and key in his house and had gone off to watch an endurance race at Snetterton on the day of the Ken Redfern meeting. Nick Jefferies said, "I told the club I was coming back and reminded them that they had the trophy. It's a shame that David didn't get presented with his first Ken Redfern – the daft buggers!"

Just three-tenths of a second separated DJ and the Honda FireBlade-mounted duo of Steve Plater and Paul Brown during qualifying for the second round of the Powerbike series at Snetterton. But come race day, Jefferies dominated once again, leading all but one lap of the 25-lap race. "I thought the race at Snetterton would really suit the power of the Yamaha," he said afterwards, "but I have to say Honda nearly caught us out. They had done a lot of private testing and had special engines developed by the factory for Paul Brown and Steve Plater."

But it seemed that no amount of work done by the mighty Honda could stop Jefferies's onslaught on the awesome new Yamaha, and in May he shipped it over the Irish Sea in a bid to give the bike its first ever win on a public roads circuit at the North West 200.

With no Superbike or 600cc Supersport rides, Jefferies was only entered in the Production race but the brute power of the R1, even in near-standard trim, was demonstrated during practice when he reported seeing 188mph on the speedometer. It was perhaps just as well that the Yamaha had so much grunt for its tiny dimensions coupled with Jefferies's solid build may not have been a match made in heaven otherwise. As it was, any detrimental aerodynamic effect or loss in the power-to-weight ratio of man and machine were more than made up for by the R1's incredible power. In a bid to improve the aerodynamic flow over his broad shoulders, Jefferies had an extra 'bubble' fitted on top of the bike's screen and noticed a huge difference straight away. "It's incredible what a two-inch high piece of plastic can do," he said. "My head was no longer being ripped off my shoulders and the grit – which feels like boulders when thrown up at you at such speeds – flew straight over the top of my head."

In fact, the bike was so good that none of the standard Honda FireBlades ridden by the likes of Ian Simpson, Steve Plater or Iain Duffus could live with it. Only the factory-prepared Blade – which had been intended for Phillip McCallen but was taken over by Michael Rutter after McCallen was injured – could match the R1 for sheer speed. Consequently, it was Rutter who took the battle to Jefferies as the pair pulled out an incredible 18-second lead over the rest of the field. They passed and re-passed each other throughout the race but Rutter finally sneaked the advantage on the last lap to win by less than two-thousandths of a second.

Because Jefferies was without a Superbike ride, he missed out on valuable track time during practice and even on race day. The other leading riders had got up to speed with more sessions on more bikes and most had taken part in the opening Superbike race before lining up for the Production event. "I just wish I had some more track time," Jefferies bemoaned. "With the long wait from Thursday practice, it took me a while to get into the groove, whereas the other riders had already had a race."

The R1 had come agonisingly close to achieving its first real roads win and Jefferies might well have delivered it had he been a touch more race-sharp. Even so, the North West 200 meeting had proved invaluable practice for the biggest road race of the year – the Isle of Man TT. As Jefferies explained, "There is no other way of testing the handling of a bike at speeds in the 180mph area, even on a track in England, and the first indications for the bike are good.

"We still have some work to do as the back end was floating around a bit on the high speed corners and I would like it more stable for the TT. You don't ride as hard at the TT but you have a lot more bumps."

Because of his wealth of racing experience in so many other arenas, it's easy to forget that 1998 was only David Jefferies's second year at the TT. Having missed the previous year's event through injury, he had to relearn the course during practice week and, by the end of it, he still wasn't convinced he knew his way around the 300-odd corners that make up the world's longest road race course. "The secret to going well at the TT is knowing the circuit," he said following practice. "I've been quite fortunate this week, even with losing the Wednesday of practice week I've got quite a few laps in. I still don't know where I'm going enough yet to start winning races. I missed last year because I had an accident at a track day a week before the TT, which was a bit unfortunate, so I wasn't fit to ride – I broke my collarbone.

"I'm really enjoying myself – I'm learning my way round and I enjoy riding the Production bike – it doesn't do anything silly; it handles really well, so I'm just going to go out and enjoy myself and see how we do."

Jefferies had entered four races at the 1998 TT and had a varied stable of machinery to see the job through. The Formula 1 he would contest on a Honda RC45, the Junior on a Honda CBR600, and the Production and Senior on the Yamaha R1. The Formula 1 race produced his best result to date with an eighth place in what was his first ride on a Superbike at the TT (in 1996 he had only competed on a 600cc machine).

DJ mirrored that result in Wednesday's Junior race on his Honda, meaning he was really starting to know his way around by the time the final race day approached. It would be a tough day with two races to contest – the Production and the Senior. That meant a total of nine laps, almost 340 miles at racing speeds, which is the equivalent of almost five Grand Prix races.

Jefferies really made the paddock sit up and take notice with a stunning ride to fourth place in the Production TT. It was the only race all week where he was on equal machinery to his rivals, and he had the advantage of knowing the bike inside out from racing it on the mainland all season. The race was won by Jim Moodie from Nigel Davies and Michael Rutter, but David's R1 was the first Yamaha home.

After the Production race, and before the afternoon's Senior event, DJ reflected on his best TT result by far and speculated on how he might fare in the Senior. "I didn't expect any amazing results and, like I say, fourth place in the Production race.... I mean, Jim Moodie and Nigel Davies and Michael Rutter – they're all really fast people round here so, yeah, everything's gone really good. This afternoon in the Senior it's the R1 again, but it's on slicks, so I think we should go alright on that but I wouldn't have thought I'd finish as high up because there's a lot more people – all the big Hondas, and it's quite a competitive class, so, hopefully, if I could finish in the top ten I'd be really pleased."

He did far more than finish in the top ten. In the oldest and most prestigious TT race of them all, Jefferies finished fourth and fired a warning shot across the bows of all the top competitors that he was on the verge of TT greatness.

By the end of the week, DJ had racked up two eighth places, two fourth places, a 100% finishing record, and a fastest lap just short of 120mph. If this was what he could do in only his second TT, and after a year missed out through injury, it was clear that he was capable of great things the following year.

Following the TT, Jefferies was leading the third round of the Powerbike series at Donington Park in July when misfortune struck. He had just overtaken Paul Brown and looked set to record his third straight win in the championship when he lost control of the R1 and crashed heavily, breaking his pelvis. As the pelvis is the largest bone in the human body, the injury was enough to rule him out of racing for several months and ended any hopes he had of winning the Powerbike championship which he had dominated up to that point.

It was a sad way to end a season that was only half way through, but Jefferies wasn't about to give up. The enforced lay-off allowed him to focus his mind on the 1999 season, but even he couldn't have dreamed of the impact he would make in the coming year.

Chapter 8

DAVID AND GOLIATH

"I'm a fighter at this game and I wasn't going to be stopped."
David Jefferies

It was at the North West 200 in 1999 that David Jefferies finally found his true vocation in motorcycle racing and the one that made him a star. His exploits in World Superbikes, Grands Prix and in British short circuit racing meant that his name was already well established, but it was the way in which he took pure road racing by the scruff of the neck and proceeded to dominate it for the next four years that made him a legend. And that legend began at the NW200 in 1999.

For once, Jefferies had the bikes to match his talent. After years of running Honda RC45s, V&M racing's Jack Valentine had finally abandoned the marque after a fall-out with Honda UK bosses. For 1999, he decided to tune a brace of new Yamaha R1s, convinced he could coax enough power out of them to trounce his former employees, the mighty Honda. "We'd had a particularly bad year in '99," explains Valentine. "We had a fire at the workshop and by the time we got that all sorted out it was too late to get a budget together and do BSB. So we said, 'Right what shall we do? We'd better do something – we'll do the TT.' So we started looking at riders and we had always got on with DJ, so we looked at his results on his previous bikes – Superstock bikes – and knew he could win without any question. We thought, 'This guy's gonna be the next star over there.' So, we had a chat and he came down to the workshops. We went through what we could do, and that's how it all started."

The V&M team might have had a rider sorted but the road racing season was fast approaching and Valentine and his partner Steve Mellor only had a matter of weeks to prepare their bikes. "We knew we could make the horsepower with them, so Steve got to work on the engines," says Valentine. "We had previously run the factory

127

Hondas so we knew what horsepower they made, and they were the only competition we had.

"In the end we had 30bhp more than they had, so I said, 'Right, as long as it goes in a straight line to start with [because we were going to the North West first] we'll be alright.' But we didn't know. We had never had it on a track or anything. We went straight to the North West and finished building the bikes there."

With the bikes only completed on the morning of the first NW200 practice session there was no time for any testing on a proper race circuit, so Jefferies found himself having his first ride on a V&M R1 round the back roads of County Antrim. "DJ had to run the bikes in on Irish country lanes," remembers Valentine. "It was pissing down with rain and David came back covered in cow shit, horse shit – everything! A brand new bike, first time out, and it was covered with shit off these Irish lanes. But he said, 'Yeah, yeah – it feels alright,' so we headed to the North West paddock.

"The first practice session was that same day and the bike was like a missile; it passed everything and David put the bike on pole position. I always remember him chatting to his dad Tony on the phone. His dad was asking, 'How's it handling?' And DJ said, 'Dad, I could take my hands off the handlebars and I could eat my dinner off the tank.' And after that he just cleaned up – he just cleaned up. We knew we were home and dry then for the TT, and of course the rest is history."

Jefferies's pole position was an awesome achievement, both for him and his last-minute team, and one that rightfully caught the paddock's attention. But Jefferies's performance in practice was overshadowed by yet another reminder of how dangerous the NW200 can be. Former Grand Prix rider and North West winner Donny Robinson was killed in practice following a crash at the Mill Road roundabout, 13 years after his brother Neil had also lost his life at Oliver's Mount in Scarborough – another of Jefferies's favourite tracks.

Having led the Production race for most of the way in 1998, with only a lack of race-sharpness letting him down in the end, Jefferies made sure he contested three races in 1999 – both Superbike events plus the Supersport 600 event – in order to get more track time and increase his chances of success.

With practice over, Jefferies set out from pole position in the opening Superbike race of the day only to be flagged back into the paddock along with all the other riders when Paul Dedman crashed into a marshal's post and broke his own leg as well as one of the marshal's. In the restarted race, Jefferies, his team-mate Iain Duffus, and Honda's Jim Moodie conducted a battle royal for the top spot with the lead changing constantly. On the final run along the coast road towards the chequered flag, it looked like Jefferies would have to settle for third spot as the two Scotsmen pulled away at the front. But unknown to the huge crowd – as well as Moodie and Duffus – Jefferies was riding in agony as an old motocross injury had played up and resulted in his kneecap popping out of joint. He told *Ireland's Saturday Night,* "On that last lap going into Portrush I felt my knee go. I thought I might have to stop and lose what chance I had but I was determined that this was going to be my big day and I just kept going although I was in dreadful pain."

Incredibly, Jefferies managed to push his dislocated knee back into place while still travelling at racing speed but, as he explained afterwards, he simply wasn't going to accept second best on the day. "On the run from Portrush to the finish Duffus was in front and then Moodie passed me and I thought then that the best I could achieve was third. But I'm a fighter at this game. I've been trying to win here since 1994 and I wasn't going to be stopped. I took the lead again at the Juniper Hill chicane and it would have taken an awful lot of pain to have stopped me after that."

It was a superhuman effort that resulted in Jefferies reaching the finish line ahead of Moodie and Duffus to take his first North West 200 win, and he was understandably ecstatic with his victory. Others were less pleased however. Jefferies's team-mate Iain Duffus was upset with some of the moves that had been made in the closing stages of the race. He complained "Jefferies came across me along the road and with Moodie on the other side I had nowhere to go."

Usually one of the most relaxed men in the paddock before a race, Jefferies admitted that nerves had got the better of him for once as he lined up on the V&M R1. "I don't normally get nervous before a race," he said, "but because I had so much power and knew I could win I was shitting myself!"

Jefferies was in tears after the race for two reasons: firstly because of what he had just achieved (a North West 200 win had always eluded his father), but mostly because of the pain from his dislocated knee.

This was easily the biggest win of Jefferies's career, but he wasn't about to rest on his laurels for the remainder of the day. As he had learned the year before, maintaining a race-sharpness throughout a multiple race day can reap rewards. And it certainly did on this occasion as DJ went on to win the Supersport 600 race after another epic flag-to-flag battle, this time with Moodie and local star Phillip McCallen.

McCallen was, and remains, a legend in the sport. As an 11-times TT winner – and the only man in history to have won four TTs in a week, a feat he achieved in 1996 – McCallen had also won an incredible, record-breaking five North West 200 wins in one day back in 1992. Although no-one knew it at the time, this was to be McCallen's last year in racing as he had been warned that one more awkward fall on his back, which he had broken at Thruxton in 1998, could leave him paralysed. On top of that, the Irishman had also recently suffered a serious shoulder injury that meant he struggled to hold onto his bike at the high speeds reached round the North West course. Hard as it may have been on a man so wholly committed to road racing, McCallen knew when to quit.

But not before putting up one hell of a fight in his swansong NW200. He and Moodie did everything humanly possible – and then some – to stop Jefferies's onslaught, but the big man was on a roll and gave as good as, and better than, he got, taking the win by 0.8 seconds from McCallen with Moodie, just 0.25 seconds farther back.

By the end of the race, DJ had chalked up two wins from two starts and set a new 600cc lap record round the North West course at 117.41mph. Too big to ride a 600cc machine? No-one told Jefferies. "McCallen and Moodie are just unbelievably hard men to ride with," he gasped after the race. "It was bloody enjoyable though – I really did enjoy that race and I'm just so glad I won."

And still he wasn't finished. No-one had managed a treble at the

NW200 since Robert Dunlop in 1994 but as Jefferies lined up for the feature event, the North West 200 Superbike race itself, there seemed no reason why he couldn't rewrite the record books. Usually laughing and joking before the start of a race, this time Jefferies seemed to be feeling the pressure as both he and Moodie dashed behind the race organisers' caravans to relieve themselves before the off!

The race was another stunner with strong challenges from local hot shot James Courtney on the Red Bull Ducati, McCallen again on the Yamaha R1, Duffus on the other V&M machine, and Moodie ever present on the Honda RC45. In the end only Moodie had the pace to go with Jefferies, but a new absolute lap record from DJ at 122.26mph proved too much for the Scotsman and Jefferies, who'd eaten breakfast without ever having won a North West 200 race, ended his afternoon with three international wins under his belt.

He was understandably elated at winning the feature race of the day. "Everything worked out perfect. It's unbelievable," he said after the race. "Neither bike missed a beat which is a great credit to the V&M team. You've also got to hand it to Jim Moodie. He must have ridden his balls off to stay that close. I only had one slide all day – after Mather's Cross on the fourth lap of the big one.

"Before the race I kind of fancied myself for one of the Superbike races, especially after I had been fastest in practice. I thought a top three position would be my best on the 600, but half way through the race I was still with them and I thought I was in with a chance of victory. I went under McCallen at the Metropole and he didn't get me back, so I was pleased. I rang my dad after each race. He seemed pleased too. We both planned a good pint or two on Saturday night."

Jefferies had become only the third Englishman in the North West 200's 70-year history to win three races in a day and his utter domination of the meeting meant that it was the first time since 1975 that an Irish rider failed to win a race. It was also the first Superbike double for a Yamaha rider since 1984 and, aside from the sporting accolades, Jefferies's performance had also earned him a handsome pay day – he netted around £10,000 in prize money alone for a day's work, not to mention the additional bonuses he received from his personal sponsors, like helmet and leather companies.

The significance of what he'd achieved that weekend didn't truly sink in until some time afterwards as Jefferies later admitted. "It didn't really hit me until after I went home. In racing everyone was saying 'Well done', but they always do. When you get home and all your mates who don't really know about racing are saying 'Brilliant, well done' when you go out for a beer, that's when it really hits home. It's going to go down in history. Very few people have won three in a day. Very few."

The 1999 North West 200 may have been the making of David Jefferies as a bona fide star of the pure road racing scene but it was just one meeting in a busy 1999 schedule. Tony Jefferies produced a glossy pre-season brochure aimed at attracting sponsors for the coming season and it offers an eye-opening insight into the costs of competing in the British Superbike Championship and the Isle of Man TT. It stated that 'The minimum budget for one rider to compete in the British Superbike Championship is £196,000. The amount required from a major sponsor is £100,000. The TT may be treated as a separate sponsorship package – the cost of TT sponsorship is £25,000.'

The plan behind the brochure had been to raise enough sponsorship money to run two new, ultra-exclusive WSB replica Yamaha R7s in British Superbikes and selected World Superbike rounds. The bikes, which were homologation specials made for the specific purpose of winning the WSB championship, were to be supplied by Yamaha UK together with some factory back-up. But the whole deal depended on the Jefferies drumming up enough sponsorship for the season and this has never been an easy task in bike racing. So it proved for David and Tony. When the reality dawned that the requisite money was not forthcoming, alternative plans had to be made. One of them was most bizarre – David decided to enter the Aprilia RS250 Challenge, which meant squeezing his considerable frame onto a tiny, lightweight two-stroke machine after years campaigning big four-stroke Superbikes. But the series was high profile, cheap to enter, and rewarded riders with reasonable prize money. What also made it attractive to Jefferies was that he'd be on exactly the same bike as all his rivals so he wouldn't suffer from the machinery disadvantage that had always held him back at British Superbike level.

The Aprilia class had been fully subscribed by the time Jefferies made his late bid for an entry but he was lucky to be given a slot on the grid when another rider pulled out through injury. And as things turned out, Jefferies's size didn't prove to be a problem at all as he romped away to win the first race, in March, at Cadwell Park by over 10 seconds from Matt Llewellyn, using all his considerable experience to deal with the treacherous damp conditions. Unfortunately, a carburetion problem on the Allan Jefferies-sponsored Yamaha R1 forced DJ out of the opening round of the British Sports Production Championship at the same meeting, and another DNF at Mallory saw Jefferies with no points at all after two rounds of the series. But a sixth place on the RS250 kept him in the points in the Aprilia Challenge.

On 2 May Jefferies won the opening round of the new Axo Superstock European Championship at Donington Park but was not eligible to score points since he was over 24 years of age. He was, however, permitted to keep his prize money, which was the intention all along – as well as proving he could win races at European level.

After Donington, Jefferies had sailed to Ireland to dominate at the North West 200 and immediately after that it was time to catch another ferry, this time to the Isle of Man. When he returned, he would be a legend.

* * *

Now the biggest motorcycle manufacturer in the world, Honda had first entered the Isle of Man TT races in 1959, much to the amusement of many British riders and race fans who thought the Japanese would never be able to build bikes capable of beating the then all-conquering British and Italian marques. Honda soon proved the doubters wrong and won its first TT in 1961 with the legendary Mike Hailwood at the helm. Over the next few decades, the Japanese firm came to dominate the TT and, in particular, the Formula 1 race which it had won for 18 consecutive years since 1982. It was practically Honda's race.

Even though the firm wasn't running a factory-backed effort in British Superbikes in 1999, it still maintained a strong presence on the Isle of Man because its founder, Soichiro Honda, had vowed to win there in a statement made back in 1954 when he began producing motorcycles. Because Honda's first TT win had effectively made the company in the eyes of the world, and because of Mr Honda's recognition of the part that Isle of Man success had played in building his company, the firm continued to view the TT as a hugely important event and continued to support it even when most other manufacturers pulled out in the 1990s.

The 1999 TT was no exception and HRC – Honda's legendary racing arm – had prepared and shipped over two exotic RC45s for Joey Dunlop and Jim Moodie to race. The bikes were the same spec as those campaigned in that year's World Superbike Championship by Aaron Slight and Colin Edwards and were extremely rare, not to mention expensive. *Motor Cycle News* estimated that each machine was worth £500,000 and reported that Honda had turned up on the Island with another £1 million worth of back-up. That meant a £2 million assault on the TT with the chief aim of retaining the Formula 1 crown it had held for the best part of two decades. Everyone else was racing for second place – everyone, that is, except for Jack Valentine and his V&M team.

Valentine still had a bitter taste in his mouth after splitting with Honda the previous year and he dearly wanted to get one over on the firm. But to do that – without the vast financial resources that his rival had at its disposal – he needed an extraordinary bike and an extraordinary rider. Incredibly, he found both – and at a bargain price to boot.

David Jefferies and the Yamaha R1 had proved their potential at the North West 200 but had yet to win at the TT. It was Jefferies's third year at the event and he still felt he didn't know his way round properly. Podiums were perhaps possible, but beating the might of Honda seemed a step too far, especially since he would be going up against the £500,000 RC45 on a £20,000 modified street bike. Odds don't come much more stacked. But then, the Isle of Man is a place where fairy tale victories are not unheard of. In 1978, Mike Hailwood had come out of an 11-year retirement to win the Formula 1 race in what has been described as one of the greatest moments of 20th Century sport. The TT is that kind of race.

Practice week followed an all-too-familiar pattern and this time it was popular Englishman Simon Beck who paid the ultimate price when he lost his life following a 140mph crash at the 33rd Milestone. His death cast a dark shadow over the week but, with the grim acceptance displayed by all motorcycle racers and their teams that fatalities can and will happen on occasion, the paddock went about its business, respectfully and professionally, though saddened and subdued.

Jefferies ended practice week with the third fastest time overall behind Jim Moodie and Iain Duffus and ahead of the man generally accepted as the greatest TT racer of all time, Joey Dunlop, who had already notched up 23 of his ultimate tally of 26 wins.

As usual, the Formula 1 race kicked off race week and an eventful race it turned out to be. Just minutes after the start, pre-race favourite Jim Moodie stopped at Glen Lough with a suspected cracked crankcase (although Honda officially blamed a failed engine management unit) and his race was over – or so it seemed. Just moments later the race was red-flagged for the first time since 1954 when Paul Orritt suffered the longest and most horrendous-looking tank-slapper at full speed down Bray Hill. He wrestled with his Honda FireBlade for as long as humanly possible but was eventually thrown from the violently bucking machine and was lucky to escape with just a broken leg. Debris from the crash littered the road and left the organisers with no option but to stop the race.

Sensing he may be in with a chance of making the re-start, Jim Moodie performed a feat of almost superhuman endurance by running three-and-a-half miles back to the paddock (much of it uphill) still clad in heavy leathers, boots and gloves and with helmet in hand, and in scorching conditions too. His heroic efforts were in vain however, when he realised Honda had no spare bike ready for him. Needless to say, he was "bitterly disappointed", not to mention exhausted.

When the race was restarted one hour later, it had been cut to four laps instead of the usual six but that still meant a distance of 150 miles – more than two Grand Prix distances. Jefferies's V&M team-mate Iain Duffus took an early lead before being overhauled by Joey Dunlop on the last remaining factory RC45. Dunlop held the lead until the mid-race pit stop where he was forced to replace his worn-out rear tyre that he had shredded during his charge to the front of the field. The tyre change was to cost Dunlop 20 seconds. Jefferies gambled on continuing with the same tyres and left the pits in the lead.

Jefferies still held a 17-second lead on the last lap but Dunlop wasn't finished. He posted the fastest lap of his life (123.06mph) in pursuit of his younger foe but even that wasn't enough to defeat Jefferies who maintained his pace to win by 15 seconds from the acknowledged 'King of the Mountain' himself. David Jefferies had won his first TT, even if he couldn't quite grasp it. "I can't believe this," he beamed. "I never thought I'd win, despite knowing how good the bike is. I just didn't think I had the experience to do it. I can barely tell you how good it feels to take a win on a bike that costs £20,000 in front of those expensive factory Hondas.

"It might sound daft," he added, "but I don't really know my way around much of the course. I was all over the place at some of the corners and I don't think I got the line around Verandah right more than once."

It was ominous news for his rivals. If Jefferies could defeat the TT's greatest rider without even knowing the course properly – and come within 1.9 seconds of setting a new outright lap record – what would he be capable of with some more experience?

Although it wasn't completely obvious at the time, Jefferies's David and Goliath win over the might of Honda changed the face of racing, both at the TT and in other aspects of British racing. If modified road bikes were good enough to beat hand-built specials from the most advanced racing workshops in the world, then why bother hanging out for a factory ride? DJ's win suddenly opened the door for any amount of riders to put together their own teams in the knowledge that if both they and their team were good enough, they too could humble the giants of racing who had called the shots for so long. As *MCN* reported, "For Honda, the result was a massive slap in the face."

Jack Valentine agreed. "It was very satisfying to beat Honda after they had dropped us from running their factory team. I heard lots through the grapevine after that win. I think the genuine people in Honda were happy for us – but yeah, for sure, it really pissed others off big time, and obviously helped with the R1 sales."

Incredibly, all the parts used on Jefferies's winning V&M bike were available to the man in the street and not exotic one-off factory items which are completely unattainable to anyone except factory riders. To emphasise the point, Jack Valentine announced straight away that he would build a replica of DJ's bike for anyone who wanted one at a cost of just £20,000 – and that included the £8,299 price of the standard bike.

Speaking years later, Jefferies would still remember that first TT win as his favourite. Not because he'd beaten Honda, not because he'd earned a nice pay packet, and not even because he'd finally made a real name for himself. It was simply because of the joy his win brought to his family. It was, "Because my mum and dad were so pleased, and my sister was up at the Creg, waving and cheering as I went past – it was a mega feeling."

The Junior TT was next up and, despite the jibes about his size not being suited to a 600cc machine, Jefferies proved his doubters wrong again with a strong ride to second place. Jim Moodie was clearly in no mood to be beaten following his F1 disappointment and even when he lost his clutch on the first lap and had fuel splashed into his eyes at the pit stop, he simply dug deeper and won the race with one good eye and without the aid of a clutch!

After a relatively slow start which saw him in sixth place at the end of lap one, Jefferies found his pace to such a degree that he looked like he could even win the race. His last lap charge saw him come within 0.4 seconds of Ian Simpson's lap record but Moodie held on to his hard-earned lead and took the win by 18 seconds. Jefferies was still pleased with the result. "I knew that last lap was a good one but I rolled off near Ballacraine because there was an accident," he explained. "I think I would have beaten the lap record if I'd had a clear lap – still, second isn't too shabby is it?"

There was no shortage of drama in the Production race on the Friday morning before the curtain-closing Senior. It's easy for non-racers to underestimate the difficulties involved in switching between different bikes at meetings like the TT. In GPs, WSB and BSB, riders race the same bike all year and become intimately familiar with its power, speed, handling and braking abilities. Not so at the TT where riders might race as many as four or five bikes in a week, varying from 125cc two-strokes to 1000cc four-stroke Superbikes. This can cause all kinds of problems. Speaking of the difference between his tuned Formula 1 R1 compared to the near-standard Chesterfield Motorcycles Production race version, Jefferies explained, "The speed at which things arrived was the biggest difference. It was easy to switch from the F1 bike to the Proddie – that felt slow and forgiving by comparison. But swapping the other way was tricky because the F1 bike was so much faster that it wheelied in places you wouldn't expect, and the braking points were much different. I hit the bales in the Proddie race because I misjudged my braking."

Jefferies crashed into the bales at Ballacraine and lost precious time as he tried to back his R1 out of them. The steering lock on the bike proved to be so limited that he ran straight back into the bales as he attempted to restart. He explained the cause of his mishap. "After riding the tuned R1 in the Formula 1 race I just forgot that this was basically a stock bike with road tyres and standard brakes. I started braking at the usual mark and then realised I was never going to make the turn so I drifted wide into the bales."

Eventually getting back on his way, he chased his team-mate Iain Duffus hard, but the Scotsman looked to have the race sewn up with an eight second lead on the last quarter of the last lap, having slashed six seconds off the lap record. Then more drama. Duffus was reported to be touring, having run out of petrol at Cronk-ny-Mona just two miles short of the chequered flag. "No words can describe how bad this feels," Duffus said. "To have a certain win taken away like that hurts so much."

Jefferies saw his team-mate standing forlornly by the side of the road as he coasted past to inherit the lead and, ultimately the win. He would be on the receiving end of such bad luck at the TT himself in years to come and couldn't help but feel for Duffus. "I know I won," he said after the race, "but I feel really sorry for Iain."

Duffus's fate had been decided at the pit stop when his team miscalculated the amount of time they'd need to refuel his bike to the brim and it had cost him the race. One more second in the pits would have handed him the victory. Jefferies almost suffered the same fate, his petrol warning light having come on with 17 miles of the last lap still remaining. But the Manx fairies had been on his side in that particular race and he'd made it to the flag to claim his second TT victory. "That's fairly special is that," he said afterwards, "because I could see I was 'Plus 1'. And then going into the second lap at Ballacraine I used the same braking marker as the other (F1) bike and overshot. When Duffus came past I thought 'Oh well, that's it.'

"I thought he would pull away, but I found I could keep with him. Then my fuel light came on so I had to roll it a bit all the way over the Mountain. He must have had a bit of a mess-up in the pits or something – I don't know – but then I was right with him and thought, 'Right, last lap, let's really, really try,' and it worked."

Two more Yamaha R1s rounded-out the rostrum, proving the dominance of the bike in the Production class. Jason Griffiths inherited second place after Duffus's demise and Phillip McCallen finished third in what would prove to be his last TT race. He retired shortly afterwards, his body too battered and beaten to continue racing.

As soon as he descended the rostrum, Jefferies started preparing for the final race of the week – the Senior TT. Despite its loss of World Championship status, the Senior is still regarded as one of the world's great motorcycle races and for a rider to add his name to the base of the famous Senior trophy is to have his name included in a who's who of motorcycle racing. Stanley Woods, Geoff Duke, John Surtees, Mike Hailwood, Phil Read, Giacomo Agostini, Joey Dunlop, Steve Hislop and Carl Fogarty – all have silver plates attached to the base of the trophy, recording their victories. David Jefferies would now face off the might of the Honda factory on his converted road bike in a bid to add his own moniker.

Jim Moodie had other ideas and set such a scorching pace from the drop of the flag that he arrived at the first commentary point on the course some 20 seconds earlier than expected and caught the Manx Radio race commentators off guard. It was clear that the outright lap record was under threat if Moodie could maintain his pace.

That record had been set by Carl Fogarty back in 1992 in his pursuit of Steve Hislop on the rotary-engined Norton in what is now considered one of the all-time great TT races. It was testimony to how hard Hislop and Fogarty were racing each other that the record still stood, seven years later, despite the huge advances in motorcycle and tyre technology.

As Moodie completed his first circuit, his lap time stunned everyone – it was 7.4 seconds inside Fogarty's landmark and worked out at an average speed of 124.45mph. Sadly for Moodie, his race ended just a few miles up the road when his rear tyre shredded under such a punishing pace. Tongues immediately started wagging and suggesting that Moodie had fitted a super-soft rear tyre just to have a crack at setting a new lap record. It's an implication that the Scotsman angrily dismisses to this day. "I think it was just a bad tyre," he says, "but quite a lot of people stupidly thought I'd put a qualifying tyre on just to have a go at the lap record.

"Some time later a guy at a chat show handed me a fiver and said, 'That's for that lap record – I watched you do it and it was amazing.' That's how much I got for breaking the lap record – five quid. Winning the race would have been worth about £15,000 and yet people thought I'd forego that to win a fiver?"

Moodie's demise left Jefferies in a relatively comfortable lead, although he was chased hard, first by Joey Dunlop, then Ian Lougher, before Iain Duffus secured second spot and handed the V&M team a 1–2. It was the first time a private team had ever secured the top two places in a Senior TT.

After the race, both Jefferies and Duffus revealed that they'd had problems throughout. Duffus, with a broken steering damper, had achieved the seemingly impossible task of physically manhandling a 190mph bike over the Island's bumps without one, while Jefferies had to guess when to change gear based on the noise of the engine alone. "I didn't have a rev counter for the whole race," he said. "I pulled up on the start line and the rev counter was just sitting in the same position the whole race – it didn't move. So I was guessing gear changes, but it worked well."

After coming home in a distant fifth place, the usually reticent Joey Dunlop finally broke his silence and criticised his Honda. "It's the end of the RC45," he said. "It's time for something new. The bike has been outclassed by the R1 after five years at the top. We'll just have to wait and see what comes out next year."

Ian Lougher, who finished third on a two-stroke 500cc Grand Prix bike, backs up Dunlop's thoughts on the performance of the R1s. Even his purpose-built thoroughbred was outclassed by the modified street bikes. "I got on the 500 at the wrong time really because the Superbikes had just gone from 750cc to 1000cc," he says. "The 500 wasn't that fast on top end speed – the V&M bikes had about 10–12mph on me. I knew the R1s would be fast because they were such fast road bikes but no one knew how well they would handle. We hoped that poor handling would be their downfall and that my 500 GP bike would be much better in that respect. It did handle great and I loved riding it but it was a really 'short' bike and difficult to ride. The R1s were probably easier."

Although Jefferies had always enjoyed a few beers – and despite the fact that he had more reason than most to sink a few after becoming just the fifth man in history to win three TTs in a week – there was no big celebration on Friday night. "It was pretty quiet really," Jefferies admitted. "I had a few drinks and a meal with the team and my family. But I had to have a quiet one because I was flying to Ireland to race at Mondello Park early the next day. Besides, I hadn't been drinking for a month before the TT so it would have been too easy to get totally bladdered!"

Jack Valentine was simply too exhausted to get drunk. "It's funny really," he says, "but I don't necessarily have a party at the end of a TT – even a successful one. You're too tired so you just chill out, have a few beers, then maybe a couple of nights later you might get hammered."

Two weeks after the TT, Jefferies told *MCN* just what his wins had meant to him. "I know it's a big achievement and I'm really pleased," he said, "but the best thing was seeing my mum and dad's faces when I came in after the Formula 1 victory. I got more from them – it was something really special. And I couldn't believe the reception I got in the beer tent after the race. I felt like a celebrity! Everyone was clapping, saying it was a brilliant ride, but I told them to calm down – I just went as fast and as safely as I could, and that was good enough."

He also admitted that his wins had come as something of a surprise. "I didn't expect to do what I did at all. Everyone said that after my North West 200 wins I could do it. I thought I had the best chance in the Proddie race and after practice things looked good. But I was still learning the course and didn't think I ever had a chance of actually winning anything."

Jefferies insisted he had no intention of being labelled a 'roads specialist' as the likes of Joey Dunlop had become, and was keen to remind BSB race bosses that he was still around following a few bleak seasons in which he'd had little support. "I'd love to go back [to the TT] next year," he said, "but I don't want to become known as a roads specialist. Getting back into the *MCN* British Superbike Championship is my top priority. And hopefully my wins on the Island have woken up some team bosses. I think they forgot about me over the last few years."

If there was anyone prouder than David Jefferies at the close of the 1999 TT meeting it was his father Tony. Having come so close himself to winning a treble in 1971, he watched with immeasurable pride as his son finally achieved what he himself had not. "I was unbelievably proud when he won his first TT. I remember the eye contact when we saw him. Half the team were in tears – you get really emotional about it, I find – very emotional. Everybody did some crying over everybody else but I think with your first win, that's the way it happens.

"For him to win, and then to win again, and then to win *again* in one week, just made it probably the most momentous occasion in my life. It was certainly better than my win – I think that probably qualifies it. Dave winning the TT was better than me winning the TT without a shadow of a doubt."

Chapter 9

THE MAN WHO WOULDN'T GIVE UP

"When I turned round to point her out she had her tits out, waiting for Dave to sign them!"
Adam Evans, David's friend

When David Jefferies caught the ferry to the 1999 TT races he was a well-known motorcycle racer who had enjoyed considerable success at various levels of motorcycle sport. By the time he returned from the Island, he was a TT legend.

Cast adrift from the rest of the world's top motorcycling championships since losing World Championship status in 1977, the TT has ever since had a tendency to create its own stars, and rightly so. The event is unique and it takes unique riders to win round such a demanding and dangerous course. But one thing's for sure – a TT winner is guaranteed respect from his peers in any racing paddock. And since Jefferies had become one of literally just a handful of men to win three in a week, he commanded more respect than most. It was also the way in which he had humbled the mighty Honda with his home-brewed special that had captured people's imagination and support. He had proved that if you had the talent – and the courage – to race at those kinds of speeds, you didn't need a bottomless wallet to win. DJ had won an entire army of new admirers and it would only grow from here.

He had also won a new admirer in the female form in 1999 and David's relationship with Susan Lloyd would prove to be the most serious of his short life. Susan was the daughter of George Lloyd who owned Lloyd Lifestyle, a motorcycle clothing import and distribution business. He was, and remains, a close friend of Tony Jefferies, so he could hardly have disapproved of the relationship.

Typically, DJ's mates never missed an opportunity to take the Mickey when he first expressed an interest in Susan. Karl Smith remembers "Susan was a bit young in the beginning – just over 16 –

so we used to bring bottles of milk round to DJ when he was going to see her, just to wind him up."

"David saw Susan for about three years from 1999 to 2002," says Tony Jefferies. "I think it just went a bit stale in the end but they remained good friends."

Despite his lifelong obsession with motorbikes, Jefferies had always managed to find time for girls. "He always had to have a girlfriend on the go," says Tony. "If he didn't, he seemed to be a bit lost until he found a new one. There was never any talk of marriage though – he never got anywhere near that."

Part of the reason for Jefferies's lack of urgency in wanting to get married was probably down to the 'Boy's Own' lifestyle that he led. When he wasn't racing bikes, he was preparing them, and when he wasn't doing that, he was working on his 'toys' that ranged from quad bikes to a Russian army Zil truck. He also owned a Volvo F12 truck cab, had more cars than even his father can remember, and had an obsession with collecting tools.

There was nowhere he was happier than working in the garage just adjacent to the Jefferies's family home. So much so that David converted a room above the workshop area and called it home. Just 20 yards across the lawn there were all the comforts of a beautiful house but DJ was happier living above his garage. There, he could invite his similarly obsessed petrol-head friends round, get some music pumping, crack open a few beers and set to work on any number of mechanical projects. There was even a toilet downstairs, so he was completely self-contained. Well, almost. Conspicuous by their absence in his living quarters was any form of cooking or washing equipment. After all, mum's kitchen was just seconds away – and it had a washing machine too!

"Our David always thought that living cost £50 a week cos that's what he paid my mum," says Louise Jefferies. "For that, my mum cleaned his room, washed his clothes and cleaned and stocked his motor home. He used to chuck his dirty washing through the French window and it would reappear the next day on the kitchen chair all ironed. She used to Hoover it, clean it, stock up the fridge with home-made meals – the lot. He was the most spoiled brat in the world."

Tony Jefferies smiles when he remembers that his son's meticulous preparation of machinery spilled over into his preparation of food. "He was very fussy about how he prepared his food," he says. "If he was buttering a piece of toast, it would have to be spread right out to each edge perfectly equal. He'd turn the slice round four times to make sure each edge was buttered neatly. He used to have salad cream on everything and even that had to be spread out neatly with a knife. And he'd also have to cut his sandwiches in perfect halves or quarters. If you nudged him on the way past and moved the sandwich out of shape he'd go bloody nuts!"

For DJ, the living arrangement was ideal. He had his own space where he could entertain his mates or girlfriends, but his family was nearby and that was just as important to him. It may not have been the most romantic setting to bring girlfriends back to – 'Mind the spanners love. Sorry about the Page 3 calendar' – but DJ never struggled when it came to finding girls.

His lifelong friend Adam Evans remembers, "He liked the fuller figure when it came to the top half of girls, if you know what I mean. We were out one night and got chatting to two girls. One of them liked David but I think he preferred the other, who was playing hard to get. It turned out they both lived in my street so he ended up playing this sort of tag-team game where he'd nip up to one girl's house and see her then go and see the other. The girls were close friends so I don't know how he got away with it for so long, but he eventually got caught and it all ended up in tears at bedtime."

In later years, Jefferies's fame as a motorcycle racer proved to be a plus point when it came to attracting attention from the opposite sex, as Evans recalls. "The first time I went to the Isle of Man with Dave, we went to Colours bar/nightclub and they tried to usher us into a roped-off VIP area because of who Dave was. But he didn't like that, he preferred to just stand around and have a few beers along with everyone else. So we were stood drinking at the normal bar and a girl nudged me and said, 'Is that Dave Jefferies? Can I get his autograph?' and I thought, 'Right, I'm in here. If I can arrange for her to meet DJ, I'll be able to pull her.' So I tapped Dave and told him what she said and he obviously thought 'Right, *I'm* in here' and he thought *he* was going to pull her. But he got more than he bargained for. When I turned round to point her out, she had her tits out, waiting for Dave to sign them! Of course he obliged, but it turned out she was a bit of a racer groupie so it never went any further than that."

On other occasions, DJ preferred to remain anonymous, if only so he could get up to mischief without anyone knowing who he was. Evans again: "One time we'd both come out of long-term relationships and had gone into man-whoring as a profession. We'd go out around Ilkley and just get up to mischief. Neither of us were real clubbers but if we wanted to carry on drinking, sometimes a club was the only option. He liked Ilkley because nobody recognised him. It's a bit of an upmarket town so no one really knew about bikes and that meant David could get up to all sorts. Otherwise it was strange because people would come up to me and go 'Is that David Jefferies?' and I'd say 'Yeah' and they'd be like 'Oh, wow', which I found strange because he was just my mate – I didn't know about road racing."

Everyone with any interest in road racing knew the name of David Jefferies following the 1999 TT, but after all the excitement and adulation he had received at the event it was back to relative obscurity the following day, at Mondello Park in Ireland, where he continued his season in the Aprilia Cup Challenge. From racing against such established names as Joey Dunlop, Jim Moodie and Phillip McCallen, DJ found himself clashing fairings for points with relatively unheard of riders in the one-make series. But to Jefferies, that meant little. He simply loved riding bikes of any make or size, whether on a purpose-built short circuit, a pure roads course like the Isle of Man, or even on everyday roads crowded with traffic.

It was this down-to-earth attitude that won Jefferies so many fans. He didn't suffer from any affectations or ego, and he would happily chat or sign autographs for anyone who asked. This endearing side to Jefferies was not lost on the press and on 23 June, shortly after his triumphant TT, Adam Duckworth penned the following tribute to Jefferies in his editor's column of *Motor Cycle News*. Under the heading 'Raise a Glass to a Man Who Won't Give Up', it read:

If you could have a beer with anyone involved in motorcycling who would it be? Mike Hailwood would probably be on a lot of people's lists. Barry Sheene, Carl Fogarty, John Surtees, Mick Doohan and Evel Knievel would also make a fair few appearances. But you could do a lot worse than stick David Jefferies at the top of that list.

It would be wrong and unfair to even suggest that you could compare Jefferies with some of the all-time greats mentioned above. And Jefferies himself would probably colour up and shuffle uneasily at such a suggestion. But stick a pint in his hand and start talking about bikes and it would probably be one of the most enjoyable couple of hours you could spend.

This is a bloke who simply loves racing. While Max Biaggi talks about his image, his inner psyche and all sorts of clever stuff, Jefferies prefers to say things like "Nowhere at the TT really worries me because I don't take risks."

This from a man who's just lapped the course at an average speed of 123.69mph on only his third time at the Isle of Man.

And what was he thinking about as he came into the pits after winning the Formula One TT? The prize money? The kudos? The party? None of those. All he could think about was his mum and dad.

Jefferies has had his fair share of ups and downs and feels he's been forgotten about over the last couple of years. He's often been left begging for rides, always hoping for a break into the really big time. But he doesn't let it get him down. He rides whatever bikes he can get his hands on, goes incredibly fast and smiles...a lot.

And at 26, he's still got time to prove the TT is not the only place he can win races. Then, maybe, he'll get the big chances he deserves and you will be able to compare him to bike racing's genuine greats.'

It's as fine and accurate a testament to Jefferies's character as anyone has written. For whatever reasons, DJ somehow never seemed to get the breaks he so richly deserved but it was his response to that fact that made him so popular: he simply rode whatever bikes he could get his hands on and enjoyed himself regardless.

Without the coveted BSB or WSB ride that Duckworth had alluded to, Jefferies got stuck into his racing at Mondello Park and finished second in the Aprilia race. He was also classed as second in the first leg of the British Sport Production Championship after the race was stopped prematurely. The second leg was also stopped due to changing weather conditions and Jefferies again finished in second place, perhaps not quite finding his short circuit pace after two weeks of riding on the Isle of Man.

Another second at Silverstone the following week left him 33 points behind Mick Corrigan in the Sports Production Championship, though the Aprilia series was an altogether tighter affair. The standings after the Mondello round showed Martin Johnson tied with Matt Llewellyn on 76 points at the top of the table, while Jefferies was tied on 68 points with Marty Nutt.

Using the same Chesterfield Motorcycles R1 that he won the Production TT on, Jefferies won the Sports Production race at Donington Park over the British Grand Prix weekend just ahead of his old GP team boss Peter Graves.

If DJ had already been a hero at the Oliver's Mount circuit in Scarborough, he now returned to the seaside resort with a new aura surrounding him. He was a triple North West 200 *and* triple TT winner, and the man most likely to succeed Joey Dunlop as the 'King of the Roads' when the 47-year-old Irishman retired, which most felt he surely soon would.

Continuing his blistering form at the circuit, DJ won three Superbike races and two 600cc races. His only defeat was in the feature 'Cock o' the North' race itself. He finished second to John McGuinness on a 500cc GP Honda that proved ideally suited to the tight, undulating course. While he lost out in the feature race, DJ still left the weekend as overall points scorer ahead of McGuiness and Ian Lougher.

McGuinness remembers that meeting as the only time the two friends came close to falling out. "We had some good races around Scarborough and places like that – the North West 200 was usually wheel-to-wheel stuff too, but Dave would always get the better of me. He would always beat me, but I remember beating him at Scarborough – I was that determined.

"The Gold Cup was over two legs – two ten lap races – and in the first one he passed me over the jumps and scared the shit out of me.

To be fair, he didn't elbow me, but he came up the inside of me. I was on my little 500 two-stroke and he were on the big R1. He bloody ran me onto the grass and I was doing about 120mph. I thought, 'You bastard!' It was probably the only time I'd ever fallen out with him a touch – there was a little bit of a needle there, you know?

"He came into our truck and he were like, 'What were you doing going so slow without jumping over the bumps?' and I was like 'I was doing my best' and we had a bit of a handbags-at-dawn session. I then beat him in the second one. I got the overall win. It was an aggregate time over the two races. To be fair though, it was probably the only time I ever did beat him apart from at Macau, but that wasn't real wheel-to-wheel stuff."

Despite this one incident McGuinness testifies that Jefferies was a safe rider to race against, and one who clearly enjoyed the buzz that racing gave him. "When Dave made a move on you it would always be hard but fair. But if he was coming through, he was coming through, and if he was on one, he was on one. When he passed me at Scarborough it was a bit over the top, but that was the only time. Normally, you'd be going down a straight at the North West 200 or somewhere at 190mph and he'd be looking across giving you the 'V' sign or grabbing hold of your leg and pulling daft faces through his visor. He'd always be up to something daft."

In the week following the Scarborough races, Jack Valentine, still flushed with his team's success at the TT, announced that he was to run Yamaha R7s in the following year's British Superbike Championship. "I still have some unfinished business and a lot to prove," Valentine said at the time, and, although he stopped short of naming riders for the team, it seemed likely that he would retain the services of Jefferies and Duffus who had handed him so much success on the road circuits.

Jefferies made a return trip to the Isle of Man in July to take part in a road test feature and video shoot. He was joined by TT legend Steve Hislop, future World Superbike Champion Neil Hodgson, and former Grand Prix racer turned TV commentator, Keith Heuwen, for what turned out to be a complete hoot. The riders were handed a collection of the fastest sports bikes in the world and told to go and play on the Mountain section of the TT course where, even outside race week, there's no speed limit for ordinary traffic. The bikes consisted of a Yamaha R1, a Honda Super Blackbird, a Kawasaki ZX-9R and a Suzuki Hayabusa, and in these experienced hands they really were tested to the limit. The *Manx Independent* reported that 'Hislop hit a claimed 180mph on the Mountain Mile aboard the Suzuki Hayabusa with the rear tyre still laying black lines' and added that the boys were 'pulling wheelies galore and generally acting like a bunch of end-of-term schoolboys.'

The video was eventually released under the title '*The World's Fastest Bikes*' and, despite the various contracts held by the riders, was intended to give a review of each machine by some of the fastest men on two wheels. It's clear to see, simply by watching the video, how much fun all the riders had making the film. Here was a chance for them to do what they liked best – messing around at ridiculous speeds on different bikes without the pressure of winning races or pleasing sponsors. Jefferies was in his element. *MCN* road tester Pete Wilson noted how, 'At every brow of every hill Jefferies would hoist whichever bike he was riding onto the back wheel."

A former Canadian racing champion himself, Wilson was no slouch, but even he was gob-smacked at just how fast Jefferies and co. were, even when they were ostensibly just fooling around. He wrote, 'I'm focusing so hard my brain feels like it's about to burst through the front of my helmet. I later learn that TT winners Hislop and Jefferies are fooling around the whole time and still keeping up with me easily.'

Jefferies showed his world class during the World Superbike meeting at Brands Hatch on 1 August. He had entered the European Superstock race which featured an arrowhead formation grid for the first time in international racing history. From second on the experimental grid (which was eventually dropped because it spread riders too far down the start/finish straight) DJ dominated the race, taking the win from Karl Harris and Peter Graves, though he was not eligible to score any points as he was over the age cap limit of 24. But on a weekend when British fans had nothing to shout about in the main WSB races, Jefferies gave the home fans something to cheer.

He had something to cheer about himself when news came through that, as a reward for his triple TT wins, Yamaha had arranged for him to have a test on the R7 ridden by Niall Mackenzie in the British Superbike Championship with a view to DJ joining the Scotsman for the last few rounds of the series.

This was the chance Jefferies had been waiting on for years and one which showed just how much his TT wins had meant to Yamaha, especially since they had been achieved at the embarrassing expense of arch rivals Honda. After being overlooked so many times by the top teams in BSB and having to accept whatever ride he could just to keep on racing, Jefferies was finally being given the chance to see what he could do on a top machine. Well, sort of.

After winning three consecutive BSB titles for Yamaha from 1996 to 1998, Mackenzie was struggling on the sweet-handling but under-powered R7. And if a triple BSB champion and former Grand Prix star couldn't post competitive times on the bike, it was unlikely that Jefferies could either. Still, it was a step in the right direction and DJ spent an hour on the bike at Donington Park under the watchful eye of Virgin Yamaha team boss, Rob McElnea.

Jefferies hadn't ridden in BSB since 1997 when he finished a lowly 19th on a privateer Ducati 916, and he was impressed with the feel of a pukka factory bike compared to his own R1. "I just can't believe how much better the R7 is compared to the R1," he said. "Don't get me wrong, the R1 is awesome but you can feel this bike was designed just for racing."

Indeed it was. In an era when the upper capacity limit for four-cylinder machines in BSB and WSB was 750cc, the 1000cc R1 was not eligible for competition, so Yamaha built the ultra-expensive R7 as a homologation special just to go racing. "I'm really pleased I've been given the chance to test the bike," Jefferies added, "and hopefully some races can come out of it at the end of the year."

Team boss Rob McElnea said, "We wanted to give Dave the chance to show us how well he can do and we have enough engines and parts to allow that to happen. This is just reward for Dave's outstanding rides at the TT this year. Hopefully he can take that success onto the short circuits."

In another cruel twist of fate, Jefferies didn't get the chance to ride the R7 at Mallory Park in late August as planned. He high-sided the V&M Yamaha R6 in the British Supersport race at Knockhill and smashed his hand and dislocated a wrist, ruling himself out of his factory debut in BSB. After his wrist had been wrenched back into place and two pins had been inserted into his hand to speed up the healing process, Jefferies explained, "It's not the comeback I wanted. I don't know what happened. I wasn't pushing any harder than I had been the previous lap when the back just snapped round and spat me off. I shouldn't be out much longer than a month," he added optimistically. "I'll be back."

The injuries meant Jefferies looked a doubtful starter for the final major road race of the year, the Ulster Grand Prix. He was under doctor's orders to rest the hand for at least four weeks but, like every other motorcycle racer, he opted to defy doctor's orders and attempted to race. While the plaster had been removed by 16 August and Jefferies said he was in no pain, the two pins were clearly visible as they poked through the skin on his hand. It may have looked gruesome, but Jefferies was not to be stopped in his bid to dominate all three of the major road races in 1999 – the North West 200, the TT and the Ulster Grand Prix. "As long as I can hold onto the bars," he said, "nothing will stop me racing the R1 and R6 in Ulster."

Broken hand or not, Jefferies was involved in two of the greatest battles ever witnessed around the Dundrod circuit at the 1999 Ulster Grand Prix, both times against Joey Dunlop and his own team-mate, Iain Duffus. At what was Dunlop's home circuit, Jefferies set out to prove that he was the new king of the roads and that it was time for the legendary Irishman to step aside and enjoy his retirement. But Dunlop didn't become a legend by going down without a fight and his performance at the '99 Ulster is rightly regarded as one of the finest of his career.

Surprisingly, for two seemingly similar characters (both Dunlop and Jefferies were quiet, salt-of-the-earth types who were happier to let their riding do the talking), Dunlop and Jefferies didn't always see eye to eye. While each had respect for the other's speed, Dunlop felt the new generation of road riders spearheaded by Jefferies were

ABOVE: *Red 1 cleared for takeoff. DJ sits in a Red Arrows Hawk.* (David Jefferies Family Archive)

BELOW: *Leader of the pack. A 15-year-old David in schoolboy motocross action at Tadcaster.* (David Jefferies Family Archive)

LEFT: *Viva Knievel! DJ was initially scared of making big jumps on his motocross bike but soon mastered the art. June, 1987.* (David Jefferies Family Archive)

ABOVE: *Year one. DJ negotiates Cadwell Park on his Yamaha FZR600 during his first year of racing, 1990.* (Miss L. Pepper/Tony Jefferies Archive)

BELOW: *Me and my shadow. David being followed round Donington by uncle Nick in 1992.* (Nick Jefferies Archive)

LEFT ABOVE: *In at the deep end. Jefferies landed a Grand Prix ride on the unsponsored Peter Graves Yamaha YZR500 in 1993. He was the youngest British rider ever to compete in 500cc GPs.* (Double Red)

LEFT BELOW: *For a big lad, DJ could get well tucked in on a bike, as this shot from his 1995 season in World Superbikes proves.* (Double Red)

ABOVE: *The start of it all. DJ leaves the line during his first ever visit to the Isle of Man TT in 1996.* (Tony Jefferies Archive)

RIGHT: *The champ. Jefferies proudly displays the trophy he received for winning the Triumph Speed Triple Challenge in 1996.* (Tony Jefferies Archive)

ABOVE: *The all-conquering V&M team at TT 2000, from left: Ian Lougher, Michael Rutter, Jack Valentine and DJ.* (Pacemaker)

BELOW: *A triple TT winner in his own right, Tony Jefferies also masterminded his son's hugely successful career.* (Tony Jefferies Archive)

ABOVE: *The power and the glory. Speeding past Barregarrow Crossroads on his Yamaha R6 during the 2000 TT.* (Dave Collister)

BELOW: *Masters of the Mountain. Two of the all-time greats of road racing, Joey Dunlop and David Jefferies, shake hands after the Senior TT in 2000. David's mum Pauline watches with pride.* (Pacemaker)

ABOVE: *All for one. DJ is flanked by his proud mum, dad, and girlfriend Susan Lloyd at the 2000 TT where he set the first 125mph lap.* (Pacemaker)

riding the roads in a super-aggressive short circuit style and taking too many risks. While Dunlop was never a fan of fairing-bashing clashes, he was quite prepared to prove that he could win races in that manner if he had to, and that set up a mouth-watering scrap between the two greatest road racers in the world at that time. What's more, there were all sorts of other factors that ensured the contest would be evened out. For example, Dunlop had already notched up 23 wins at the Ulster Grand Prix (and 48 at Dundrod in total) so his knowledge of the circuit was second to none. Jefferies, on the other hand, had never been to Dundrod before and would have to learn the circuit during practice. This would clearly go in Dunlop's favour. The Irishman was, however, 21 years older than his Yorkshire rival in a sport which is usually considered a young man's game. Dunlop was also on a 750cc machine while Jefferies enjoyed the luxury of the more powerful 1000cc Yamaha. But then, let's not forget that he still had a bad injury and would be riding with two pins in his wrist. It was a mouth-watering prospect to see who would gain the upper hand – the old school Dunlop with his intimate track knowledge and legendary smooth riding style, or the new pretender – the aggressive, short-circuit-style Jefferies who was young enough to be Dunlop's son.

Jefferies explained to *Road Racing Ireland* magazine how he had managed to learn the daunting and super-fast 7.4-mile course in preparation for this clash of the titans. "Iain Duffus showed me around the circuit in a car but I went out in practice and tried to learn it by myself. It's tricky and fast and I'll not learn it in six laps. Plus I'm taking it easy with my hand in mind. I don't want to hurt it."

When asked which parts were the trickiest, Jefferies's complete lack of circuit knowledge became all too apparent. "The wriggly bit up the hill...I don't know the names," he replied. "And the bit from the hairpin.

"Come race day I might be all right but I don't want to go home thinking I should have backed off and just learned it this year. I'll be happy to come back again after learning it this year and being fit."

The opening Superbike race was sensational with a slow-off-the-line Dunlop recording his fastest ever lap around the Dundrod circuit at 125.14mph to battle through to join the leading trio of Duffus, Jefferies and Ian Lougher. When Lougher later pulled out with gearbox problems, it became a three-way fight for the win. Dunlop passed Jefferies to take second spot but DJ then responded by passing both his adversaries to take the lead. Elbow-to-elbow and fairing-to-fairing, the two V&M Yamahas mugged Dunlop all the way round the circuit, sending Joey's loyal local fans into a frenzy.

Jefferies set his fastest lap of the race on the final circuit and came round the final corner with both wheels drifting across the road to take an emphatic victory in his first ever visit to Dundrod. It meant he had won all three major road races and beaten the acknowledged master, Dunlop, at his own game. Dunlop admitted of the two Yamaha riders "I just couldn't live with their speed. Even when I did move into second they came blasting past down the straight again." His thinly disguised anger at the two younger riders' styles was revealed when he said, "On the last lap I didn't dare take any chances because I didn't know what line they were going to take. I saw what you could call some 'interesting moves' around Dundrod."

Unperturbed, a jubilant Jefferies openly admitted to having the time of his life drifting and sliding his R1 with complete mastery. "It was great fun," he beamed. "I dived in a few times to get ahead of Duffus and pushed hard on the penultimate lap. On the last lap I had the machine weaving everywhere and round the last corner I was showing off."

It was round one to Jefferies but Dunlop approached him in the paddock afterwards to have a quiet word. It has not been recorded what was actually said but it appears that Dunlop was warning his younger rival of the dangers of the Dundrod course and telling him to calm his riding down before someone got hurt. Tony Jefferies disputes this version of events. "They didn't really have strong words," he says. "Dave was having to push really hard because he was on Pirelli tyres and he couldn't get the drive out of the slow corners. Joey was pulling away out of those on his Michelins so DJ had to ride really hard to catch him up again.

"It was really frustrating for Dave because he knew he could go as fast as Joey but his tyres were spinning up and he kept losing time.

So to stay with Joey, he had to pull a few moves that were pretty close. Joey was pretty philosophical about it. He was like 'Well, that's what you've got to do sometimes I suppose.' He'd had days where he had to do the same."

Jack Valentine says he heard lots of partisan Irish fans branding his rider 'a complete nutter' because of his riding style but he offers an alternative explanation. "There were a lot of Irish fans coming over and saying 'Aye, yer man's crazy.' We used to get that a lot because nobody on the road racing scene had seen a bike with proper horsepower before, and even at the TT David was coming out of corners leaving big black lines, just power-spinning the tyres, and it was the same at the Ulster. They had never seen it – they said he was just crazy. I had a few of the regular Irish teams and team owners saying 'Your fuckin' man's crazy – slow him down' and all that. Again, it was just his handling of the bike."

Nevertheless, some observers recall Dunlop being in an extremely rare, furious mood after that race and seeming more determined than ever to beat Jefferies in the second encounter – no matter how hard he had to ride to do it.

Jefferies himself hinted at the frosty relationship between the two in an interview for www.ttwebsite.com in 2001, saying, "If you totalled up all the times I've spoken to Joey and said 'Hello' it would come to about four minutes. He was a very shy sort of guy and I think he looked at me as the young, new, idiot. He was even quiet around friends who knew him well, so someone who turned up and started doing what I did – he wasn't going to be my best friend. He wasn't that sort of person. I respected him as a rider of course."

Whatever the state of their relationship following race one, Jefferies may actually have done Dunlop a favour by getting his back up. There was no more dangerous opponent than Joey Dunlop when he felt he had a point to prove, and it was clear from his steely gaze as he took to the line in race two that he was intent on teaching the two young upstarts a lesson.

The Supersport 600 race – held in between both Superbike events – had gone some way to backing up Dunlop's claims that Duffus and Jefferies were closer to the edge than they should have been. As

Jefferies dived up the inside of his team-mate to take the lead at the fast Wheeler's Corner, he clashed fairings with Duffus and the Scotsman crashed out, his V&M machine careering into a road traffic sign while Duffus himself tumbled to a halt unscathed. And the carnage didn't stop there. As Jason Griffiths swerved to avoid the fallen Duffus, Adrian Archibald had no choice but to run into the back of the Welshman and he too went down in a heap. Dunlop, who managed to navigate the crash site safely, must have been shaking his head and thinking "I told you so."

The incident caused the race to be red-flagged and the results were taken from the last time all riders had crossed the start/finish line, meaning that Duffus, although laid out on the grass, was declared the winner. In any case, the accident did nothing to deter Duffus or Jefferies from resuming battle in the second Superbike race and Dunlop refused to back off either, leading to one of the greatest battles ever seen around Dundrod.

Clerk of the Course, Billy Nutt spoke to Jack Valentine before the race to ask him to remind his riders that the Ulster Grand Prix was in fact a road race as opposed to an elbow-bashing, no-holds-barred sprint around a relatively safe short circuit. It would appear none of the riders took the slightest bit of notice.

Dunlop fluffed the start but was soon hunting down the yellow and red V&M bikes at the front of the field. When he eventually took the lead, the partisan crowd went wild to see this silver-haired old fox taking the fight to the two wild young guns. After biding his time in third place, Jefferies made his move past Duffus and set about attacking Dunlop, but even he admitted scaring himself, such was the pace the old master was setting. "I ran wide, almost hitting a telegraph pole at Budore, and gave myself a big fright," he said.

With a monumental effort he finally caught Dunlop on the penultimate lap but had to set a new outright lap record of 126.85mph to do it – and this on his first ever visit to the track. But Joey was having none of it and responded by lapping Dundrod quicker than he had ever done before (126.80mph) to just edge the win from Jefferies who showed how much he had enjoyed the race by pulling a monster wheelie out of the final corner. "I was trying and was going to pass him into Wheeler's on the last lap," he told *Road Racing Ireland* magazine, "but just as I was going to, I realised I was too fast and shut it off. Then at the hairpin I had too much power to give it a handful coming out of the corner."

Whatever their differences, Jefferies paid tribute to Dunlop after the race and openly admitted he simply could not find a way to beat him in such form. "Joey is an unbelievable rider," he said. "Going into fast, blind corners he knows when to hold it flat-out and when to open her up at other corners. I just couldn't do that."

Fittingly, it was a draw between Jefferies and Dunlop with each rider taking a Superbike win apiece. The older man from another era of bike racing had shown he still had the mettle to mix it with, and beat, the very best of the young road racing hot shots. Joey's incredible win had even more poignancy when it turned out to be his last ever meeting at Dundrod. He couldn't have made a finer exit, or handed the torch to a more worthy challenger.

For David Jefferies, the Ulster Grand Prix had capped an absolutely unbelievable season on the roads. From having started the season never having won one of the big three road races on the calendar, he finished it with three wins at the North West 200, a treble at the TT and a debut victory and outright lap record at the Ulster Grand Prix. When all other things were even, only the great Joey Dunlop had beaten him fair and square in a road race during the 1999 season. It seemed that after trying his hand at so many forms of motorcycle racing, from Grands Prix to World Superbikes via BSB and even some World Endurance racing, he had finally found his niche. This was where he belonged – on public road courses riding production-based machinery at utterly astonishing speeds.

After finishing second to Karl Harris in the European Superstock Championship race at Assen, it was back to Oliver's Mount in a bid to win another Gold Cup. Jefferies won his fair share of races at the three-day meeting, taking two Superbike and two 600cc race wins, but he lost out on the cup which went to his close friend John McGuinness by two-fifths of a second – the cup being awarded on aggregate times over the weekend.

Now fully recovered from his broken wrist, Jefferies had another crack at a British Supersport 600 race on the V&M R6 at the last round of the BSB championship at Donington Park. He surprised everyone by qualifying second and finishing in an impressive fourth place in what was only his second attempt in one of the most fiercely competitive classes in Britain.

Jefferies ended his British racing season in third place in the Sports Production Championship and lost out to Matt Llewellyn in the 250 Aprilia series, but there was still one big event to go before he hung his leathers up for winter – the Macau Grand Prix.

True to his present form, Jefferies won the race on only his second visit to the circuit after a close battle with Swiss World Superbike rider Andy Hoffman and his old sparring partner, Michael Rutter.

The Guia circuit in Macau makes the TT look safe, running, as it does, completely through Armco-lined city streets and alongside the harbour where a crashed bike can easily end up in the sea. And it's not slow either, as Jefferies related. "On the fast part along the sea front we were reaching speeds of about 175mph," he said, "and that really makes you concentrate!"

Elated to have added yet another victory to his amazing tally in 1999, DJ overdid things on the drink after the race, as Jack Valentine remembers. "Ha ha. Yes, when he won Macau the first year, I remember seeing him with a monstrous hangover all the way home on the jetfoil. He was clutching his trophy and looking absolutely shit."

Tony Jefferies admits his son wasn't the best man at dealing with hangovers. "He used to get so ill after drinking heavily," he says. "Next day he would throw up for hours. I had to stop on the way back from Donington once to let him be sick outside the car. He didn't get drunk on a regular basis but when he did, he really suffered for it."

Jefferies's Macau victory meant he had won at least one race at every road circuit he had been to in 1999. It was a year to savour and Jack Valentine looked back on it with fond memories. "It was a fabulous year. I think we ended up with lap records at the Ulster when he was there in a novice jacket – he got some stick over that. It was on the front page of – I think it was the *Belfast Telegraph* – 'Jefferies qualifies pole', and a picture of him in a novice jacket. So we ribbed him about that. He wasn't happy about that. But I think he got the lap record there, the lap record at Macau, and he was right on the lap record at the TT, so it was a fabulous year on the roads."

The crowning moment for the V&M team came at the prestigious *Motor Cycle News* awards in Birmingham when they were presented with the award for Bikesport Team of the Year. Jack Valentine, Steve Mellor, David Jefferies and Iain Duffus – all resplendent in custom-made yellow and red V&M dicky bows – strode onto stage to accept the award that marked their stunning year of racing.

Valentine paid tribute to his team saying, "To get an award like this makes it all worthwhile. Everyone in the team, from riders to mechanics, deserves this because of the hard work they have all put in through the year. The wins at the TT were special, especially as the bike we were racing were not that far from stock. We spent months preparing them but no one expected the production-based R1 to be so capable on the road."

No one had expected David Jefferies to be quite so capable either.

Chapter 10

RECORD BREAKER

"You're going down those straights at 180mph looking over at each other and having a little snigger and a wee wave."
Iain Duffus

David Jefferies's all-round performances in 1999, both on the roads and on short circuits, were enough to convince Yamaha that he was worthy of some serious machinery for the 2000 season. The firm announced it was prepared to supply Jefferies and the V&M team with factory R7s – the same as those ridden by Niall Mackenzie in '99 – for an assault on the British Superbike Championship.

Jefferies was delighted. It seemed he had finally achieved his dream of landing a competitive Superbike ride. He said "Superbikes are where I want to be next year. People may forget I was in Superbikes when I was just 19 and then I rode in World Superbikes in 1995. I've learned a lot since then and now I want to show people I've got what it takes to win on the short tracks. All I need now is a decent bike and it looks like I've got one."

Jack Valentine was just as thrilled to be receiving factory support again after his split with Honda in 1998. "To have bikes as good as Mackenzie's with help from Japan is crucial," he said. "Anything less and you don't stand a chance. Having these machines makes us a much more attractive package for sponsors."

Valentine would live to regret those last words. After months of trying to find sponsors to bankroll the team – and coming very close to signing up BT Phonecards as their main backer – the Jefferies Superbike jinx struck again and Valentine had to admit he simply couldn't find the money to run in BSB. No sponsors meant no bikes and the deal, which had looked so promising, was off.

Failing to find sponsorship for their 2000 campaign was doubly hard to accept for the V&M team. Not only had they done enough to secure a promise of factory bikes and support from Yamaha Japan, but winning the *MCN* Bikesport Team of the Year Award had proven just how professional and successful the team was. To have both manufacturer support and approval from the industry – as well as the results sheets that showed just how many wins the team had achieved in 1999 – seemed to put V&M in a perfect position to secure sponsorship. After all, what more could a potential sponsor want from a team? And yet the money was never forthcoming. Did Jefferies's face simply not fit? Were potential sponsors put off by the fact that V&M had stated their intent to contest the TT again? Did that pose too much of a PR-unfriendly risk?

Jefferies for one thought the TT may have been a factor. Speaking in 2002 he said "Two of the teams I've spoken to this year said, 'Well, if you're going to do the TT we're not interested because we don't think you're going to give 100% commitment in the UK,' which is a load of rubbish. I mean, the way I look at it is the more you ride bikes, the faster you're gonna race, whether it's on a road circuit, a motocross bike or a road bike – you're just on bikes all the time. I wanna race bikes, it's what I love doing. I love the Isle of Man, I love short circuits, and I think you can do both. Hislop proved you can do both, John McGuinness has done both, Jim Moodie does both, so if people are so short-sighted that they won't give me a ride because of the Isle of Man, well that's their decision."

Just as quickly as Jefferies's season seemed doomed, it turned around again with the formation of Team O2+. On paper at least, it looked like the perfect set-up; the same factory Yamaha R7s that had been offered to V&M, big bucks sponsorship, and even the backing of bike-mad movie star Ewan McGregor who put himself forward as a team figurehead.

The two-rider team would see Jefferies teaming up with old sparring partner Matt Llewellyn. The team principal, Tim Ford, had already run a squad in the British Supersport Championship but had decided to move up into the big league for the 2000 season, even if he wasn't sure why. "I really don't know why we decided to expand from running in Supersport," he said at the time, "we just knew that we had to do it and, more importantly, that we could do it and do it very well."

For Jefferies, there was even the added bonus of being able to continue his association with V&M as they were to be contracted to look after the technical side of the 02+ team. Although he woudn't be running his own set-up as originally planned, Jack Valentine seemed happy enough to be going racing again. He said, "Tim approached us several months ago. Other people have approached us before and since but we have faith in Tim's concept and we are more than happy to work with him and the people he's put together. It's not at all easy to run a Superbike race team – just ask any team manager how difficult it really is – but Tim and ourselves are really starting this entire team from scratch and it's going to be tough, very tough."

Jefferies himself was understandably delighted to be thrown a lifeline at such a late stage in the year, as the racing season was only a couple of months away. "I'm really pleased to get a proper crack at the British championship," he said. "Some people have got me tagged as a road racer who can't mix it on short circuits, but look at my record – since 1991 I've done more short circuit stuff than the roads. I'm going for it this year. I always go for it and working with Jack again is terrific. I just want the season to start right now – I can't wait to get out there."

Despite Valentine's warnings about the difficulties of running a BSB team, Tim Ford remained undaunted at the prospect and was oozing confidence for the year ahead. "You could say it's a challenge, but it's that and more. Not only do we have an unshakeable passion for the sport, we have a lot of faith in David Jefferies – he truly has the talent and potential to become a great success. We intend to do a professional job and be treated as equals. We've secured some major backing, bikes that we know are good enough, and we have the talent and skills in-house to make sure that we don't fold."

Those last words would come back to haunt Ford sooner rather than later. Little more than a month after making so many bold predictions, he had to announce that his new dream team had indeed folded due to lack of sponsorship – exactly the same problem that had shattered V&M's plans – and that the best he could offer Jefferies and Llewellyn were rides in the British Superstock Championship. He said, "We had to make the decision in the best interests of the team so we'll be in the

Superstock class with Yamaha R1s instead. Luckily we were able to keep both riders. They're disappointed, but they understand the reasons and we're confident we'll win the Superstocks."

Jack Valentine remembers the frustration of the whole doomed affair. "They were going to put this big team together in British Superbikes and they had all these ideas. We had the bikes there but there was nothing coming through – no money, no sign of it. They did the pre-season television work at Donington with no sponsors names on the bikes, apart from O2+ which was the team name. So we just never touched the bike. I said to the guys, 'Look, we're not touching the bike until we see spares coming through and a percentage of the money' but, of course, it never happened. We were going to be the whole technical side of the set-up. They ended up running Superstock bikes and they did a pretty good job but used up all their budget doing it. They were nice people – genuinely nice people – but I think they got a little bit above themselves with the PR side."

Once again, Jefferies's dream of a competitive BSB ride had been scuppered. If there was a silver lining to this latest cloud, it was that V&M were now free to contest the major road races once again and since this didn't clash with the O2+ team's plans (road racing had never figured in their calendar), Jefferies signed up to head their assault which would begin with the North West 200 in May.

Before that, Jefferies finished third in the opening round of British Superstocks with his O2+ team-mate Llewellyn taking the win ahead of Glen Richards on a Honda FireBlade. With both O2+ bikes on the rostrum first time out, Jefferies must have wondered just what he could have achieved if the funds had been found to contest BSB.

There was to be no repeat of his 1999 hat-trick at the North West as Jefferies's new V&M team-mate Michael Rutter took all the glory. Rutter, who was deputising for the injured Ian Simpson, won both Superbike races and the Supersport 600 event to complete his own hat-trick. Iain Duffus had signed for Honda for the 2000 season and was to have another coming-together with Jefferies following the incident at the previous year's Ulster Grand Prix. This time around it was Duffus who tangled with Jefferies in the Production race and brought both riders off, though neither suffered serious injury.

Despite the two seeming to have a penchant for knocking each other off their respective motorcycles, Duffus and Jefferies had immense respect for each other, both as riders and as people, and they thoroughly enjoyed racing each other at the North West. "You're going down those straights at 180mph, looking over at each other and having a little snigger and a wee wave," Duffus said when asked about his NW200 duels with Jefferies. "David was the absolute worst for that, you know – he'd give you the finger and the 'Vs' and all sorts of daft stuff. Richard Britton was the same – they were two comedians, on and off the track. Then the last lap, the body language changes and you go and see if you can win."

Jefferies clearly enjoyed racing against Duffus too. "That's when you really build your respect for other riders; when you're sat there at 180mph, about a foot away from somebody, and looking across and smiling at them. That's when you have the fun side of it as well – it's quite enjoyable."

Two seconds in the Superbike races and a third in the 600 event meant Jefferies didn't exactly have a poor day at the office at the North West in 2000, but after his triple the previous year it certainly felt that way, though DJ was magnanimous in defeat. "Last year it was my year," he said, "this year it looks like it's Michael's."

It wasn't until the fourth round of the British Superstock series that Jefferies managed to take a win, but when he did, it was in what was widely regarded as the race of the year up to that point. But for a time, even his Superstock ride had seemed in doubt as the troubled 02+ team lost its main sponsor just four rounds into the season. This time around there was a happy ending as the squad landed a title sponsor that was sure to impress the paddock – from now on, Jefferies and Llewellyn would be riding for the Page3.com team!

Not only would millions of web surfers now be able to read all about the performances of the team's two riders, but the pit lane garage would now be an altogether more glamorous place to be thanks to the presence of a bevy of Page 3 promotional beauties. It's no wonder that Jefferies and Llewellyn were grinning like naughty school boys in the promotional pictures which announced the arrival of the new team sponsor.

As if inspired by the injection of fresh cash and added glamour to his team, DJ rode a brilliant race at Oulton Park to claim his first Superstock win of the year. In a fairing-bashing battle with his team-mate Matt Llewellyn, Kawasaki-mounted Steve Plater, and future MotoGP star Chris Vermeulen, Jefferies gave it his all to win by just 0.195 seconds. The racing had been so close that DJ had completed the last few laps without a clutch lever after a clash with Plater had broken it off. Plater himself had to contend with a flapping fairing that had also been broken in the heat of battle, but he had clearly enjoyed the experience, saying afterwards, "That was brilliant. I haven't had so much fun in ages. I just love riding the 900 and the battle with David was the best sort of racing – fun with a capital F!"

Jefferies had also enjoyed the scrap and the win that moved him to within four points of the championship lead after he had scored a second at Donington and fourth at Thruxton. "Oulton is my favourite circuit," he said after the epic clash, "and even more so now. It was a great scrap. No one could make a break and I really enjoyed it. Great fun."

The quality of the opposition was something to be considered too. Anyone who said that David Jefferies couldn't cut it on short circuits needs to be aware that he was beating men of the calibre of Chris Vermeulen who has gone on to win in MotoGP for Rizla Suzuki. It was an impressive performance from Jefferies and timely too, as it filled him full of confidence for the trip over the Irish Sea to the Isle of Man where Honda would pull out all the stops to make sure the young upstart on a modified road bike would not repeat his success of 1999.

* * *

Quite naturally, considering his treble win of the previous year, David Jefferies started the 2000 TT as hot favourite for the big races. But he admitted in *MCN*'s TT preview supplement that the days of being a happy-go-lucky unfancied 'novice' TT racer were over and that he felt a lot more pressure in 2000. "To win three races last year was unbelievable," he said. "It just blew my mind to be honest and it didn't really sink in for a while. I think I did so well there because I really enjoy racing the course. You've got to enjoy it and I do. Last year I just rode at my own pace and let the results come, but I know damn well this year I've got to push all the way because everybody wants to beat me.

"There's a hell of a lot more pressure this year and there's still loads to learn about the course. I still don't know how to do a good lap there on a 600 – it's not as simple as taking exactly the same lines as the big bikes and riding as hard as you can. I've got to concentrate on how to improve and learn from last year. To win three again would be nice – well, that's a bit of an understatement! I'd love to do four and get the lap record too, though I'll settle with just being faster than last year."

Jefferies knew his main opposition in the Superbike races would come from his V&M team-mate Michael Rutter (especially after the form he showed at the North West 200), and the Honda-mounted Iain Duffus and Jim Moodie. But the real dark horse was Joey Dunlop. Openly critical of the SP-1 that Honda had supplied for the North West, Dunlop had taken the unthinkable step of considering riding for another manufacturer for the first time since 1981. Honda, who had always appreciated Dunlop's loyalty, got the message, and last minute arrangements were made to supply Joey with the very latest factory-spec engines being used by World Superbike star Aaron Slight. To underline the seriousness of Honda's challenge, three Japanese engineers were also sent over to the Isle of Man to look after Dunlop's bike. It was a measure of how desperate Honda was to both hang onto Dunlop and to prevent Jefferies taking another Formula 1 win that it took such steps to ensure victory.

Dunlop might have been fully grey-haired now and approaching 50 years old but Jefferies knew better than to discount the wily Irishman if he was in the right frame of mind. As the most successful and experienced TT rider of them all, you only discounted Dunlop at your peril. "What can you say about Joey?" Jefferies said. "Course knowledge is paramount and he knows every bump, crack, kerb and hedge of every corner. If he gets out of bed on the right side he can still take wins. I tried everything I could to beat him at the Ulster GP last year and couldn't – he was riding as hard as ever. He might be 20 years older than me but he pushes just as hard. If he rides at his best, he can beat anybody."

Joey *was* to ride at his best in the Formula 1 race. So was Jefferies. And the battle turned out to be one of the best ever seen in TT history.

Jefferies's own bike had come on leaps and bounds since the previous TT and now had about 10bhp more. And even though the V&M R1s were making 182bhp on the firm's own dyno compared to the standard model's 132bhp, Steve Mellor was confident he could easily coax more power out of the bikes by simply changing the carburettors, but had opted not to as 182bhp seemed more than enough. In comparison, John McGuinness's 500cc V-twin Grand Prix bike was only making around 130bhp, which led to DJ predicting it would get "hammered down the straights."

The bikes were now dubbed 'R71s' because they were a hybrid of Yamaha's R1 and the exotic R7. Steve Mellor explained the rationale. "Last year's bikes went well to a point. They accelerated hard but hit a wall around 185mph. Getting past that was a struggle. The problem is the R1 looks very nice but it isn't aerodynamic. We thought the R7 would be better and it was – a lot better than we hoped."

So Jefferies would line up on an R1 engine coupled with sleek, aerodynamic R7 bodywork to start the defence of his F1 crown. The scene was set for a terrifyingly fast race in which the magical 125mph lap could finally be set. The Isle of Man TT course is unique in that an outright lap record can almost be more important than a win and it's one of the few – if not the only – bike racing circuit in the world where the majority of fans could tell you what the current lap record is, who set it, and when. It's that important. The current lap record holder at the outset of the 2000 TT was Jim Moodie with an average speed of 124.45mph. It seemed likely that, if weather conditions were favourable and a battle royale erupted between Jefferies, Dunlop, Moodie and Duffus, a real landmark would be reached in TT history.

Jefferies dominated the practice week leader boards and came within 5.6 seconds of setting the first 125mph lap when he posted an average speed of 124.43mph.

As usual, Jefferies's family had travelled to the Isle of Man to help in any way they could. Each had their own little routine worked out by now. His sister Louise would always give her brother a signalling board at Creg-ny-Baa to keep him informed of exactly where he was in the race in relation to other riders; Pauline would invariably be found in the pit lane with a stopwatch to hand and polish at the ready to clean her son's visor and bike screen; while Tony – who had been through the TT as a rider and knew intimately the difficulties his son faced out on the course – would usually try to find a quiet spot to be alone with his thoughts; not an easy task since he is so well known in every racing paddock.

Speaking to Greenlight Television in 2003 for a DVD tribute to David, Tony gave a fascinating insight into his thoughts at the start of one of his son's races. "I always used to be out on the start line to watch him go. There's one thing I remember which was a real emotional moment. On only a few occasions when I started the TT did I set off as number 1 or number 2. We set off with dead engines then and had to push-start the bikes. It was very different to what it is now because there was an eerie silence before the start of a TT race. So when you set off, the flag would drop and nothing would happen because all you could hear was the patter of tiny feet – or in my case, big feet. All you could hear was the bike starting, and then off we'd go. But that silence and looking down the Glencrutchery Road at the top of Bray Hill – no other bike in sight and no noise, is something that you cannot repeat. There isn't anywhere in the world that could have that sort of situation.

"When David first rode as number 1 (the year 2000) I remember looking down the road as he was waiting. It was completely empty and I couldn't look at anybody. I had to look straight ahead because I knew if I looked at anyone I would burst into bloody tears. It was just the waiting and watching – but, suddenly, off he went. I watched him go then wheeled my way to the back, out of the way, and cried my bloody eyes out."

David was always grateful to his family for the help and support they offered throughout his racing career. "It's really nice to have the support of my family," he said. "There are so many people who go racing because their dad won't let them have a bike or something, which is hard work, so I'm fortunate to have that support and I really do enjoy it. My dad's my manager and my mum and sister are my biggest fans, so it's really good."

Conditions were far from perfect for the start of the Formula 1 race. Damp patches prevailed under the many trees which lined the course and, while the roads were drying fast, the first few laps were clearly going to favour Joey Dunlop with his unrivalled course knowledge in such conditions.

For many years Dunlop had said that he would know he had his 'race face' on by the bottom of Bray Hill (a terrifying flat-out drop about half a mile into the course) on the first lap and was capable of challenging for the win. Today, he clearly did. Dunlop sped off into an early lead, displaying his mastery of the course in such tricky conditions. Jefferies, Rutter and McGuinness chased hard but Dunlop maintained his lead and completed lap one with an advantage of 0.2 seconds over Rutter. But after Rutter suffered several massive slides on damp patches and lost his confidence, and John McGuinness dropped off the pace, the race became a straight fight between Jefferies and Dunlop.

On laps two and three, Dunlop held a slim advantage but as Jefferies became more familiar with the course conditions, he gradually upped his pace and began reeling in the maestro. "The conditions were ideal for Joey," David would later say. "He knew every bump, rut and wet patch on the road. He went off from the start at full pace – it took me several laps to get up to race speed."

After posting the fastest lap of the race on lap four, Jefferies briefly snatched the lead only for Dunlop to regain it again with a quicker pit stop.

The duo were neck and neck in the early part of the fifth lap, with both men clearly giving it everything they had, when suddenly the race was over: Jefferies was spotted by the helicopter camera grinding to a halt just before Ballig Bridge, about eight miles into the course. "Something just went bang on the fifth lap," he said once he got back to the paddock. "I had just drawn level with Joey prior to the second pit stop, but he had a better one than me, gaining six seconds. The problem is something internal. We don't know what, so we'll just put a new engine in for the Senior race and try and sort it out when we get back home."

The problem turned out to be a clutch basket destroying itself which, in turn, shattered the R71's engine casing. Understandably, Jefferies was gutted, but he took nothing away from Dunlop's achievement after the Irishman had gone on to record his first F1 win in 12 years. Jefferies was even man enough to admit he would have struggled to beat his inspired rival. "I'm not sure I could have kept up that pace in the conditions," he said. "Joey deserved the win. I'll just have to get it right on Friday in the Senior."

Jack Valentine echoed the views of thousands of fans who had been deprived of a dramatic last lap showdown between the two fastest TT riders in the world. "It's a real shame," he said, "not just for us, but for the fans. If David had stayed out, that would have been a hell of a last lap and I don't know who would have won it."

But Valentine had been seriously impressed with his rider's maturity in such trying conditions. "That was a sad race for us to lose but, again, it was a good measure of how professional David was as a rider," he said. "There'd been a lot of rain. There were damp patches and a hell of a lot of leaves under the trees round the Laurel Bank section; and the same down through Glentramman. So when David set off he wanted to have a look at the circuit. But Joey being Joey, he always excelled in those types of conditions and really turned the wick up, getting a lead on David as they came through the first lap. But once David had looked at the track and could see where everything was, he started to turn it up on the second lap and closed up on Joey. Then I think one of the guys made a little bit of time up on the pit stop and unofficially we were, I think, 1.5 or 1.6 seconds in front after Ballacraine. Then a clutch basket broke."

There was a humorous end to the tale however, as Jefferies's mechanical curiosity got the better of him. Valentine explains: "Typical David – he pulled in at Ballig Bridge and, being bored waiting for a lift back, he thought, 'Oh, I'll take the fairing off the bike and have a look at it,' and burned his head on the exhaust pipe. He came back with a big blister on his head and promptly got told by our guys that it would teach him a lesson for messing! All week he was walking around with a big blister on his head."

Asked in an online interview for www.ttwebsite.com in 2001 if he could have beaten Dunlop had his bike held out, Jefferies revised his earlier opinion and said, "Yeah, I think I would of done. But by putting this on the TT Website, a load of Joey fans will read it and say that Joey would have won. Everyone is entitled to their own opinion. I didn't, he did, and he was the better man on the day. It's all hypothetical, but yes, I do think I would have beaten him."

With one race lost, DJ would have to win all three of his remaining events if he was to repeat his TT hat-trick of the previous year. It was a tall order, as any rider knows, that to win a TT you need generous helpings of luck on top of uncanny riding ability and technical sympathy for the bike. But Jefferies wasn't afraid of tall orders and he set about his task with renewed vigour after the disappointment of the F1 race.

Next up was the Junior TT on the Wednesday of race week and DJ was keen to win the same race that his father had won back in 1971, though the race was then for 350cc machines instead of the current crop of 600cc Supersport bikes.

Jefferies led the race at the first timing interval but it was just by a whisker from his by now regular nemesis, Joey Dunlop, who had spent the morning winning yet another TT, this time the Ultra-Lightweight 125 event.

As he flashed across the start/finish line, it was announced that Jefferies had set a new lap record for the 600 class from a standing start – one-fifth of a second inside Ian Simpson's three-year-old benchmark. His speed of 119.88mph showed not only how determined he was to make up for his DNF in the F1 race, but also that he had mastered the very different art of riding a 600 round the TT course. Both he and Adrian Archibald, his closest challenger once Dunlop dropped off the pace (exhausted after already winning three TTs that week – the Formula 1, 250cc Lightweight and 125cc Ultra-Lightweight events), would both up their speeds and lap at over 120mph as they battled for the win – the first men ever to achieve the 120mph mark on 600cc machines at the TT.

Going into the final circuit, Jefferies held a 10 second lead, but Archibald – an up-and-coming young Irish rider from the same hometown as Joey Dunlop – whittled it down to just seven seconds before the final run over the Mountain. It was an inspired ride but he couldn't catch DJ over his favourite section of the course and Jefferies held on to take his first TT victory of 2000 and his fourth in total.

It was a matter of family pride that David had now won one more TT than his father, and three more than uncle Nick, and his Junior win came exactly 29 years after Tony had won the same race. It was also DJ's first Junior win which now meant he had won in every class he had ever entered at the TT – Formula 1, Production, Senior and Junior – and broken Honda's five-year stranglehold on the event as well as giving Yamaha its first win in the 600cc class. For good measure, DJ also shaved more than half a minute off the Junior race record.

After the race Jefferies said, "I just got my head down and got on with the job. The bike worked brilliantly and it was a great race. I wanted to get this one under my belt to get over Saturday's disappointment and get me in the right mood for my two races on Friday."

No one was in the right mood come Friday morning's Production race. Conditions were as bad as they had ever been round the course and the riders were pulled off the line just as they were due to set off for the four lap race. A five-hour delay ensued and the event, when it finally did get underway at 4.30pm, was cut to just two laps. Riders braved standing water and mist on the Mountain but many pulled in after just one lap claiming conditions were too dangerous. Neil Hanson, in his first year as Clerk of the Course, came in for some serious criticism, with most of the top riders saying the race should never have been run. It certainly would not be run in such conditions today.

And to make things worse, the rules governing the Production race did not permit riders to use full wet tyres – they had to run on road legal street tyres which don't offer anywhere near the same grip as full wets.

But Jefferies saw an opportunity to add to his growing tally of TT wins and splashed on through the mist and rain as quickly as he could manage in relative safety. After the first lap he held a commanding 26-second lead over local hero Richard 'Milky' Quayle, with acknowledged wet weather supremo Michael Rutter a further five seconds back in third. Jefferies's opening lap of 99.34mph proved just how bad conditions were, since he had posted a lap at

120.94mph on the same bike in dry practice. But even that paled into insignificance compared to the top speed registered as Milky Quayle broke the timing beam over the start/finish line. He was credited with a top speed of 483mph after rain had affected the electrics in the timing equipment!

Eventually finishing 17 seconds ahead of Quayle – who was making an impressive TT debut after winning the Manx Grand Prix – Jefferies added his voice to the protest that the race should have been postponed. "They shouldn't really have run it," he said. "The conditions were bloody awful. There was a lot of standing water about. At the end of the Mountain Mile I was getting wheelspins at 140mph so it's pretty scary."

Third place finisher, Michael Rutter, agreed. "I'm just glad to have finished in one piece. It was *very* frightening."

There was relief for the riders when it was announced that the Senior race, due to get underway after the Production, had been postponed until the following day. The only losers were the fans, many of whom were booked onto ferries and flights back to the mainland on the Saturday.

For those who did manage to stay, the weather was much kinder and there was the mouth-watering prospect of a final Senior showdown between Joey Dunlop, who had scored his third TT hat-trick that week, and Jefferies, who had taken two victories.

As hoped for, the pair were inseparable at the first timing checkpoint at Glen Helen, eight miles into the course, but then Jefferies piled on the coals and surged ahead to lead Dunlop by nine seconds by the time he got to Ramsey. Dunlop was clearly tiring after a week that would have exhausted a man half his age, and Michael Rutter took over second spot. From then on, it was Jefferies's race all the way and the only question that remained was whether or not he could crack the elusive 125mph lap barrier in the perfect conditions. With only one chance at a 'flying lap' (the first lap is from a standing start, the second includes a pit stop, the third is a standing start from the pit stop, the fourth is interrupted by slowing for another pit stop and the fifth is slowed by another standing start as the rider leaves the pits, meaning the sixth lap is the only one when a rider crosses the start/finish line at full speed both at the start and finish of their lap), Jefferies and the crowd knew the sixth lap would have to be the one.

Naturally, when a rider has a commanding lead in a race as important as the Senior TT, the temptation is to protect that lead without taking any chances that could lead to either a crash or a mechanical malfunction. But racers are racers and concentration is often best kept by applying maximum effort rather than riding at nine-tenths when mistakes can too often be made. In Jefferies's case, he decided to go for it. The weather was perfect – he was on form with two wins already in the bag, and he held a secure lead over his team-mate. More importantly, this would be Jefferies's last lap around his beloved TT course for a whole year. There was never really any question of *not* going for it. Jefferies buried his head behind the bubble, tucked his considerable frame in as tight as he could and wound the throttle back to the stop. He used every ounce of course knowledge he had learned in his four years of racing at the TT and set about earning a place in the history books.

All round the course, spectators held their breaths as the flash of red and yellow swept past them, travelling faster than any motorcycle had ever gone round the Island's roads – and there had been no shortage of fast men who had pitted their skills against the TT circuit over the years.

Suspension bottoming out at Bray Hill, knee dragging along the tarmac at Braddan Bridge, helmet brushing the walls at Handley's, Jefferies kept piling on the pace. Faster, faster, faster. Inch-perfect, drifting the rear wheel out of the long, fast bends on the Mountain, howling past spectator's legs as they sat on the bankings watching in awe. For precisely 18 minutes and six seconds, David Jefferies was the very definition of concentration – well, almost. In the final few straights he seemed almost casual as he waved to the fans cheering him on from the side of the road.

As he hurtled closer and closer to the finish line, his full ten years of racing experience were channelled into that one magnificent lap. And as he blasted out of the shadows at Governor's Dip and screamed along the final few hundred yards of Glencrutchery Road towards the chequered flag, he not only took the Senior TT win, but stunned the grandstand crowds as it was announced that David Jefferies had become the first man in history to lap the Isle of Man TT course at 125mph. His exact speed of 125.69mph guaranteed Jefferies a place in the TT history books that can never be taken away from him. The great Jimmy Simpson had been the first man to lap the course at 60, 70 and ultimately 80mph back in the 1930s, Bob McIntyre had broken the magical 100mph barrier in 1957, John Williams achieved the first 110mph lap in 1976 and Steve Hislop became the first to clock a 120mph circuit in 1989. Now, 11 years later, David Jefferies had raised the bar yet again with an astonishing average of 125mph.

He would later explain his feat in quite nonchalant terms. "I must admit, I wasn't pushing it that hard. I think I did it to try and show myself what I could do, but I wasn't pushing to the limits. I just enjoyed myself. I never set out to do 125mph, but it's nice to be the first person to do it. I knew I had a big lead and I had lost all my tear-offs. I used two of them on the first lap and rode the next four laps with one on which I left until the Nook on lap five. Then I thought, 'Riding within my limits, what sort of speed can you do here?' and that was it.

"It was one of the best laps I'd ever done because it just seemed to flow together. I just had to concentrate. I basically thought one corner ahead. As I came out of Quarterbridge, I thought, 'Right, get into the right position for the next corner.' Then as I came out of Braddan Bridge I thought, 'Right, get ready for Union Mills.' I just basically thought one corner ahead all the way round. I don't think you can do that for six laps. I just really concentrated.

"In all the other successes I've had, everyone said, 'Oh brilliant, you've won a race but you just missed out on a lap record.' So this time I thought, 'Right, I'll see what I can do.' It was more for my own personal interest really – to see what I could do. It was probably the most enjoyable lap I've ever done."

Typically, Jefferies was also very modest about setting a new outright lap record on the longest, toughest and most dangerous course in the world and was quick to point out that Carl Fogarty's lap from 1992 was just as impressive. "I ride relatively safely over here," he said. "I know there are a few other people who won't think so, looking at it, but I still say that Fogarty's lap in '92 was more impressive than my lap because he had a bike with a lot less horsepower and he rode it a lot, lot harder. I mean, I know I've still got to hang on to mine even though it's got a lot more straight-line speed, but he rode his bike a lot harder than I rode mine to get the lap record."

The list of Jefferies's achievements at the 2000 TT are impressive: The first man in history to win three races in a week on two consecutive years, the first man in history to break the 125mph lap, and he also set new lap and race records in the Junior and Senior events. In just two meetings, he had gone from being an unfancied TT novice to a six-times winner – more wins than many top riders achieve in their entire careers. As DJ himself said, "To be the fastest man round here and the first to do 125 – it's pretty special is that."

John McGuinness has no idea of what made Jefferies so good around the TT course and wonders if his friend ever really knew himself. "DJ did it on his own naturally; he just took it in his stride. It wasn't even an effort for him. He'd just ride – he'd ride anything. Put him on a trials bike, a Supermoto, anything, and he could ride it. When he started winning the TT he didn't even know why himself. People would ask him and he were like, 'I don't know really, I just enjoy riding my bike, you know?' He would get off the bike and there wouldn't be a bead of sweat on him or anything. A red hot day – do six laps of the TT and it was effortless. I don't know how or why. I don't know."

Tragically, that Senior TT proved to be Jefferies's last battle with Joey Dunlop and also Dunlop's last ever TT race. After an incredible career in which he recorded 26 TT wins – a tally never likely to be equalled, let alone bettered – Dunlop was killed on 2 July at an obscure race in Estonia. Just a few weeks after one of his most successful TTs ever, the legendary Irishman had gone back to his roots and entered a little-known event where he was as far out of the limelight as he could hope to be – just the way Joey liked it. Still at the top of his game at 48, Dunlop had taken the Honda RC45 that hung from the ceiling of the pub he owned in Ballymoney and won the Superbike race at Tallin before crashing out of the 125cc event – whilst in the lead – and hitting a tree. He died instantly and the entire world of bike racing went into mourning.

It's a world not unaccustomed to tragedies but Joey had seemed invincible; so safe, so reliable and, most believed, so close to retirement and the safety that would bring. After such a stunning TT, in which he had finally achieved his dream of another big bike win in the F1 race, it was widely believed that Dunlop would hang up his leathers at the end of the season.

Joey's tragic death stunned everyone in motorcycling, including Jefferies, who simply couldn't believe that he was gone. "I was at Silverstone when news started going around in whispers about his death," he said. "At first I just thought, 'These are only rumours, they can't be true.' When I found out it was the truth I was in total shock. I couldn't believe it had actually happened."

Dunlop's death proved that even the safest and most experienced riders could be caught out by the dangers of road racing. Jefferies may not have been close to Dunlop – few people were, given his extremely quiet and reclusive nature – but he had the utmost respect for him as a racing rival. "Joey is simply a miracle man," he said after the Formula 1 TT in 2000. "He can still show us youngsters how to handle a Superbike around the world's most demanding road circuit." There could be no finer tribute to a racer's skills than such words from a rival.

The tragedy was compounded in 2008 when Joey's brother Robert lost his life during practice for the North West 200. Racing was so much in the brothers' blood that both separately admitted they had no idea how to stop, or what they would do with themselves if they did. No punishment short of death itself could tear them away from the sport that had given them a reason for living in the first place. They remain Ireland's best-loved and most famous road racers.

* * *

After fifth and third places in rounds five and six of the British Superstock Championship, Jefferies was back to winning ways in round seven at Oulton Park. The series had become hugely popular with fans as they could watch only slightly modified versions of their own bikes battling it out on track. The championship had now become a regular tussle between the Honda FireBlades of Aussies Chris Vermeulen and Glen Richards, and the Yamaha R1s of Jefferies and Matt Llewellyn, with the occasional guest appearance from the likes of Steve Plater on his Kawasaki. *Bikesport News* commented on the popularity and professionalism of the series, saying, 'Far from being just a support race, the Superstock class has matured into an enthralling and entertaining series in its own right. The racing is close and hard fought and the teams are professional and well presented both on the track and in the paddock. The Page3.com Yamaha team is stealing all the limelight off the track, but on it the Sanyo Honda duo of Glen Richards and Chris Vermeulen are ready to match them.'

The Oulton race was red-flagged following an incident in the first leg and restarted as an aggregate race. But so close was the action in both legs that Jefferies only just took the win from Llewellyn by less than a tenth of a second to close within 11 points of the championship lead.

That gap was further reduced at a very wet Knockhill round where Jefferies rode to fourth place ahead of Llewellyn to slash his lead to just 9 points. Both riders were overshadowed by the sensational wet weather riding skills of Chris Vermeulen who took an easy win and gave an early display of his mastery of the wet which he would later use to devastating effect in MotoGP.

The Ulster Grand Prix started under a dark cloud in 2000. Not only would it be the first time in decades that local hero Joey Dunlop would not take to the grid, but there had been a double tragedy just seven days before at the Monaghan road races where Gary Dynes and Andy McClean were killed. Many people, including the mayor of Ballymoney – Joey Dunlop's home town – were calling for the Ulster to be boycotted in the wake of the tragedy but race organiser Billy Nutt told the *Belfast Telegraph*, 'Ulster motorcycling is a large family and everyone feels one another's hurt. Of course we are saddened by the events of Sunday – we have lost two well-respected competitors. But it would be their wish that the show should go on. That's the way it has always been.'

Nutt's final words are a truism: no matter how dangerous road racing is and no matter how many lives it has cost in the past – and is sure to do in the future – it has always continued as long as there are riders who are prepared to take the risk and spectators and sponsors who want to watch, or even pay for them, to do so. Only in most recent times has this simple equation been under threat as the health and safety brigade gain ever more powers to stop people exercising their own free will.

David Jefferies defended that freedom of choice vehemently; nothing was more guaranteed to get his back up than someone insisting that road racing, or the TT in particular, should be banned. He hated those who criticised the sport without having any understanding of what a man like himself got out of it. "I think you've got to be able to accept what can happen – you have got to be able to accept the consequences," he said. "I get really annoyed with all these do-gooders, saying, 'Ban the TT – it's bloody disgraceful, blah blah blah.' Nobody is forced to go to the Isle of Man. I am pro-TT if you like it, but if you don't like it, then don't go. But if you don't go, then don't start slagging it off."

"The people that keep saying that it's dangerous are all these arty-farty bastards who live in the bloody countryside and ride horses. And when you look at the number of people that get hurt riding horses – that really winds me up. The TT gets taken out of context. The press love it – 'Woooo – the TT – someone has been killed.' Unfortunately they don't glorify the fact that Lady so-and-so's daughter got hurt on a horse because horses are lovely, super. The establishment likes horses.

"And rugby as well – people get injured doing rugby or fencing, you know. There are so many other sports which are dangerous, but I've chosen to do the TT. No one is forcing me to go there. Yeah, people might say that I'm thick – 'Bloody silly bastard, riding at the TT' – but that's what I want to do and at the minute I'm the best in the world at it."

Personal experience had taught Jefferies that one didn't need to be engaging in dangerous sports to suffer serious injury or even death – he was aware that both outcomes could occur in the most innocuous circumstances. "I think life's dangerous," he said. "My uncle was changing a light bulb years ago and he fell and broke his neck, and he's now paralysed from the neck down; can't breathe on his own, can't eat on his own properly. He was changing a light bulb in his garden.

"I know another guy who dived into a swimming pool and broke his back. Life is dangerous no matter what you do. There's a girl I know, she comes to race meetings. I saw her recently and she was a bit upset. She said, 'My best mate got killed in a car last night driving home from Leeds.' It can happen."

David's sister Louise remembers his very matter-of-fact approach to racing on the roads, and at the TT in particular. "It was in 2002 and we were all sat there in the pub talking about the TT. Someone asked Dave if he ever worried about the TT. Dave said 'No – I know if it goes wrong I come home in a box.'"

With this very realistic acceptance of the dangers of life in general and motorcycle road racing in particular, Jefferies set pole position for the Ulster Grand Prix ahead of his new V&M team-mates Jason Griffiths and Ian Lougher. His blinding turn of speed was testified to by top Irish rider Richard Britton who said, "In the first practice period I was able to stay with Jefferies on the straight sections of the course but when it came to the corners he just left me standing."

On paper at least, Jefferies looked like he should dominate the meeting. After all, he had scored a win and two second places in his first visit to the circuit in 1999 and that was with an injured hand and against the might of Joey Dunlop. Now his fiercest rival was sadly no more, his hand had healed, and he knew which way the course went. Surely there could be no stopping him?

An added incentive for DJ was that while he'd won trebles at both the North West 200 and the TT, he hadn't yet managed to do so at the Ulster. Having only entered three races however, there was no margin for error and he'd need to win every one to do the treble.

Things got off to a good start with Jefferies winning the opening Superbike race by 1.15 seconds from Griffiths, with Adrian Archibald just five hundredths of a second behind the Welshman. While DJ led throughout, it had been a close-fought battle and not without its problems, as he explained afterwards. "My visor was filled with splattered flies," he said. "I lost the two tear-off strips which clean the visor on the very first lap, and in the closing stages I had almost double vision. I just couldn't see where I was going. On one occasion I saw what I thought was a rider only to find it was a straw bale!"

Jefferies's hopes of a hat-trick were ruined in the Supersport 600 event when he could only manage a fourth placed finish behind Lougher, Griffiths and Adrian Archibald – Ulster's new hope following the loss of Joey Dunlop. A bad start saw Jefferies having to battle his way through the field that allowed the leading trio to put themselves out of reach.

The second Superbike race was almost a carbon copy of the first, with DJ leading from flag to flag, but there was one scary moment as he started the final lap. Harold Crooks reported in *The Guardian* that, 'As he [Jefferies] came through to start his last lap, two slower riders were right on his line. He had to put the big Yamaha right down on its side as he cut inside them, almost colliding with the official putting out the last lap flag.'

Fortunately no harm was done and Jefferies completed a Dundrod double. The *County Down Spectator* highlighted Jefferies's crowd-pleasing antics as he crossed the finish line on the back wheel. It reported that, 'The victory was nothing more than a formality but the wheelie that he produced exiting the new chicane on the last lap was nothing more than an act of pure genius. It came straight from the Randy Mamola school of wheelies but was ten times better as he negotiated the right hander on the back wheel to the delight of the crowd.'

Jefferies's performances had helped to save the Ulster Grand Prix. After a safe day's racing held in brilliant sunshine and with DJ's antics keeping the 10,000-strong crowd on its toes, Irish road racing recovered some of its former glory and people were reminded just why – despite its dangers – they loved the sport of road racing in the first place. With Jimmy Walker writing in *Ireland's Saturday Night* that, 'David Jefferies, the flying DJ, provided a rescue act for Ulster road racing when he sizzled to a sun-soaked double in the Ulster Grand Prix,' and *Sunday World* reporting that, 'Yorkshire's David Jefferies gave Irish road racing a timely tonic yesterday with his first double success at the Ulster Grand Prix,' it was clear that Jefferies was being seen as the saviour of road racing and that he had greatly improved the image of the sport following a dark 12 months in which seven competitors had lost their lives.

In spite of the positive press that surrounded the Ulster in 2000, there was one dark footnote. Promising Irish rider Uel Duncan crashed heavily in practice and has been confined to a wheelchair ever since. But his subsequent career as a successful road racing team owner proves that riders enter road races knowing the risks and accepting them and that, even when they lose their mobility, they never lose their love of the sport.

On his return from Ireland, Jefferies finally got the chance he had been striving to get for years – to ride a factory bike in BSB. His test on the Yamaha R7 had clearly impressed all the right people and DJ now received the welcome news that he would actually get a chance to race the bike since both the regular team members, Steve Hislop and Paul Brown, were sidelined with injuries. Needless to say, Jefferies was delighted at the prospect. "I rode the R7 in a test last year but only got about nine laps," he said in the run-up to his debut on the bike at Cadwell Park. "I'm really looking forward to this to prove what I can do on a Superbike. I think I'm at the point in my career where this is right for me. The team is brilliant too – just look at the names it has brought on over the years."

The names that Jefferies was referring to, who had ridden factory Yamahas in BSB, included Niall Mackenzie, Steve Hislop, Chris Walker and Jamie Whitham, so he knew the bike and team were as good as any in the UK paddock. But no rider can expect to enter any top series, whether Grands Prix, World Superbikes or British Superbikes, at such a late point in the season and expect to challenge for wins straight away. To be amongst the consistent front-runners required several months of pre-season testing and race experience on the bike to develop it to suit the rider's own particular style. By the time Jefferies jumped on the bike at Cadwell, the other front runners in BSB like Neil Hodgson and Chris Walker, had almost a full season's racing on their respective bikes and had them fine-tuned to such a degree that they only had to think to make them turn, stop or slide. Jefferies had had nine laps on the bike the previous year and even then it was set up for Niall Mackenzie's unique style. It was a golden opportunity and a great shop window for Jefferies but it would clearly take more than one meeting before he could feel comfortable enough on the bike to challenge at the sharp end of the field.

Even so, Virgin Yamaha team manager Rob McElnea seemed confident in his stand-in rider. "I rate David as a rider," he said, "and he's a natural choice for Yamaha after the TT, and doing so well on the R1 in the Superstock series. He's capable of running with people like Steve Plater and John Crawford. If he does that I'll be more than happy."

Jefferies did run with Plater and Crawford and finished in 9th and 10th places, but got a bit of a shock at just how tough BSB had become since he last raced in the series. "The races have really showed me that this is a step up," he said. "The bikes are a step up and so is the competition. I know I need to work on my fitness."

It may have been an eye-opener for Jefferies but his results were as good as could have been expected with so little time on the bike. The R7 had never quite succeeded as a race bike, and if riders of the calibre of Niall Mackenzie could only manage two podiums in a whole year of racing it (as he did in 1999), then there seemed little hope for a one-off stand-in rider.

As Hislop and Brown needed still more time to recover from their respective injuries (Hislop had only just discovered on a second check-up that he had actually broken his neck following a crash at Brands), DJ was given another chance to shine on the R7 at Mallory Park. This time he would have an unlikely team-mate in the form of Aussie bad boy, Anthony Gobert.

A former WSB race winner, Gobert had been fired from his Suzuki Grand Prix ride after failing a drugs test, and a succession of scandals and drink-driving charges had followed him to his new racing home in the American Superbike Championship. He was fast running out of options when Rob McElnea took a chance by offering him the stand-in ride on the R7, a move which would at least guarantee the Yamaha team a surge of publicity, if nothing else.

Jefferies improved in the first leg at Mallory to take a fine seventh place but dropped back in leg two to finish 11th. His results were good enough to earn him a final outing on the R7 at Brands Hatch where he again took a seventh before crashing out of race two. "There was something on the track," he said afterwards. "I'm sure of that because the front tyre tucked under and there was nothing I could do. I managed to hold the bike up with my feet but once we ran into the gravel trap at Paddock Hill Bend there was nothing I could do."

Despite the disappointment of crashing out of his last race, Jefferies's outings on the Virgin Yamaha had proved two things. One was that the use of a factory bike did not instantly guarantee podium places, and the other was that, at this level of the sport, a rider needs to be settled into a top level team for a full season if he is to get the best out of his bike. Sadly, Jefferies would never get that chance.

There was more glory in store at Scarborough in September where the stars had turned out in force to celebrate the 50th running of the Gold Cup meeting. The programme for the parade lap read like a who's who of motorcycle racing. From Geoff Duke, the first winner of the Gold Cup back in 1950, to John Surtees who hadn't been back to the circuit since winning the cup in 1957, others in attendance included 15-times World Champion Giacomo Agostini, eight-times World Champion Phil Read, Jim Redman, Tommy Robb and Mick Grant. As the winner of the 1970 event, David's father also took part in the parade lap riding a Yamaha quad.

The current master of the circuit was undoubtedly Jefferies who won both Superbike races and the feature Gold Cup event, under the watchful eyes of bike racing royalty, to draw level second with Barry Sheene in the list of all-time Gold Cup winners. Only Geoff Duke, with five wins, now stood ahead of him.

As well as riding the factory R7 in the last few rounds of the 2000 season, Jefferies still had to contest the Superstock championship, meaning he was riding in three races at each round. A third place at Cadwell Park left DJ still trailing his Page 3.com team-mate Matt Llewellyn who had led the championship all year. But when Llewellyn crashed out on the penultimate lap at Mallory Park and DJ went on to win the race, he found himself right back in the title hunt. And after a second place at Brands Hatch, Jefferies went into the final round at Donington needing just a top six finish to clinch the title.

It sounded easy enough, but a bad tyre choice saw him slump to the fourth row of the grid for the race while his main rivals, Llewellyn and Glen Richards, would be starting from the front row. It was a difficult situation. If he rode steady and circulated without taking any risks, he would lose the championship on points. Yet if he rode too hard and clashed with other riders, he could easily crash out and still lose the title. But in a calculated display of riding, Jefferies did exactly what he needed to, scything his way past at least ten other riders to claw his way up to fifth place, just one place higher than he needed to be, and secured his third British championship by four points from Glen Richards who had leap-frogged Llewellyn in the last two rounds. With good pit signals telling him exactly where he needed to be, Jefferies overtook enough rivals to ensure a top six finish but refused to get involved in any unnecessary battles. "When Rob Frost came by I knew I was high enough to win so I just let him go," he said after the race. "Rob can be a bit hairy to fight with and I didn't need that."

After winning the British Superstock title, Page3.com boss Tim Ford revealed his squad would not be defending it in 2001 as he had landed factory Ducatis for an assault on the British Superbike Championship. Matt Llewellyn signed up immediately but Jefferies baulked over the team's reluctance to allow him to contest the TT. He had also impressed with his rides on the R7 and was waiting to discover if there would be any other offers from established BSB teams for 2001.

Eventually, when no better offer was forthcoming, Jefferies agreed to ride for the Page3 team but revealed that he was still trying to reach an agreement on the TT. "I've already agreed with Page3.com to race on the short circuits but I'm still keen to race on the Island," he said. "We've still got a lot of talking to do about that. I'm looking forward to having a crack at the British Superbikes on a competitive machine. It was too good an opportunity to miss so I thought I'd have a go at it. I've never been so far advanced for a season."

Jefferies should have learned from bitter experience to be more cautious. Incredibly, just as a BSB deal finally appeared to be in place, it would all fall through again, through no fault of Jefferies himself. It seemed he was destined never to compete in a top team in BSB.

But before all turned to despair yet again, there were still some races left to round off the 2000 season. One was in Ireland where, as a North West 200 and Ulster Grand Prix winner, Jefferies was revered. For the International Sunflower Trophy at Kirkistown, Jefferies would be partnered with Jim Moodie on V&M R1s. Moodie had wrapped up the British Supersport Championship on a V&M R6 after splitting acrimoniously with Honda at the TT where he refused to ride a specially prepared FireBlade after branding it uncompetitive.

It was a meeting to forget for Jefferies. After being beaten into second place by Michael Rutter in the opening Superbike event, he crashed heavily in the feature Sunflower race and his bike landed on top of him. Despite walking away with nothing more than a damaged finger, the tumble was big enough to rule him out of the 600cc race meaning that, for once, he left an Irish meeting without a win. But, however, DJ was soon heading back to the Emerald Isle to take part in an altogether different form of two-wheeled sport – the Irish Supermoto Championship.

An increasingly popular sport, Supermoto is contested half on tarmac and half on dirt using specially-designed hybrid bikes. Jefferies had entered the first two rounds of the series on a 426cc Yamaha decked out in V&M colours, primarily for the fun of it but also as a means of staying 'bike fit' during the winter break from road racing.

As usual, Jefferies wasn't there to make up the numbers and he finished second to the Ulster champion, David Tougher, in his very first Supermoto race at Nutts Corner. Unfortunately, DJ failed to finish either leg in the second round of the series before jetting off to Macau for the Grand Prix, but he stated his intent to try again in 2001.

John McGuinness remembers requiring Jefferies's assistance to make it through the airport in Macau that year. "I had broke my leg at Oulton Park in July and had been out of action, but I really wanted to ride at Macau. After the 13-hour flight, though, I was fucked and my leg was in agony. So DJ carried me and put me on a luggage trolley and wheeled me through the airport."

DJ once again came to the rescue when McGuinness got into a threatening situation with a burly and highly-agitated German biker. "We'd hired some scooters and went motocrossing on them, completely wrecking the things, blowing the tyres up, the lot. Anyway, I carved up some German bloke who was riding one of those big chopper bikes and he started chasing me. I had my bad leg and I was flying in and out of the traffic but he eventually caught me and started giving me a lot of pain. I was like, 'Whoa, whoa, whoa – I've got a bad leg,' but he was saying, 'Where is your passport?' DJ just came up and said, 'Hey pal, you'd better get going lad – get yourself away.' And that nipped it in the bud. A handy lad to have around in a tight spot were DJ."

While there are many temptations in Macau, particularly of the female variety, and the paddock abounds with many sordid, unprintable tales of riders taking full advantage, Jefferies wasn't one of them. McGuinness claims he was too shy. "We had some good nights," he says, "some drinking sessions and we always had a good crack together. We did the Go-Go bars and saw all the sights and delights, but Dave was cautious about the whole prostitute thing. He was never interested in all that. He liked to go and have a look, he was intrigued by it all, but he was too cautious to take advantage."

After finishing second in Macau, Jefferies dropped the bombshell that he was turning his back on road racing in 2001 in favour of racing full time in British Superbikes. Suddenly, the North West 200, the Isle of Man TT and the Ulster Grand Prix would be deprived of their biggest star. Having already lost Joey Dunlop for very different reasons, the future looked bleak for pure road racing. Jefferies had almost single-handedly saved the sport during some of its darkest hours, but now he'd been forced to make a decision he hoped he'd never have to make – road racing or British Superbikes. And road racing lost.

Chapter 11

FOOT AND MOUTH

"Bloody hell, he's bigger than me and can push me wherever he wants to!"
Ian Lougher

For the best part of 100 years, race organisers in the UK had always left a slot at the end of May and beginning of June to allow for the Isle of Man TT. It had always made sense when most of the top riders in the UK raced at the TT but now there seemed little need to avoid date clashes. Since most of the top BSB runners didn't race on the Island, it was decided that staging a BSB race on the same weekend as a TT race wouldn't affect too many people. One man it did affect was David Jefferies.

In order to be competitive in BSB, riders cannot afford to miss any rounds, and with sponsors pouring hundreds of thousands of pounds into backing each BSB star, they expect them to finish as high up the championship table as possible. So when David Jefferies finally bit the bullet and signed with the Page3.com team to race Ducatis in the British Championship, he was also signing away the chance to race on his beloved road circuits. Since they now clashed with BSB, he would not be permitted to race at them.

Jefferies had long said, as a token of his commitment to a career in BSB, that if he ever had to make the choice between a ride in the British championship or a season on the roads, he'd forsake the roads. Now he'd been forced to back up his words with actions at the insistence of team boss Claire Ritchie. 'We've put the cards on the table,' she told *MCN* in late 2000. 'We'd like to work with David but he has to choose. He can get injured so easily doing the road races – he injured his hand at the Sunflower races in Ireland recently.'

Despite the fact that Kirkistown is a short airfield circuit and *not* a public roads course, Ritchie's point was clear – the team viewed road racing as being too dangerous and if Jefferies wanted a career in BSB, he would have to forget about it. Ritchie, whose husband Graeme had sadly been killed in a crash at Brands Hatch in 1997, added, "Also, doing the TT would mean riding for Yamaha again. We won't be taking the Ducatis there so it's a big no-no. We would want our riders to concentrate on the British championship."

Jefferies was, at that point, clearly still struggling with the decision, as he refused to make any comment to *MCN*, but when he did break his silence he defended what must have been the toughest decision of his racing career. "02+ offered me the ride on the condition that I did not compete anywhere else except the BSB championship. I had to do a lot of soul searching to say 'Yes.' I'm a bit upset because the TT has been very good for me and I really enjoy racing there. But this is a great opportunity and I'd be daft to turn it down. I've got to move on and, without wanting to be big headed, I've proved what I can do on the Isle of Man with six wins and the outright lap record there. All I can do there now is notch more wins whereas Superbikes are a completely new challenge for me."

That may have been so, but another issue for Jefferies surrounding the TT was the money that it earned him in a successful year. "It's going to sound very mercenary is this," he said, "but the problem is that the career span of a racer is quite short relative to other jobs. No one is earning big money in BSB but the TT can earn me £75,000 in prize money, and as a professional racer that's a considerable amount of money."

The headlines over Jefferies's decision said it all: *'Jefferies Bombshell'*, *'Jefferies chooses Superbikes over TT'*, *'BSB or TT? Tough choice for Jefferies.'* Such was Jefferies's standing at the TT that the organisers even considered taking the unprecedented move of switching the date of the Senior race to avoid a clash with the Brands Hatch BSB round. That at least would have given the likes of Jefferies, Michael Rutter and Jim Moodie – the few stars who contested British championships and the TT – the chance to compete in both events. The Manx government also ploughed a further £100,000 into the prize fund in the hope of attracting a better entry.

In the end, neither Jefferies nor the Manx authorities should have spent so long agonising over the 2001 TT – Jefferies because, once again, he was about to lose his BSB ride at the eleventh hour, and the Manx authorities because for the first time since World War II, there wouldn't be a TT to worry about.

By late January of 2001 the 02+ team was in trouble again. News International, the company which owned title sponsors Page3.com, had been restructured and there was no place in the new-look firm for a bike racing team. Despite winning a British championship in its first year of involvement and receiving much publicity for doing so, the sponsorship package was pulled and 02+ found itself without financial backing. Claire Ritchie admitted the future for the squad looked bleak. "We're in negotiations with a couple of sponsors. If they say no, time's running out, and it could go either way."

Team owner Tim Ford remained confident saying, "As far as I'm concerned we will be racing in BSB this season with two riders on Ducatis and support from Italy. We've lost a lot of time but we're working flat-out to make that up."

But the writing looked to be on the wall for the team and, yet again, Jefferies had had the rug pulled out from under him just weeks away from the start of the season. He must have been wondering what he'd done wrong in a previous life.

By mid-February, Jefferies and Llewellyn were officially given the news that the 02+ squad had folded, at least as far as the 2001 season was concerned. By then, it was too late for either rider to find an alternative competitive ride in BSB as all the slots had long been filled. It looked like being a wasted year at the prime of Jefferies's career and he was understandably distraught, if not a little angry. "I am really pissed off that I have been left in this situation," he said. "Basically, Matt and I were taken off the market in October and constantly reassured everything was going to be fine. As it turned out, it wasn't, and we have been left with nothing. I'm in a far better position than Matt because I can go to the TT and other road races and earn a good wage doing that. Matt has nothing."

Jefferies quickly came to an arrangement with the V&M team to contest the major road races and also the British Superstock Championship, while Llewellyn was thrown a lifeline with the chance to ride the V&M R6 in the British Supersport Championship.

Jim Moodie was still recovering from a big crash in pre-season testing in Spain.

It wasn't the BSB ride that Jefferies had been hanging out for but at least he had gainful employment for the season and could expect to make decent money from competing in the major road races. Few riders, if any, race for the money – after all, there are thousands of easier and safer ways to make a living. Yet while they race for the thrill – the challenge and the chance to prove themselves – racing careers are short and riders must earn as much as they can for their futures, as they can be forced to retire at any moment in the event of a serious crash.

Then things went from bad to worse as far as the 2001 season was concerned. Already denied a BSB ride, Jefferies received a second blow when it was announced that the North West 200 and TT meetings were under threat because of the foot and mouth outbreak on the UK mainland. Suddenly it looked like even his second line of defence, when it came to earning a wage, was about to crumble.

For many, the very idea of the TT being cancelled was unthinkable. After all, the only events which had caused its cancellation since the inaugural meeting in 1907 had been two world wars. While the Island itself was free from the foot and mouth outbreak which had seen tens of thousands of cattle being culled on the mainland, Manx authorities wanted to keep it that way and the potential damage which could be done by thousands of UK visitors tramping through Manx fields and spreading the disease was too much of a risk to take. When it was decided that there was no time to instigate a foolproof means of disinfecting every visitor, the writing looked to be on the wall for the TT.

To add to the problem was the fact that thousands of race fans had already booked time off work, as well as ferries, flights and accommodation, and had little choice but to travel to the Isle of Man or have no holiday at all that year. Many fans still turned up at the North West 200 when the racing was cancelled in May but that was primarily a weekend event, as opposed to a two-week commitment. TT organisers were hoping against hope that people would still throng to the Isle of Man to enjoy all the peripheral events that went alongside the racing, since the Manx economy relies so heavily on the fortnight which brings in upwards of £50 million a year.

The announcement, made in late April, that the TT would indeed be cancelled, met with a mixed reception. Chief amongst the most aggrieved – apart from Island hoteliers – were the race teams who had already invested huge sums of money in the event. One such team was V&M. Jack Valentine raged, "We've bought £80,000 worth of equipment just for the TT. We've spent £20,000 alone on updating the Formula 1 bikes and we've got two new Proddie bikes plus two 600s. Our total budget – with transport, ferries, hotels and food – must be around £125,000."

Valentine understood that the reasons for cancelling the TT were sound, but his argument was that the decision should have been taken much earlier so that teams could have avoided such costly preparation. "They should have called it off months ago when foot and mouth started," he said, "or they should have run the races instead of leading everybody along, thinking it was still on."

Jefferies, who stood to make upwards of £100,000 if he had enjoyed a typically successful TT, bemoaned the loss of what was effectively his annual wage. "I'm gutted about the North West and the TT being called off," he said. "I was planning to make my year's wages at the two races. Now I'm not getting any."

Another blow for Jefferies was that he'd miss the chance to add to his tally of TT wins. He'd already lost a year in 1997 due to injury and for any rider to miss two TTs was to seriously damage their chances of getting amongst the all-time greats in terms of absolute wins.

TT stalwart Ian Lougher remembers how frustrating it was to be slouching on the sofa at home when he should have been hammering down Bray Hill. "It was absolutely awful sitting around when the TT should have been on. Not only that, it was hard on the wages too because the TT was the biggest earner of the year for a lot of us. It was shite and I was really disappointed."

Jefferies spent most of what would have been TT week on the Isle of Man where he busied himself instructing on Duke track days at the Jurby airfield circuit. It wasn't until some weeks later that he realised how much he'd missed the races themselves. "Initially I didn't think it had affected me that much," he said, "but it was other team members in the British racing paddock that noticed I wasn't particularly happy and it affected my racing a little bit until I got my head back into gear properly."

But Jefferies did take at least one positive from the cancellation. Reflecting on the matter in 2002, he said, "I think in a way it proved a lot of the sceptics wrong. A lot of people said the TT could survive without the racing and I think last year really proved it couldn't."

The closest either Lougher or Jefferies got to racing on the Isle of Man that year was during a road test photo shoot for *Two Wheels Only* magazine. After testing the leading sports bikes of the year, the pair lined up against John McGuinness and racing journalist Gus Scott for an egg-and-spoon race in pit lane – clad in their full racing gear! Lougher had to retire when he dropped and smashed his egg and Scott lost control of his spoon, blaming a poor silverware choice. So after the pit stops, where each rider had to stop and change eggs, it was McGuinness who applied the pressure for the win, but Jefferies's steady hand and course knowledge saw him emerge triumphantly and the take the honours atop the genuine TT podium.

The cancellation of the centrepiece of Jefferies's year meant all he had to focus on in 2001 was the British Superstock Championship, and it was clear from the off that it was going to be a struggle. Just as he himself had enjoyed an advantage when the R1 was first launched in 1998, now the riders of Suzuki's new GSX-R1000 were reaping the rewards and the R1s were struggling to keep up.

From the opening round at Donington, it was clear that the Suzukis were going to be the bikes to beat as Australian Paul Young rode his to a 12-second victory and Jefferies could only manage fourth on his Yamaha. But he blamed his performance, at least in part, on his own lack of aggression in what was becoming an increasingly competitive class. "I was just too gentlemanly," he said afterwards. "I need more aggression in my overtaking moves. I didn't want to upset anybody but it looks like that's what it needs. The Suzukis are fast – it's going to be a tough year."

There was drama for Jefferies in the second round when he was hit by John Crockford on the approach to Maggots at Silverstone.

MCN reported that 'Crockford went down while Jefferies showed great skill to keep the bike upright while hanging on with one foot over the seat.'

Jefferies finished seventh after losing time and said, "Everything was going well when I suddenly got whacked in the leg. It was enough to take my breath away but I got going straight away and charged as hard as I could."

Even Young admitted the advantage his GSX-R1000 had after the top six slots on the grid were taken by Suzukis at the ultra-fast Snetterton circuit. "If David Jefferies gets his Yamaha on the podium I'll buy the guy a beer," he said. "He'll do well to get among the Suzukis."

In the race itself, Jefferies got punted off line by another rider and lost so much time he could only finish 12th, while Young went on to win yet again and Suzukis filled the top seven places.

It wasn't until the sixth round of the championship at Thruxton that someone other than Paul Young won a race, but once again it was a Suzuki pilot – this time John Crockford. Jefferies was finding more pace on the Yamaha and managed to take second spot, his best result of the year to date. After the race he said, "This is a track where horsepower isn't the biggest factor so it's good to see the R1 can still cut it against the Suzuki."

At the seventh round of the championship at Oulton Park, DJ finally took his first win of the year and headed-up a podium which, for the first time all season, didn't feature a single Suzuki. Things might have been very different if runaway championship leader Paul Young hadn't lost a footrest and been forced to retire while holding a five-second lead. But Jefferies had his problems too; he was riding with a heavily strapped left knee after dislocating the kneecap during a Supermoto race in Ireland two weeks previously.

The result reduced Young's 65-point lead over Jefferies to a more encouraging 40 points and, while his win was fortunate, Jefferies was happy to take points any way he could get them, saying, "If someone wants to give me that amount of points then I'm not going to argue."

Young rode superbly at Knockhill, storming through the field from 27th place to finish third after a woeful wet qualifying left him near the back of the grid. He even managed to pass Jefferies who could manage no better than fifth at a circuit that had usually favoured him.

With the North West 200 and TT having been cancelled, there remained just one major road race left in the British Isles in 2001 – the Ulster Grand Prix. And when the organisers announced it would go ahead in August, the V&M team made hasty arrangements to take part. "The mechanics will have their work cut out in the run up to the meeting," said Jack Valentine, "but we're all looking forward to going over to the Ulster GP. The atmosphere is unique and the Irish fans are so enthusiastic about their racing. I'm really pleased we've been able to reach an agreement to take David over, and I'm sure he won't disappoint them."

For David, as well as most other top UK road racers, it would be his first outing on the roads all year and he was clearly looking forward to the prospect. "I'm over the moon to be going back to the Ulster," he said. "I've enjoyed a lot of success on the V&M bikes on the Dundrod circuit with two wins last year and a win and a lap record in 1999. It would be nice to keep the record going in 2001."

Jefferies was entered in both Superbike races as well as the 600 event but, for the first time in his Ulster GP career, he failed to take a victory. Three second places was the best he could manage after some ferocious racing with the likes of Ian Lougher and Adrian Archibald. Lougher, who won the opening Superbike encounter, remembers just how close things were. "David and I were absolutely elbow-to-elbow at the Ulster Grand Prix in 2001 and I was determined to beat him. My Suzuki was finally a match for the V&M bike that had been dominant for the last few seasons. We were round the back of the circuit on the last lap and were elbow-to-elbow from Joey's Windmill right the way through all the fast corners to Wheelers. Then he levelled and got in front of me going into Tornagrough, but I passed him on the outside again. I knew I was faster through the Quarries and when DJ just got caught slightly with a backmarker I won the race.

"That's when I knew I could actually beat him in a square fight and I was mad keen to get to the TT the following year on the Suzuki.

"The Ulster had been a real short circuit-style race and while we were elbow-to-elbow throughout that last lap, it was all very fair and we just gave each other enough room to make it safe. In 1999, Joey Dunlop had had an epic race at the Ulster with David and Iain Duffus and thought they were both a bit wild. He said he'd never seen so many funny lines around Dundrod. I always found DJ to be fair and safe in his racing but during that race I remember thinking, 'Bloody hell, he's bigger than me and can push me wherever he wants to!'"

Sadly, the meeting ended under another dark cloud after Lougher's bike left the track and struck a flag marshal during the 600cc race. The marshal, Gerry Allaway, died from his injuries. Lougher escaped without injury but was clearly shaken up by the encounter. "The bike clipped a kerb and I lost control," he said. "I was flung down the road but the bike bounced into the air."

Ironically, the tragedy occurred at a new chicane that had been installed in a bid to improve safety. This latest death prompted new calls for road racing to be banned after a particularly tragic two years for the sport. In May 1999, one of Ireland's most popular riders, Donnie Robinson, had been killed at the North West 200. Three months later, Joey Dunlop's protégé, Owen McNally, was killed at the Ulster Grand Prix. Then in July of 2000, Dunlop himself lost his life in a far-flung road race in Estonia and the whole of Ireland grieved. One month after that, Gary Dynes and Andrew McClean lost their lives in a crash at the Monaghan road races in Ireland and now it seemed even the volunteer marshals weren't safe.

The string of tragedies led to some of Ireland's smaller road races being cancelled in 2001, notably the Carrowdore 100 meeting. A task force was set up to investigate ways of making the sport safer but some had simply had enough and high profile race organiser, Billy Nutt, decided to quit his position and step down from his organisational role in road racing. The future for the sport looked bleak and with the cancellation of the NW200 and TT delivering a further body blow to the sport, many wondered if the time had come to admit that road racing had had its day.

Jefferies returned to the relative safety of British championship racing and found himself being gifted another win at Cadwell Park after race leader John Crockford crashed out on the last lap. But Jefferies had to work hard to inherit the lead and pushed his way determinedly through the field after a poor start saw him languishing in fifth place. *MCN*'s race report backed up Jefferies's claim that the Suzuki GSX-R1000s had outclassed the Yamaha R1. It read: 'It was a race that perfectly summarised the season so far for the Yorkshire man – he had to ride the wheels off his Yamaha to keep up with the GSX-R1000s and hope one of their riders made a mistake.'

Jefferies had played his cards perfectly and used the only weapon left in his armoury to beat the superior Suzuki – he had piled so much pressure on to Crockford that he finally made a mistake and crashed out. "It's great to get a win, not just for me and Yamaha, but for everyone," Jefferies said. "It does get a bit boring when the same person wins all the time. I'm riding my bollocks off every time I go out just to keep up with the Suzukis."

Paul Young took a flag-to-flag victory at Brands Hatch to extend his championship lead to 54 points after Jefferies could only manage fifth place despite again 'riding the wheels off his V&M R1,' as *MCN* reported. He was clearly riding harder than ever but was simply being outpaced by superior machinery, and Jefferies must have begun thinking that he needed to be on a Suzuki in 2002.

Young should have wrapped up the title at Mallory Park but was taken out of the race by Gary Mason. Jefferies finished third but had resigned himself to the fact that he would not be able to hold on to the title he won in 2000.

A seventh place at Rockingham was enough to wrap up the title in Young's favour but DJ hadn't gone down without a fight and this time he quite literally rode the tyres off his bike just to net sixth place. After relinquishing his Superstock title to Young he said, "I had to ride so hard just to keep on terms with the Suzukis that by the end of the race the tyre was right down to the canvas and I couldn't get any drive."

Jefferies's seventh place in the final round at Donington Park was enough to secure second spot in the championship but it was clear the R1 had had its day, at least in its current guise. If he wanted to regain the Superstock title in 2002, he knew he needed to be on a Suzuki.

But his performances on the under-powered Yamaha had really impressed team boss Jack Valentine who says, "2001 was a good year for David on the short circuits because the GSX-R1000 Suzuki was really, really strong – they were absolute missiles out of the box. The R1 was way down on horsepower and I always remember going to the first meeting at Snetterton and David got his arse kicked. He got a bad start and then he was trying to make up for it on the brakes, but all these lads on the Suzukis were in his way and he just couldn't get through. So I think he finished about fifth and he was well pissed off.

"When we got to Silverstone I said, 'Look, get yourself sorted out because it ain't going to change. You can ride this bike – just get stuck in.' So he put it on pole at Silverstone, if I remember rightly, and from there on he was always a challenger. I think he had a win at Oulton Park and a win at Cadwell. They were tremendous rides and to motivate him, I said, 'Right David, we're in the GSX-R cup, but with you on a Yamaha. If you finish second, then that's like a win. Everybody in the game knows that you're totally underpowered.' And after that he really picked up his game and rode fantastic that year."

David had managed to collect some wins in 2001, most notably at Oliver's Mount back in September when he equalled the great Geoff Duke's record of five Gold Cup victories. He won every single heat and race he entered on his Superbike to stand joint top of the all-time winner's list at what was one of his most successful circuits.

The final road race outing of the year was once again the Macau Grand Prix but it was to be a tough meeting for Jefferies. Just five laps into the opening free practice session, his V&M engine blew up and he was forced to share his team-mate Jason Griffith's bike for the remainder of practice. Despite managing just four laps in qualifying, DJ was able to set a time good enough for third spot on the grid before Griffiths jumped back on the bike and suffered the same fate – his engine also blew up. Now both riders were without a bike for the race itself and, while Griffiths was forced to sit out the event, DJ took up his rival Ryan Farquhar's offer of a loan of his spare engine. It was a generous gesture that Jefferies gladly accepted, even though Farquhar had made it clear that it wouldn't be nearly as fast as the V&M motor.

Jefferies scored an impressive third using the spare motor and was delighted with the result after all that had happened. "Given the circumstances I'm over the moon with the result. Ryan told me the engine wasn't as quick as the one in his bike, let alone my regular one, but I really want to thank his sponsor, Winston McAdoo, for letting us use it. Mind you, the race was nearly over when one of the Americans, Vincent Haskovec, tried to punt me off at the first corner. He fell but I couldn't believe that they tried to blame me for it. Do they really think that I'd try to brake test someone at 170mph?"

With that result, although he didn't know it yet, David Jefferies's hugely successful career with the V&M Yamaha team was over. And while a switch to Suzuki would ensure further success for Jefferies, the move came as something of a shock to Jack Valentine.

Chapter 12

THE NEXT LEVEL

*"He was competitive everywhere he went but when it came to the roads DJ
just took it to the next level."*
John McGuinness

The TAS (Temple Auto Salvage) Suzuki team was formed in its
current guise in the year 2000 but team owner Hector Neil had
been involved in road racing since the 1970s when he worked with
legendary Irish rider Tom Herron.

In 2000, the team had opted to run just one rider – Ian Lougher.
He remembers those early days as being something of a re-learning
process for everyone involved. "The TAS team was a good team to
ride for. I started with them in 2000 when they came back with the
Yamaha R71 after years of not being involved in racing. The team was
very inexperienced to begin with so they employed me as a mechanic
too during the winter of 2000/2001, which is when I moved to
Northern Ireland. In 2000, we did just the three main road races –
the North West 200, the TT and the Ulster Grand Prix – but in 2001
we had four Suzukis and I was really looking forward to the TT that
year, but of course it never happened."

Hector Neill takes up the story. "When we switched to Suzuki in
2002 we decided to upgrade to two riders, so we started looking
round. There were two or three names mentioned and David
Jefferies's name came up. Philip (Hector's son and team manager)
rang up Tony Jefferies. He was interested so agreed to meet with us
to discuss things further at the Ulster Motorcycle Show. When we got
to the show, Suzuki kept asking us if we had decided our rider line-
up and we said 'No, we're still talking.' Suzuki was scheduled to
launch the team at ten o'clock and we were still arguing terms with
Tony. He was hitting us with a price and we said 'No, you're too
expensive'. At five-to-ten the Suzuki boys were looking over nervously
so I said 'Okay, give him what he wants.' I handed over a contract

and said 'Quick, sign it now' and nodded at the guys from Suzuki so that they could go ahead and announce the two-rider team as being Ian Lougher and David Jefferies. It was as close as that."

Jefferies had already signed a deal to race a Suzuki GSX-R1000 for the Tech 2 team in the British Superstock Championship but had looked certain to ride for V&M again in the major road races. His last-minute decision to sign for the TAS squad surprised Jack Valentine. "David leaving us has come as a shock," he said at the time. "But that's life and we've got to get on with it. We'll still be at the TT and we're intending to win it."

Looking back now, Valentine admits it was a frustrating and senseless loss of Yamaha's top roads rider. "Obviously by then David was like a superstar at the TT – he wanted a bit of money. So I told Yamaha that he wanted a retainer – I think we were talking £20,000. That was absolute peanuts for what he was doing, but they were like 'It's a bit much' and I said 'I don't think it is.'

"Then Suzuki came along and said £20,000 wasn't a problem – so, I mean, what do you do? We'd had a gentleman's agreement with David but there were no bad feelings or anything.

"I went back to Yamaha and told them that Suzuki had made him an offer but they were still humming and harring, so we had to let him go to Suzuki. Simple as that. The annoying thing was that after he'd gone with Suzuki, Yamaha found the budget and I had to scurry around then because I had to get two replacement riders, which turned out to be Jim Moodie and Iain Duffus. Okay, we got on the podium at the TT, but the thing was, we wanted David. They just screwed it up for themselves there, did Yamaha."

Jefferies himself had clearly struggled to make the right decision, as loyalty to his old team had to be balanced with finding the most competitive and financially rewarding package for 2002. "It was quite a difficult decision to make," he admitted. "I've been with V&M for a long time and had all my success in the Isle of Man, but things can't last forever so I got an offer and it was quite a nice one. There's no hard feelings at all between myself, Jack and V&M, we still get on well and it was just one of those things – it was just a decision I had to make so I'm quite looking forward to it. The Suzuki is the only bike that's passed me in a straight line while I've been riding the V&M Yamahas, so the bike's certainly quick enough."

Jefferies's 2002 plans were used as the opening entry on his newly set up website (www.davidjefferiesracing.com) which would, from that point on, keep his fans up to speed with all that was happening in DJ's world. The opening diary entry read:

Hi Everyone

2002 starts with new teams all round. The big surprise is that I have joined a new team for the road circuits and have moved from V&M. I know this is a shock to many but I felt the opportunity of being with the TAS team was too good to miss, given their association with the Suzuki Crescent BSB team and their experience on the pure road racing front. The Suzuki has been the all-powerful Superbike and the prospect of riding the 180bhp Superbike on the road circuits is going to be a real challenge.

TAS are based in Northern Ireland and have a wealth of experience, run by ex-racer Hector Neil and his son Philip. My team-mate will be Ian Lougher, a rider with years of road racing experience, and together we believe we will make the most formidable team going to the Isle of Man for the 2002 TT.

On the short circuits I'll be with the Tech 2 race team riding in the Performance Bikes Superstock Championship, again on a Suzuki GSX-R1000. The team are full of enthusiasm and, like me, want a championship win. They have assured me nothing will be spared to help me win the championship and I will be doing everything I can to make it happen.

So it's all new, lots to learn and very exciting. I feel just like a player who has changed premiership clubs and I really welcome the new challenge.

The new website will keep you posted on what's going on and the guys from Legend have done a great job. I hope you enjoy the site and hope to see you around during the 2002 race season.

David Jefferies

DJ's 2002 season kicked off at Mallory Park with the Race of the Year meeting where he rode his Superstock GSX-R1000 to second place behind Glen Richards who was riding a full BSB-spec Kawasaki ZX-7RR.

Jefferies also took second place in the opening round of the British Superstock Championship at Silverstone behind the similarly-mounted Chris Burns. He was then offered a stand-in Superbike ride at Brands Hatch in the second round of BSB, deputising for the injured John Crawford in the ETI Superbike squad. Again, with no testing on the bike – which in full Superbike trim was vastly different to Jefferies's Superstock Suzuki – it wasn't an ideal situation, but DJ's determination to impress in the class meant he never turned down any opportunity in BSB. After finishing 13th in the opening leg then improving to 11th in race two, Jefferies admitted he'd found the switch between bikes demanding. "Getting confidence was the hardest thing," he said. "Learning to let off the brakes and really commit that front end to the corner."

After another second in the Superstock class at Donington, Jefferies finally took his debut win on the big Suzuki at Oulton Park, his favourite UK circuit. The utter dominance of the GSX-R1000 in the Superstock class was highlighted by the fact that the bike filled the top 14 places in the race results.

Following his success at Oulton, Jefferies faced a hectic two weeks as he attempted to race at both the North West 200 and Silverstone over the same weekend. "I'm going to qualify at the NW200 on Thursday, fly back to qualify at Silverstone on Friday, fly back to race at the NW200 on Saturday, then fly back to race at Silverstone on Sunday," he said. It was a gruelling schedule by any standards but made worse by Jefferies having to change his riding style between that suited to a road race and the more aggressive, on-the-edge style required on short circuits, although he always insisted this was never a problem for him as it was for some other riders.

With such a tight schedule, flying to and from Silverstone and Northern Ireland, there was bound to be drama and sure enough, on the Friday before the NW200 race day, DJ almost failed to qualify at the Northants circuit. He explained, "We were in a light plane and flying out to Ireland took two hours and ten minutes. But coming back to Silverstone for practice, the wind was against us and we took over three hours. I just got there in time to get on the bike."

Not only did he get there in time, but DJ also racked up his second win of the year in the Superstock championship to move to the top of the points table and cap a memorable weekend. There had been success at the North West too, though perhaps not as much as Jefferies might have liked on his TAS Suzuki.

Following its cancellation in 2001, demand for the North West was huge in 2002 and more than 130,000 people came to watch the action around the 8.9 miles of public roads that made up the famous course. Sadly, they had to endure less than perfect weather conditions but Jefferies's experience helped in the opening Superbike race when a tyre gamble paid off and allowed him to take the win. In the damp conditions, most of the grid opted to run full wet tyres but DJ took a gamble on the road drying out slightly and chose to race with Pirelli Supersport tyres. When early pacesetters Jim Moodie and Iain Duffus – both riding for Jefferies's old V&M Yamaha team – were forced to pull in with shredded rear tyres, DJ was able to cruise to his debut roads win on the TAS Suzuki. As he crossed the finish line with a monster wheelie, no other rider was in sight and there would be a 17-second wait before second-placed Ryan Farquhar finally completed the race.

The rest of the meeting didn't quite go as planned – DJ lost out to Kiwi Bruce Anstey in the Production 1000 class and could only manage a fifth place in the 600cc race. Like Jack Valentine, his predecessor, TAS team owner Hector Neill partly blamed Jefferies's insistence on tinkering with his bikes for his lacklustre performances in the other races at the North West. Being mechanically minded and having spent so many years working on his own bikes, Jefferies found it hard to trust even professional mechanics to prepare his machinery and usually made further adjustments himself. "David used to like to set up his own bikes," says Neill. "We'd have the bike all ready to go and then, the next thing we know, David has gone and changed it without us knowing. The first race we did was the North West and DJ came second or third. I asked him what he had done to the bike and why he had changed it. He said, 'I didn't think that Philip and you would have the know-how to set it up.' I told him to trust us for the next race and he won it. He trusted us from that point on."

Jefferies considered another hectic fly-in, fly-out arrangement that would have allowed him to race at the Snetterton round of the Superstock championship and the Isle of Man TT. Ultimately, he decided against it as the timescale was so tight that it would only have allowed him to get to Snetterton on time if he didn't finish in the first three in the TT Production race. "There's not really a lot of point in racing if we're not trying to win," he said, "so it's just not an option anymore. If I have to go to the podium and garlanding ceremony at the TT, which is compulsory, I can't make the race at Snetterton. I realise I'll be handing 25 points to someone – probably Chris Burns who will take the championship lead – but while we have this clash of dates between the TT and British Superbikes, it's unavoidable."

DJ would once more be racing against a member of the family at the TT in 2002. To celebrate his fiftieth birthday, Nick Jefferies announced he would be coming out of retirement to ride in the TT once more. Nick proved he was still competitive round the Isle of Man with his best finishes being 11th in the Junior and 13th in the Senior in what would be his last TT – although he has still never officially retired. "I still think I can do it," he says now, "but the golf handicap's coming down so I may just concentrate on that!"

After a two-year absence, riders were keen to get to grips with the TT course again – perhaps too keen. Practice week saw a rash of crashes, though most riders attributed them to the patchy conditions rather than to over-enthusiasm and depleted course knowledge.

Jefferies himself admitted that he was a little concerned about how well he knew his way round the course after posting a poor 35-minute lap – in a pub! "Now that I've done four years, the thing with the Isle of Man is that I can sit and just do every corner in my head – but I made a fool of myself not so long ago. I went out with some friends of mine to a pub, had a few beers and then decided to talk my way round a lap, which was quite embarrassing. The disappointing thing was it took me 35 minutes!"

He needn't have worried. Jefferies picked up where he'd left off in

2000. In practice he set the fastest ever course lap on a Production machine from a standing start. His average speed of 121.48mph on a near-standard Suzuki GSX-R1000 was a portent of things to come. He was also given a good workout when the same bike ran out of fuel well short of the finish line and DJ had to push it back along the uphill incline of Glencrutchery Road. His team later admitted they had expected as much. "We didn't fill the tank right up so we sort of expected him to run out on the second lap," said mechanic Nigel Everett. "It'll do him good to push it for a bit – fitten him up."

As usual, the Formula 1 race kicked off TT proceedings and Jefferies was red hot favourite to win, even if he was on a new bike and with a new team. As the riders loitered on the Glencrutchery Road waiting for the five minute board, many went through their own private rituals in preparation for the dangers that lay ahead. Some had elaborate routines that involved lucky charms, traditional winks and handshakes, or even wearing the same pair of pants that they'd last won a race in. Anything to calm the nerves and reassure them. Not Jefferies. "I'm rarely nervous before a race," he said. "I'll just sit on the pit wall and have a crack with the lads. I'm certainly not superstitious. The only thing is my sister gives me a pit board at Creg-ny-Baa every year, but even that's more in her head than mine. I always put on my right glove before my left but that's about it, and I think that's more from habit than anything else. I'm not really superstitious but I wouldn't ride number 13 at the TT, that's for sure."

Hector Neill had already observed how calm his rider was before a race. "DJ never suffered from pre-race nerves. He'd just wander about until it was time to go and get his leathers on, then he'd jump on the bike and be away. There was no superstitious routine or anything like that. Sometimes he'd sit on the bike or sometimes he'd stand over at the wall at the side of the track."

Jack Valentine remembered that David "Always had that quiet confidence and very rarely got rattled. He just went out as if it was a Sunday morning ride. Obviously he had a screw loose, but he was good."

As he lined up for the 2002 Formula 1 race however, Jefferies was spotted walking over to the cemetery that, rather ominously, lies directly behind the scoreboard on the start/finish straight. When asked why by journalist Mac MacDiarmid, DJ replied, "Just to say 'Hi' to Lee Pullan." A former TT rider, Pullan had been killed at Spa in 1996 during a World Endurance race after a marshal had wandered onto the track during the race. He is buried in the cemetery adjacent to the TT start line.

For every rider that races, there are others close to him who need to have their own routine to get them through the anxious times when their riders are out on track – especially when it's a track as dangerous as the Isle of Man TT. Tony Jefferies was no exception. "I think smoking cigars helped me get through it," he once said. "But the main thing was that I wanted to be on my own. The most annoying thing that used to happen would be people who came up and said, 'Hello Tony, how are you? I remember watching you race at so-and-so.' And I'm just waiting, listening to the commentary – waiting to hear if David has got to Ramsey Hairpin or wherever. So I'd often just try and find a corner I could go and hide in and listen to the commentary. I was quite happy doing that. I didn't think about the dangers of it – more about the bike breaking down to be honest."

In the Formula 1 race, the bike almost did break down and it was only Jefferies's mechanical sympathy that prevented it from doing so. Jefferies had left the start line like a bullet from a gun and by the first timing point at Glen Helen – just nine miles into the 226-mile race – he had established a seven-second lead from his good friend John McGuinness. Jim Moodie, Ian Lougher and Adrian Archibald all chased hard but no one could live with Jefferies's pace. On the second circuit, he piled on the coals even more and became the first man to lap the course at over 126mph when he obliterated the lap record with an average speed of 126.68mph This was despite having to slow down to take on fuel at the end of the lap. From then on, it appeared the race was over as DJ built up a seemingly unassailable lead of one minute and eighteen seconds.

Then, as he rounded Ramsey Hairpin on the last of six laps with just 12 miles to go, Jefferies thought his race was over. "I nearly lost control of all bodily functions when I went for the next gear up only to hear the limiter cut in and nothing happen," he explained after the race. "I was really worried before I got third gear and knew it was a gear selector fault that would only get worse if I tried to bang another gear in. I just left it alone and for the rest of the lap had to make do with only third gear."

Hector Neill remembers the problem well. "There was a wee spring held in by a wee screw in the selector shaft and in our engines every one had a fault and came loose. We had to glue them all in but that particular engine had been put in the bike before we knew about the problem.

"David had experienced the problem before so he knew exactly what it was and knew not to try and change gear. If he'd tried to change it he could have ended up with no gears at all, so he just had to coax it home over the mountain. That would have been his only flying lap in that race and I still wonder what speed he might have done."

With only one gear at his disposal for the final 12 miles of the race, Jefferies had some hairy moments trying to compensate. "I was shitting myself," he admitted a few weeks later. "You've got no engine braking to help you stop as you're rushing into corners and I kept arsing them up. I also had to do battle with a back marker. That wasn't scary, it was just bloody annoying. I was like 'Oh my god I'm not going to win!' All this work and five-and-a-half laps and it's going to break on the last lap. When I pulled in to the pits I was like 'Have I won? Have I won?' and they said 'Of course you have' and I was like 'Thank God.' I didn't shit myself because I was scared – it was because I didn't bloody well think I'd won the race!"

Jefferies's win was the first for Suzuki in the Formula 1 TT since Graeme Crosby took the victory way back in 1981, 21 years previously. An incredible achievement in itself, but DJ was still disappointed that his bike had got stuck in third gear because he felt he could have gone even quicker on the last lap than the incredible 126.68mph he achieved on his second lap. He said, "The second lap didn't even feel fast to me because I had to come in for fuel, so it wasn't a full flying lap. I knew nothing about getting the fastest lap until I got back. I'm a little disappointed the bike went wrong because the last lap would have been much quicker than lap two. I reckon it might have been possible for a 17min 45sec lap (127.5mph) on the last one."

Suzuki had very little official presence on the Isle of Man in 2002 and was even reluctant to grant the TAS team official status before the event. But Jefferies's dominant win changed all that as Hector Neill recalls. "It was a big boost for us, and Suzuki, to win that race. When we were coming over to the TT, Nick Barnes from Suzuki rang and asked what was painted on the side of our trucks. When I said 'Suzuki GB' he asked me to take the 'GB' off the truck because we had new bikes and it was a new project, and if we didn't do well it would be really bad publicity. He could lose his job over it.

"I told him the trucks were all painted and they were staying painted; that he'd just have to trust us. I told him we'd had good tests with the bikes and we had two good riders.

"Well, DJ went out and won the F1 race on the Saturday and Ian won the 600 Production race on the Monday. The next thing we knew, Nick was on a flight to the Isle of Man and running up pit lane saying he couldn't believe what we'd achieved. We won four races that week for Suzuki. They were happy enough to have Suzuki GB on the trucks then. The Japanese were over the moon too. We sent them the team award – a nice piece of engraved Manx slate – and they were very appreciative of that."

Jefferies's dominance in the opening race of the week didn't bode well for his competitors and they must have realised they were racing for second place when he revealed that he was only going to get faster as the week progressed. After his F1 win he said, "Every lap I do around here allows me to get more comfortable – more confident to push harder. There are places I am able to go flat out now without even lifting off and to have even thought about doing that two years ago was a dream."

Two days after scoring his seventh TT win, DJ racked up his eighth in the Production 1000 race. On a Suzuki GSX-R1000 little changed from the street-legal model that many fans rode to the TT, DJ managed to lap at an incredible 124.31mph. That was just 2.3mph slower than on his highly-tuned Formula 1 bike, and the fact that he averaged such a speed on road legal tyres instead of special racing slicks just highlighted his incredible talent around the TT course. At such a pace, DJ was able to pull out a 13-second lead over his team-mate Ian Lougher before easing off on the last of the four laps to cruise home to win. Jefferies had clearly enjoyed the softer, more forgiving Production bike. "That race was a lot more fun than the Formula 1 because the Production bike is much nicer to ride. I was able to take some liberties with it because you can push it much harder."

No one can ride round four laps of the TT course at racing speeds and not have at least one close shave, and DJ was no exception as he revealed after the race. "Unfortunately, due to the size of the field, we were catching backmarkers really quickly. At Rhen Cullen, on the last lap, I went a little bit tighter than a backmarker and we came over the jump together, but then he decided to move to the left. I was fully committed so I had to breathe in a bit and scoop through the gap. I was already on the power so there was nothing I could do. It was a bit tight but it was 'racing tight' which usually means there's a good two inches either side!"

For once, the tables were turned as far as Jefferies's size and build were concerned. So accustomed to being told he was too big to be successful on a Superbike in BSB, Ian Lougher now admitted Jefferies's size actually *helped* him to win the race. "I tried my best to catch Jefferies," he said, "but his big arms help him keep the bike more stable over the bumpy bits. I'm only a little bloke."

A broken valve halted Jefferies's attempt to win the Junior 600 race but, as he said, "At least I managed to make it to Sulby where there's a pub and I was able to have a pint and watch the rest of the race."

It wouldn't be the last time DJ would destroy one of the smaller 600cc machines and, although it may not have been his fault on this occasion, Hector Neill says he had a habit of breaking the little bikes. "He was a big guy – he was no good on a 600. Every time I gave him a 600 he broke it. The engine would just come back in bits. Bang! He brought me back loads of engines in a million bits. He was a big rider for a big bike."

There was further misfortune in the Production 600 race when Jefferies ran short of fuel on the last lap and had to ease off to make sure he got the bike home in an unaccustomed seventh place.

But there was still one race left and it was the one everybody wanted to win – the Senior TT. This time the TAS Suzukis ran perfectly and the team scored a 1–2 with Jefferies leading Lougher home. The Welshman remembers, "David dominated every race in 2002 at the TT. I got closest to him in the Senior. We were separated by just three seconds after the first lap, then I overshot the stop box during the first pit stop and was penalised five seconds, though I didn't know it at the time. I did actually stop, but half a bike's length too late, and the next pit board I got said I was down on Jefferies by eight seconds. I couldn't understand it. The bike felt great, there had only been three seconds between us and I didn't feel like I had made any mistakes, so it was a mystery to me and that did my head in for the rest of the race. It was very disappointing."

Third-placed finisher John McGuinness remembers just how hard he tried to beat Jefferies in that race. "I tried so, so hard on that FireBlade and I *so* wanted to beat David – so badly it was painful! I remember getting out onto the Cronk-y-Voddy straight and could just see David at the end of it. I thought 'I'm catching him' but he just seemed to get himself settled in, gave himself a little bit of a shake and *boooof* – he was gone. Smashed the lap record and he was away.

"How he did it I don't know. He seemed to be able to control that pressure or whatever and was just able to switch it on – you had to admire him so much for that – he was the best round there, that's for sure."

Even now, as the TT's biggest star and fastest man, McGuinness seems to regard Jefferies's achievements on the Isle of Man with a mixture of awe and disbelief. "He was competitive everywhere he went but when it came to the roads DJ just took it to the next level. He was scary. He was lapping at 120mph-plus in his third year and beating everybody. On one side of the coin it was scary, but he obviously knew what he was doing. You can't just turn up and go that fast if you don't know what you're doing."

Not only did Jefferies win the Senior TT, he also broke more records in that one race than many top riders would in their entire careers. His Senior victory took his overall TT win tally to nine and also saw him become the only man in history to win three TTs in a week, on three occasions, and in three consecutive years. On his second circuit he set a new absolute lap record at 127.29mph, meaning he was the first man to lap the TT course at 125mph, 126mph and 127mph. He also set a new race record of 124.74mph. On top of that, earlier in the week he had set new Formula 1 lap and race records and new Production 1000 lap and race records. His new outright lap record also counted as a new Senior lap record. He became the first rider to win the F1 TT on a Suzuki since Graeme Crosby in 1981 and the first to win the Senior on a Suzuki since Rob McElnea in 1983. In short, Jefferies broke just about every record it was possible to break during the week. The TT had never seen such utter dominance by one man.

Jefferies had mixed feelings about setting the first ever 127mph lap of the TT course. While he was proud to have done so, it was winning races that meant more to him – the lap record was simply a by-product of that. But that didn't stop the press asking him how much higher he could push the absolute lap record. "I don't know what the limit is because when I did 125mph everyone said, 'That's the limit – you can't go any quicker.' But then I did 126mph, and now I've done 127mph. The limit is how comfortable you feel on the day. I mean, I don't ride beyond my limit on the Isle of Man. I try and ride well within my limits and don't take any unnecessary risks. Any sort of risks I do take have been thought about and planned, therefore it's not a risk – it's a planned move. So I don't know, it just depends how you feel on the day, weather conditions... This year they've resurfaced bits of the track that were very bumpy before, so that could give you a second. A couple of those and suddenly you could be going that bit quicker. I'm not going to break lap records; I'm going to win races."

Jefferies seemed to have an uncanny knack of doing both without too much effort. Waiting to present him with the Senior TT trophy that year was the most successful motorcycle racer of all time, Giacomo Agostini. The Italian had enjoyed a phenomenal career in the 1960s and 1970s, taking a total of 15 world titles. It was a career, however, that was rudely interrupted by Tony Jefferies who won the 1971 Junior after Ago had taken straight wins in 1968, '69 and '70, and again in 1972.

After Agostini presented David with the trophy, he walked over to where Tony was sitting and started chatting with his old rival. Tony explains – "Ago came over to me and started talking about David. He said 'He's a big man for a TT racer but he go very fast, no?'

"I said 'Yes, that's my son, David.' Ago looked amazed. It had never clicked!"

David himself said, "It was quite funny really because my mum knows Agostini, and she saw him outside the paddock earlier in the week. She asked 'Can I have a picture with you and my son?' And Ago sort of said 'Yes, okay', so we stood there and had our picture taken, and he didn't know who the hell I was. So then my mum, dad and Ago all sat on the start line for the Senior race and after he'd given me the trophy Ago said to my dad, 'Tony, that man, he is very quick but he is very big, no? And then my dad said to him 'That's my son'. It was a really special moment – special for me and for my dad."

Agostini had been a hero to Tony Jefferies before he had started his own racing career so it was with great pride that he watched his son receive not only the winner's trophy but also high praise from the man himself. "To see race speeds this high is wonderful," Agostini said of Jefferies's new records, "and shows what respect should be shown for TT winners. Jefferies is a remarkable rider and will be one of the greatest."

From a man whose record of 15 World Championships is never likely to be beaten, praise doesn't come much higher. Looking back on that victorious TT now, TAS boss Hector Neill ranks Jefferies alongside the likes of Agostini when it came to riding the TT course. "I've worked with many of the greats in road racing and I rank David as one of the best," he says. "He was a super Isle of Man rider – simply brilliant round the TT course. He could just ride a motorbike superbly – he knew the place so well. There are so many fast, bumpy stretches but David just wrestled the bike through them. He could put the bike anywhere on the road that he wanted. That's a big advantage round the Isle of Man."

David Jefferies had indeed made the TT his own. He reflected on his incredible 2002 success through his website diary pages. "I have to say this has to be the highlight of my racing career. I just get such a buzz out of riding round the TT circuit. I love the big bikes and I think that is where I have the advantage. I can move the bike around at really high speeds when all the forces are working against making the bike turn.

"On each lap I usually find a way to improve. It's a slow process and a matter of building confidence. This was only my fifth year at the TT and on the big bike I managed to get Bray Hill absolutely flat-out in the Senior race by the end of the week. I have always had to roll it just a little bit before, but actually holding it against the stop all the way over the top of the hill and through the dip at the bottom creates an incredible speed difference and you really feel it at the bottom. The G-forces on the bike must be terrific. I would love to have an accurate speed gun on me there because I reckon I must be doing at least 175mph, possibly 180mph.

"I wanted to win three this year and I knew the best chances were the Formula 1, Production 1000, and Senior. I was having a bit of a struggle with the 600 as I just didn't seem to get the balance right with the power and the gearing. There's so little margin for error as I'm a bit big for a 600. The Suzuki was quite different to the Yamaha I had previously ridden. The power characteristics made me have to really work at it to make sure it didn't drop off the power band. Regrettably, during the race it touched a valve and that was that, so I never really knew what I could do on that bike.

"The 600 production Suzuki was a real toy to play with. It felt that nearly all the corners were flat out – I mean the fast ones. It was really close racing and my anxiety to get fuel in to save time nearly cost me a finish. The fuel light came on just after the Quarry Bends so I knew I was in trouble. I dropped the revs and even freewheeled from Signpost to Governor's, so I would just have enough to get out of the dip at Governor's and not have to push. It just made it.

"The guys from the TAS team were a really good bunch. Nothing was too much trouble for them and Hector Neill and his son Philip are so enthusiastic you just get swept along with the 'crack', as they say. It was a great result for them, especially as my team-mate Ian Lougher did so well, giving the TAS team a total of four wins in the week.

"Highlight of the week? Being presented with the Formula 1 trophy by the legendary Geoff Duke and the Senior Trophy by Giacomo Agostini.

"It was one hell of a week and I was absolutely knackered when I got home after two weeks of continual riding, presentations, team talks and a fair bit of celebrating. My whole family were there supporting and helping me and my sister Loubie was signalling for me with all her mates at the Creg.

"The response from all the fans around the circuit was fantastic. The signals, the cheering – which you can actually hear at some of the popular spectator spots – and the programme-waving gives so much encouragement that it really eggs you on, which just helps the TT to be such a special event. And the star of the week? Well what else – the Suzuki GSX-R1000."

As part of a bonus scheme, Jefferies received a GSX-R1000 Suzuki for every race he won at the TT that year, meaning he had three of the bikes at his disposal once he got home. Showing his generous nature, he gave one of them to Ian Hutchinson to race. 'Hutchy' had formerly worked at the Jefferies shop as a mechanic but didn't see much of David at that time. It was only when he started racing that the two became good friends. Said Ian: "He never actually helped me initially when I started club racing, but then when I came to the British championship paddock he helped with the Superstock a bit and he actually got me a bike in 2002. David bought a road bike for me – well, he didn't actually buy it. When he rode for TAS Suzuki that year, he won three TTs and he got a GSX-R1000 for each win, so he gave one to me to race and two of my friends bought the other two."

Buoyed by his TT success, Jefferies proved he could easily make the switch from roads to circuit racing at Brands Hatch on 16 June. Just days after his TT triumphs, he won the Superstock race at Brands by five seconds from similarly-mounted Chris Burns and John Crockford. He said, "Winning here was vital. I've a load of points to make up after my crash here earlier in the year and missing the last round at Snetterton due to the TT. I wanted to prove that if your head is in racing mode you can win on the roads or short circuits. But now the TT is over, my mind is solely on winning this title."

It has long been a point of contention whether or not a rider needs time to readjust to short circuit scratching after spending two weeks at the TT. The Island requires a rider to race at sustained high speeds and to settle into a smooth rhythm; hugely aggressive braking, vicious twists of the throttle and the scraping of footpegs round corners simply doesn't pay off on real roads.

The same cannot be said of purpose-built short circuits where aggression and ten-tenths riding is everything. Because of the amount of run-off and the proliferation of safety fences at most short circuits, riders can afford to crash and can therefore afford to ride at 100% on every corner of every lap. They get on the throttle earlier on the exit to corners and brake later and harder than they possibly could do on the bumpy real world roads circuit. Some riders take time to make this transition, which explains why some teams chasing a short circuit championship are reluctant to expose their riders to real road races. Jefferies always claimed that making that transition was never a problem and his win at Brands Hatch seemed to back up this point of view.

Another win at the following round at Rockingham hammered home the point that Jefferies was equally competent on short circuits as he was on the roads. "A lot of people say you can't do both, but I've just proved you can," he said. "I won before I went to the TT – I did the North West, the TT, came back and won at Brands and then won here. I've proved you can do both."

Jefferies did, however, admit that there was a short period of readjustment needed. "I noticed at Brands that I wasn't quite braking as hard into corners and things, but I was still fastest in the times. It does take a little practice."

As another reward from Suzuki for his incredible domination of the TT, DJ was given a berth in the Rizla Suzuki BSB team at Rockingham alongside his former team-mate from 1995, John Reynolds. The ride became available when Karl Harris broke his wrist at Oulton Park. Jefferies relished the chance. "People involved in the team keep telling me there's no pressure – just go out and enjoy myself," he said before the race. "But I'm well aware that after my TT success everyone wants to see what I can do on a short circuit. People look at my TT success and expect me to be in the top three here. Suddenly it's like – if I do shit, I'm a wanker!"

Jefferies didn't 'do shit.' On a bike he'd never even sat on before

ABOVE: *Flying over the Mountain at Cadwell Park in one of his rare opportunities on a factory bike in BSB. DJ rode the Virgin Yamaha at selected rounds in 2000.* (Double Red)

RIGHT: *Happy days. The Page3.com team after winning the 2000 British Superstocks title, from left: Claire Ritchie, DJ, Tony Jefferies, Pauline Jefferies, Susan Lloyd and Tim Ford.* (Tony Jefferies Archive)

ABOVE: *DJ discusses the finer points of the TT course with his uncle Nick in 2002.* (Nick Jefferies Archive)

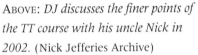

LEFT: *Tony and DJ shared a sense of humour.* (Double Red)

RIGHT ABOVE: *The TT is like no other racing circuit in the world, as this shot of David during practice in 2002 shows.* (Dave Collister)

RIGHT BELOW: *Anything you can do. Jefferies performs synchronised wheelies with his pal John McGuinness during TT practice in 2002.* (Dave Collister)

ABOVE: *No fear. Jefferies blasts past the walls at Handley's Corner at over 120mph. TT, 2002.* (Pacemaker)

BELOW: *'You went how fast?' Fifteen-times world champion Giacomo Agostini quizzes DJ at the 2002 TT.* (Pacemaker)

RIGHT: *Only DJ could hoist the massive Senior TT trophy aloft with such little effort. TT, 2002 – his ninth and last TT win.* (Pacemaker)

LEFT: *Under the Bridge. No room for error as Jefferies chases Ryan Farquhar and Adrian Archibald under the railway bridge at the 2003 North West 200. Bruce Anstey brings up the rear.* (Pacemaker)

RIGHT: *The final lap. DJ hammers through Union Mills just moments before his fatal accident at the 2003 TT.* (Dave Collister)

BELOW: *David's mum Pauline and sister Louise prepare to lead the David Jefferies memorial lap at the 2004 TT.* (Pacemaker)

ABOVE: *Respect. Some of the 5,000 bikers who turned out to commemorate their hero.* (Pacemaker)

BELOW: *Respect. Two fans visit the site where their hero lost his life in 2003.* (Pacemaker)

Rockingham, he took on a field of top riders who had been riding and refining their bikes all season long and finished in eighth and ninth places. As proof of how seriously DJ took the chance to ride a full factory BSB bike, he completed an incredible 188 laps of the Rockingham circuit over the weekend (including time on his Tech 2 Superstock machine).

Rizla Suzuki team boss Paul Denning was impressed. "It's a real challenge to mix with the top guys in Superbike when you haven't been on the bikes all year, like the other riders," he said. "Slicks do make a difference and the bike is very different from a Superstock. I think Dave did really well and we will have him back again if we have the opportunity."

DJ had clearly enjoyed the experience too, but was fully aware of the extra responsibility a stand-in rider has – not to crash a bike that isn't theirs. "There is no doubt it's a very competitive bike, but it's not easy to ride. I would like another couple of races to make a serious impression. I can run with the top guys, but I didn't want to bring Paul a pile of scrap back after throwing it down the road. I hope I get another chance to ride for the team. Crescent is one hell of a professional outfit."

Jefferies was convinced he had the pace to run in BSB, given enough time on the right bike. "With the same six months of track time these guys have on their bikes I could run with them," he said before joking, "plus if someone gave me the job the motivation would be there to eat fewer pies!"

He may have joked about it, but Jefferies's size seemed to be the only thing holding him back from achieving his dream of securing a top BSB ride. His physique was clearly something which ran in the family. "I'm just short of six foot if I could stand up," says Tony Jefferies, "and my dad was 6ft 1in. Pauline was 5ft 10in as well, so David came from quite a tall family."

Certainly most rivals and team bosses considered Jefferies had the talent to make it in BSB or WSB if he had just been that little bit smaller. Former Grand Prix star and triple BSB champion Niall Mackenzie definitely thought he was fast enough. "He was worthy of a BSB ride, definitely. He was a young rider with a massive amount of talent and everybody knew that. He was always on the top teams' shortlist. I don't know why he never got a ride.

"Maybe if the 1000cc four-cylinder bikes had been allowed to race in BSB before 2002 DJ would have got a ride. The 750s didn't quite have the same power-to-weight ratio to compensate for his size."

Hector Neill had planned to run a TAS Suzuki team in BSB in 2003 and would have had no hesitation in signing Jefferies as a rider, but his planned move into the class didn't happen until some years later. While acknowledging David's size disadvantage, he insists it wouldn't have put him off giving him a BSB ride. "We were almost ready to make a move up to BSB with David in 2003" he explains. "That was definitely on the cards, but we held back for various reasons.

"I loved pure road racing and wasn't so much into BSB, whereas my son Philip likes the TT and the North West but he's not really into road racing – he always wanted to go to BSB. So we went along those lines by setting up a team for the British Supersport championship before moving into BSB proper. But we probably would have ended up moving to BSB a lot sooner with David had he lived. I would definitely have given him a chance despite his size.

"I think DJ was probably passed up by other teams because of his size – they all want small, light riders to get the most speed and acceleration out of the bike. The way they see it is there's no point spending thousands on shaving fractions of weight off a bike then putting a big heavy rider on it."

John McGuinness is another who believes his friend never got a fair chance in BSB and he noticed how the frustration of not getting a top flight ride began to eat away at Jefferies in later years. "I don't think anyone gave him a chance – the chance that he deserved. It seemed to bother him. Towards the end he got a bit…I don't know. I saw an interview with him at Knockhill and it wasn't Dave, you know? It wasn't what Dave was all about. He was like 'I've got a white bike [unsponsored] now and I'm going to do it myself. Nobody gives me a chance.' He just didn't seem himself – but, you know, he jumped on Superstocks and hammered everyone. As far as natural ability goes, he was the most natural rider in the country. There's no question, I think."

Jefferies's former V&M team boss, Jack Valentine, now runs Suzuki's BSB team. He believes that if the current capacity limit of 1000cc had been introduced earlier than 2002, DJ would have been on every team's shopping list. "He was a big lad, David, and that's why he never got a fair chance. He wasn't fat – he was just big. And like myself, when I was drag racing, I couldn't get any lighter than 12.75 stone. It was impossible. I'd have been ill. Same with David – he could get down to around the 13-stone mark but he couldn't go any further."

"David loved riding on the roads but he was a top man on the short circuits as well. He could just ride a motorcycle – he was a natural. I mean, these bikes we've got now would have been perfect for him. The 750s I think he was maybe a little bit too big for, but when they went to 1000cc it would have been perfect for him. We tried everything to get a package for him to do the roads and Superbikes, but it just never came off."

Jefferies's rival and 2002 TAS team-mate Ian Lougher was amongst the few who had doubts. "I think David was always a bit big to cut it in the top level on short circuits," he says. "David actually did a year in WSB without much success, but he could probably have cut it in BSB, though it depends what you mean by 'cut it'. Could he have been BSB champion? I don't know. That's one of the interesting 'What ifs?' of racing that we'll never know the answer to."

Jefferies was clearly wearied of the size issue, saying in a 2003 interview "Everybody says I'm too big. I've proved that theory wrong so many times that I'm bored of doing that now."

He also suspected that his size wasn't the only factor that prevented him from securing a top flight ride – financial backing was another stumbling block. "I think, unfortunately, that's the way racing's going at the minute. I didn't have a personal sponsor this year and there are quite a few guys in the Superbikes who tend to be there because they've basically bought the ride. They've got £100,000 with them and that opens doors. So I'm still gonna be here on my Superstock bike and just keep riding round and proving what I can do.

"I'm the official reserve rider for the Crescent Suzuki team, but the unfortunate side of that is you ride only when someone else is injured, and you'd never wish that upon anybody. I wanna try and win the Superstocks again and hopefully people might notice what I can do and I'll get a Superbike ride."

When asked what his ultimate ambition in racing was, Jefferies replied, "To be British Champion on a Superbike and then move on to World Championship competition. I want to show people who say 'He's too big – he's too this, he's too that' what I can do with a competitive team who want to work with me. I'm not just a road racer, and my size doesn't matter. I've proved what I can do on the circuits, but I just want the chance to prove what I can do properly."

Jefferies's debut on the Rizla Superbike impressed team boss Paul Denning enough to convince him to give David another chance on the bike at Knockhill. Karl Harris was still recovering from his broken wrist. Denning said, "Considering that DJ has not been on short circuit slicks all year, and it was his first time on a Superbike this year, he rode very well, improving his times all weekend. In fact his fastest times were in the last few laps of the second race on Sunday. He added valuable points for the team and deserves the opportunity to have the chance of back-to-back meetings."

After a disastrous qualifying in damp conditions left him languishing in 24th place on the grid, Jefferies rode superbly in race one, carving his way through the field to seventh place. It was his best result yet on the Suzuki and proof that the more time he had on the bike, the higher up the order he finished. Sadly, any hopes of doing even better in race two were ruined when the GSX-R's engine blew up and forced him out of the race. It was a disappointing end to Jefferies's BSB career. Although no one could possibly have known it at the time, the Knockhill round was to be the last chance David Jefferies would ever get to prove himself in the British Superbike Championship.

Racing is full of 'what ifs?' But speculation as to what might have been is largely futile. It seems that most people in the paddock felt that David Jefferies deserved a full-time ride in a proper factory BSB team but, for whatever reason, it never happened and after Knockhill in 2002, he would never again get the chance to prove he was worthy of the ride which had so long eluded him.

* * *

Even with the huge amount of laps he had been completing by riding in both BSB and the Superstock championship over the last two rounds, Jefferies still couldn't get enough of bikes. As well as instructing on Supermoto track days organised by his father, he was also covering thousands of miles on the roads on an assortment of machinery, though usually a BMW of some type from the family showroom.

At the beginning of August, David joined a group of motorcycle dealers for a ride-out to the old Nürburgring circuit in Germany. The 14-mile road course is no longer used for racing but it is open to anyone who wants to ride or drive it and owners of everything from Ferraris to Suzuki Hayabusas can be found paying their cash and heading out to lap the track as fast as they dare. Needless to say, few have lapped it faster than the quickest man in TT history – even when he was on a touring BMW.

David remembered getting some strange looks from the owners of super-fast sports bikes as he turned up on a tourer for the trip to Germany. "There was a range of bikes, the majority being Supersports machines, like the GSX-R Suzuki and Yamaha R1. There were also a few Ducatis, an MV Agusta F4, and one BMW K1200RS. That was me.

"Turning up on a BMW turned a few heads on arrival but after a ride on the back roads to Aachen it had turned a few more heads. I managed to give some serious pain to the bike, much to the surprise of the R1 men, and then just unclipped my panniers and walked into the hotel whilst they had bungee straps flying off in every direction.

"Next day it was off to the Nürburgring, once again using the back roads. They do have some great biking roads over there, and again the BMW led the way. When we got to the 'Ring' I couldn't wait to get on the circuit. I had heard so much about it. I felt a bit of a prat in full Rizla Suzuki team leathers on a road bike, but I don't have any road leathers. It wasn't long before an instructor realised who I was

– the Germans are quite fond of the TT – and the next thing I knew I was getting a demo lap in his BMW M3.

"I had really set the sparks flying with the BMW, literally, and was a bit concerned about what my sister would say when I got back to the dealership with everything scraped to death. I did push it a bit hard for a tourer, much to the amusement of the crowd who seem to take up residence at the Nürburgring on Sundays. The instructor asked me to go out with some of the quick boys on his R1, which was very nice of him, and was so impressed with my lap that he had a camcorder fitted and asked me to do another quick one."

After finishing second in the Superstock race at Knockhill and taking the championship lead from main rival Chris Burns, DJ extended the lead further at Thruxton, though he was disappointed at only taking second place again. "It was a frustrating day at Thruxton," he said. "We had a plan to really go for a break on the first lap, which is just what I did, and by lap eight I had built up a four second lead. Then out came the safety car and I lost all the benefit of the early hard work.

"After the safety car went in we were all in a line, bunched up together, so it was a six lap dogfight between me, John Crockford, Kieran Murphy and Chris Burns. I managed to get the lap record but in the end Crockford out-dragged me to the line and won by 0.12 seconds. Chris Burns was 4th so I had a seven point advantage on him and although I was disappointed that I didn't win, I have extended my championship lead to 30 points."

With a growing air of inevitability, there was more tragedy in store at the Ulster Grand Prix in 2002. This time top Irish road racer Gary Jess was killed in the opening Superbike race after crashing and being struck by another rider. To compound the tragedy, Jess's wife was in attendance at the event and was six months pregnant with his child. In any other sport, a mistake costs a competitor a point, or prize money, or perhaps a sprained ankle. In motorcycle road racing it can cost the lives of competitors and completely shatter those of others around them.

David Jefferies found out at first hand just how fine the line between success and tragedy is in his chosen sport. After winning the Production

1000 race, he crashed at over 150mph on one of the most lethal tracks in racing. That he survived and Jess didn't only served to highlight the role of luck in such events. To further prove the random nature of injury and death, Jefferies suffered nothing more than a damaged thumb and general bumps and bruises, although he was in some pain the following day. "I feel as though someone has put me in a sack and hit me a hundred times with a big stick," he said.

The crash obviously ruled Jefferies out of the day's remaining races, meaning he came away with just one win in the Production 1000 event in what was to be his last Ulster Grand Prix.

It has often been remarked that TT riders must have no fear; that anyone capable of hammering between two brick walls at 190mph must be completely fearless. They would be wrong. David Jefferies was afraid of two things – rats and needles. But to have any chance of winning the British Superstock title, DJ had to overcome his fear of needles (if not rats) at Cadwell Park.

Following his crash at the Ulster, he needed two pain-killing injections in his thumb where he'd ripped the ligaments. "I really hate needles, but it was worth having the jabs," he said after the race. "My thumb is really swollen but at least I finished on the podium."

Jefferies was gifted third place after Ross McCulloch crashed out on lap six, while his main championship rival, Chris Burns, won the race by over 12 seconds from his Suzuki team-mate John Crockford. The win moved him to within 21 points of Jefferies at the top of the points table.

A victory for Jefferies at Oulton Park – his fifth in the Superstock series in 2002 – increased his championship lead over Burns to 30 points with only two rounds to go. But in bike racing, nothing can be taken for granted and Jefferies's title challenge was seriously impaired at Mallory Park when he suffered a huge high-side and dislocated a toe.

"It was just one of those days," Jefferies said. "If I knew Crockford was going to beat Burns I could have stayed happily in third place and won the championship. But I didn't know that at the time. I like winning and I knew I could get both Burns and Crockford at the hairpin. I had lined them up a couple of times and was ready to make a move down the inside. I wanted all the drive I could get and overdid it. Next I had a giant high-side which spat me 30 feet in the air. I came down with a mighty battering but luckily only managed to dislocate a toe."

With Burns finishing second, the championship lead was reduced to just ten points, setting up a final showdown at Donington Park in the final round.

Sadly for fans eager to witness a dog fight for the title, Chris Burns went out of the race early on with a lack of grip and Jefferies rode to a steady third place behind John Crockford and Steve Brogan to secure his fourth British championship. "At last I can sit back for just a moment with the Superstock Championship in the bag," Jefferies later said when reflecting on his season. "It was never in doubt in my mind but it got a bit close. I knew I would be at a disadvantage with missing a round at Snetterton because of the TT, but to have a stupid fall-off at Brands meant that I had given two rounds away. Then to go and crash at Mallory was even more stupid as I could have won the championship the way the results worked out that day.

"So at Donington it was third I required to guarantee the championship and that's just what I did. I could have gone faster if I had to do, but I just made sure I stuck neatly in third place and knew I would win. I had set a cracking pole lap of 1min 35.7sec so was comfortable lapping in the 1min 36–37sec range for the race.

"It's really good to get the number one plate back after such a struggle on the R1 against the Suzukis last year. This year on the Suzuki was really good. The bike is awesome. Tech 2 did a great job of preparing it – not one breakdown all year – and Pirelli supplied a great tyre service. I felt a bit sorry for Chris Burns getting a DNF on the last round, but experimenting with new Dunlops without having tried them in practice is always a big gamble. It's great to be number one again."

As was now customary, Jefferies rounded out his season at the Macau Grand Prix. The race was postponed from its traditional Saturday slot because of wet conditions, but they failed to improve on Sunday. Starting from pole, Michael Rutter finished over six seconds ahead of John McGuinness, with Jefferies in third. It was as good as he could have hoped for under the circumstances, as he explained after the race. "This year we've had a few problems with the clutch burning out so I just daren't give it real berries off the line. So I was steady away off the line and thought I'd try and pick my way through, and, as it happened, everything went according to plan.

"I didn't think I'd be able to beat John or Michael. They're riding really well at the minute and I'm happy for third place. It's the first time TAS have been here and we're on the podium. Pirelli have done it again with the tyres so I'm really pleased. I think John knew the lead he'd got and he was just riding a nice steady pace. I think I caught only about half a second on him towards the end, but I'm pleased enough with that."

John McGuinness has fond memories of racing against DJ at Macau. "I remember we were going down towards Lisboa – probably 170mph – and we'd been looking across at each other, flicking the V-sign, waving, and he was probably trying to hit my kill switch button or whatever. You ride against some other guy and they're just so concentrated on what they're doing, but DJ would be pulling faces and giving you the Vs. We'd be on the front row of the grid at the Macau GP and he'd be going round winding everybody up, shaking their hands and laughing at them, telling everybody to relax and to enjoy it – pull some wheelies, do some skids. Everyone else was so focused but he was just so cool and collected. He was good to have around – he had a great aura on the grid."

On his return from Macau and the racer's traditional nine-day end-of-season holiday in Thailand, Jefferies signed to ride with the TAS team again for the major road race meetings in 2003. He revealed he had been offered the chance to ride the ex-Colin Edwards's factory WSB Honda SP-2 at the 2003 TT, but turned down the offer, electing instead to sign for another year with the TAS squad, an off-shoot of which was being awarded a place as reserve rider for Rizla Suzuki in BSB. "It's good to be given the opportunity," Jefferies said, "but horrible to know you only get to compete if someone else gets hurt."

Being contracted as Rizla Suzuki's reserve rider meant Jefferies was a step closer to achieving his dream of becoming a full-time factory BSB rider but, as things turned out, it was a contract he was never called upon to fulfil. He explained his reasons for turning down Honda's offer – a position that would eventually be filled by Jefferies's former TAS team-mate Ian Lougher. "Despite the might of Honda I decided to stick with the Suzuki on which I had so much success this year. The temptation to ride for Honda was a serious problem as I know the SP-2 that Colin Edwards rode last year would be good, but I get on so well with the Suzuki I felt that had to be the bike. The TAS team, my family and me have a great relationship and we will be looking forward to riding the improved Suzuki for 2003."

But what was most frustrating about the approach of the 2003 season was that Jefferies couldn't even secure a ride in the Superstock class, despite being the reigning champion. Another winter of frustration and team searching loomed ahead. It would be the last.

Chapter 13

FULL CIRCLE

*"I'm not gonna let people say I've been beaten. I'm still gonna be there and
I'm still gonna try and win the championship."*
David Jefferies

In the winter of 2002/2003, David Jefferies really proved his all-round motorcycling capabilities with some incredible results in the British Winter Supermoto Championship. Riding a 450cc Honda he had bought and prepared himself, he humbled many British championship-level riders on much bigger and faster full factory 600 and 650cc machines.

After taking two second places at Croft in December, DJ realised he could afford to be more aggressive because falling off a Supermoto bike is not usually as punishing as falling off a 190mph Superbike onto tarmac. "You can tell these guys don't spend all their time on tarmac because it hurts too much when you crash on that stuff," he said. "So I'm going to have to get tougher on the dirt. I had a great time at Croft and was really pleased with two seconds, especially in the Open class."

With a new aggressive approach, DJ started to really get the hang of things and won six consecutive races at Snetterton including the big race of the day, the Open final – and this on only his second outing on the Honda.

There were more wins at Pembrey in Wales, notably the 450cc final, and at Anglesey shortly afterwards. 'A British championship Supermoto win for a road racer,' Jefferies wrote on his website after his trip to Wales. 'Getting to be good fun, this Supermoto game. I am now third in the 450 Championship which has come as a bit of a surprise as I only started after Christmas.'

Anyone who thought Jefferies wasn't fit should have tried competing in 16 Supermoto races in one day as he did at Donington Park for the final round of the winter series. Once again, DJ was outclassed by the factory 600cc machines but it was clear that, with the right machinery, he could easily win a British Supermoto Championship the following year. Of his day's racing he said, "I only had a problem with Warren Steele and Christian Iddon who beat me by a mile on their Husqvarna and Husaburg 600s. I did manage to beat everyone else and won the 450 final and was second in the open final along with a third in the Superfinal. So it was a hell of a busy day for me. My mechanic Spencer, from the Superstock team, came to help me with changing tyres, etc., which was a great help, because after 16 races I was well and truly knackered. But I did it and it's great training for the race season."

Running with, and beating, the best Supermoto riders in the UK may have been great training for the upcoming season but it didn't help Jefferies secure a competitive ride for the year. As the reigning British Superstock champion, he should have had no problem in securing a top notch seat for 2003. The owner of the number one plate in any championship is a big draw for teams and DJ's proven ability in the Superstock class – he had won the same title three times, although it went under a different name in 1996 – should have guaranteed him the best ride in the series.

But as usual, Jefferies's bad luck struck again during the off-season and he found himself just weeks away from the opening race of 2003 without a ride – again. And with all the rides already taken so close to the start of the season, the reigning champion was forced to return to his roots and source his own bike and run his own team to defend the number one plate. "It sort of went pear-shaped right from the start really," Jefferies explained. "I was supposed to be with Tech 2 but they let me down at the very last minute – about three weeks before the start of the season. So I had to put my own team together, hence the reason the bike's plain white. I've got Pirelli backing me with the tyres, V&J Superbikes have supplied me with the bike and the rest of it's coming from me. It's a bit of a pain really but obviously I can't *not* race – you still have to be racing and keeping yourself dialled-in, so that's what we're doing. It's a nightmare because it's me putting my own money back in but I'm not gonna let people say I've been beaten. I'm still gonna be there and I'm still gonna try and win the championship."

John McGuinness was astounded that his friend couldn't get a Superstock ride. "What more could the bloke do?" he said in 2003. "He won the Superstock championship. He beat everybody. I mean, he beat Chris Burns and he went on to ride in MotoGP. DJ won the championship and this year he didn't get his deal; he didn't get the package he wanted so he thought, 'Well bugger this, I'll go and get my own.'"

McGuinness was amazed at the enthusiasm his friend was able to muster under the circumstances. It was just like Jefferies's first season all over again – he had come full circle, preparing his own bike and running his own team. "Suzuki donated a couple of bikes and they took the engines out to be sent off for tuning. My uncle's a wagon driver so he picked the engines up for DJ, stuck them in the cab of his truck, brought them to Frank Wrathall's and Frank did some work on the engines for him.

"There's a friend of mine who paints car bumpers of all things and DJ asked me, 'Will you ask him to paint the fairings for me?' This was all real last minute stuff – weeks before the first championship round. He came across flat-out in his Shogun over the Pennines to see us and he's rubbing the fairings down into the early hours of the morning. My friend was painting them and putting the number boards on and then Dave was off to buy a van and trying to get the job all organised. The most important thing was that he had the big fat 'Number 1' on the front of his bike – he was the champion."

Such was the last minute nature of things that when Jefferies rolled down pit lane for the start of the opening British Superstock round at Silverstone in March, his Suzuki GSX-R1000 only had nine miles on the clock. In fact, Jefferies had only finished working on the bike at 7pm the previous evening.

With the GSX-R being new for 2003, DJ did well to finish second to a surprise winner. Future World Superbike star Lorenzo Lanzi took part in the Silverstone race as a warm-up for the European Superstock championship round later in the season. Although Lanzi won the race on his factory-supported Ducati, Jefferies once again proved that he was capable of mixing it with European – and future world-level – riders. Yet still his performances were overlooked.

Jefferies's old V&M team-mate Matt Llewellyn found himself in a similar situation to DJ in 2003, running his own bike in the Superstock series on a shoestring budget. Their rivalry was resumed at Snetterton where Llewellyn took his first win since 2000, with Jefferies finishing fourth. Jefferies turned the table at Thruxton by taking his first win of the season and announcing that, "Matt's series lead will be short-lived."

Both riders were furious when they were once again denied the chance to race in BSB by series boss Jos Foulston. The British Superbike grid was worryingly sparse in 2003, with only 15 riders lining up for some races. Series chiefs attempted to beef up the grids by running a Privateer's Cup alongside the BSB championship. Separate points, prize money, and, ultimately a championship title, would be awarded to riders and teams who did not enjoy any factory support. Jefferies and Llewellyn seemed to fit the bill perfectly and jumped at the opportunity of contesting the Privateers' championship on their spare Superstock bikes. Naturally, the lightly-tuned bikes would be no match for the full factory BSB machines but good rides would still, hopefully, be noticed by team bosses and could, potentially, lead to offers of factory rides. But Foulston refused to allow either rider to run in the series on the grounds that 'big names' like Jefferies and Llewellyn would 'overshadow' the rest of the privateer entry.

Jefferies was furious at the apparent double standards being exercised. "I'm gob-smacked that I've had my entry knocked back," he said.

Foulston said he would permit Jefferies a full BSB entry but, as a genuine privateer, that was not only unaffordable for Jefferies, but unrealistic too. He couldn't be expected to compete against million-pound teams on a lightly-tuned road bike. "I want to run in BSB with a full Superbike but can't get a factory ride because the teams reckon I'm physically too big for the bikes," Jefferies told *MCN*. "It's tough enough doing Superstock out of my own pocket. I'm a privateer in every sense of the word but they won't accept me because I've got too high a profile. If I went into the Privateer Cup it would be self-funded, using my spare Superstock bike."

Foulston defended his decision by saying, "DJ and any of the other top Superstock guys can run in BSB. But they are all professional racers. If we allow them in the Privateer Cup it could jeopardise the rest of the entry."

Jefferies's last attempt to gain an entry into BSB had failed. No top level team wanted him because he was deemed to be too big, yet when he tried to enter the series under his own steam, he was told he had too high a profile and was a 'professional racer.' It must have seemed at times to Jefferies that there was a conspiracy to keep him out of the championship.

DJ cheered himself up at Oulton Park with a novelty ride in the BMW Boxer Cup. The cup was staged alongside big bike race meetings in Europe and featured a multi-national line-up of riders, all bidding to win the championship and the BMW M3 car that went with it. Jefferies took part as a guest rider and finished in a highly creditable third place. "I had to change my style of riding to suit the BMW flat twin," he said, "especially with the anti-dive suspension, but I just about had it mastered in the end. I was happy to finish on the podium and BMW GB seemed pretty chuffed as well. Having stars like Andy Hoffman behind me did give me a bit of a buzz."

Jefferies was on form in the Superstock race too. "In the Superstock Championship I did exactly what I set out to do at my favourite UK circuit. Pole position and a start-to-finish win. I knew if I could get into the first corner in front I could make a break for it and that is just what happened. Now I'm back in the lead in the championship and that's where I want to stay."

From Oulton it was straight onto a ferry to Ireland for the North West 200 where he would give the new-for-2003 GSX-R1000 its road race debut. Jefferies was joined by a new team-mate, Adrian Archibald, after Ian Lougher took up the offer of riding Honda's SP-2 that Jefferies himself had declined. Judging by Lougher's testament, it proved to be a wise decision on Jefferies's behalf. "A lot of people thought I was mad to leave the TAS team after 2002 and perhaps, looking back, I was," Lougher now admits. "But I had the offer of an ex-Colin Edwards factory Honda SP-2 from World Superbikes and it was too good a chance to pass up. But I think Honda underestimated just how fast the four-cylinder bikes were going to be in 2003. Ryan Farquhar kept blasting past me down Sulby Straight at the TT on a private Suzuki. People were passing me by 5–8mph."

Archibald was being hailed as the rider most likely to succeed Joey Dunlop as the leading Irish contender on the roads. He had already proved himself with some spirited rides against Jefferies but had yet to win a TT race. "I didn't know David that well when we became team-mates," Archibald says. "I'd raced against him a lot though. When he was on the V&M bikes we had a few good races, especially in Ireland at places like the Ulster Grand Prix. We got on well together in the team. There was a bit of rivalry between us simply because we both wanted to win – everyone in the paddock wants to be on top – but most people in the pure road racing paddock tend to get on fairly well. There's maybe a bit of bitching and back-stabbing going on between certain people but I think there's a lot more rivalry in the British Superbike Championship paddock than there is in road racing."

Practice on the new GSX-R1000 at the North West proved to be a baptism of fire in less than ideal conditions. Jefferies said, "It was difficult to tell just how good the Superbike was as at top speed it was wandering all over the track with the standing water and giving me a whole load of wheelspin at speeds in excess of 160mph. So it was an experience, but we now know everything works. The 600 was probably the best test and was certainly the most improved bike from last year."

Of the race meeting itself, Jefferies said, "Our new bikes from the TAS team worked pretty well considering we had never ridden them before Tuesday practice, but a few teething problems made it hard work. The race meeting turned out to be more of a test session with all the parts from Suzuki coming so late in the year, but we finished up with a really good package in the end.

"It was a real shame the last Superbike race was cancelled because of the rain as we were really up for that one. Anyway we know we have a great bike for the TT. The power is fantastic and we now have the handling, brakes, etc., set up ready for an assault on the Island.

"The 600 felt really good as well. I had just moved up into 5th position when the race was stopped, but the new gearbox was great for me. I reckon we will be in with a great chance at the TT.

"The Production race was as normal in that only a couple of tenths separated the first three. I felt good in that one as well but I think Adrian Archibald and Ryan Farquhar rode better than I did. They've had a little bit of practice on the roads in the wet this year and it was my first race. I missed out on that one, but won't next time.

"So, all together, the North West 200 turned out to be a bit of a damp squib this year and will be a memorable event for all the wrong reasons. In the past I can remember having barbecues in the evening, looking at the sun setting over the sea. This year it would have taken an age to light a barbecue."

The Knockhill round of the British Superbike Championship on 18 May would prove to be the last race meeting that Jefferies would complete. In damp conditions, he was battling for the lead with Steve Brogan before heavy rain started falling and overwhelmed his intermediate tyres. Suffering a lack of grip, DJ dropped back to fifth place in the last laps of the race and fell five points behind Brogan in the championship chase.

Jefferies updated his online diary after the race:

'When it's nice at Knockhill it's very, very nice – but when it isn't, it's horrible. And that's what it was like this weekend. On Friday it was freezing cold with an east wind blowing off the North Sea. Just getting changed into freezing leathers was bad enough, never mind racing. On Saturday the good news was that the wind changed but the rain came so it was a pretty horrible day, especially getting pipped for pole in the last minute.

'Race day was not much better. Any sunshine only lasted a short while before a downpour, which is just what happened in the race. I gambled on intermediate tyres and the gamble all but paid off with me dropping behind and then clawing my way back to take the lead. But the heavens opened before the end of the race and I dropped to fifth. The only good thing is it caught out a load of other riders who didn't finish, but Steve Brogan had gone for a full wet set-up and it paid off for him with a win. So now I'm only five points behind in the championship.

'Roll on the TT. I've just got back from Knockhill and hopefully should have everything ready for departure next Friday."

The TT now beckoned and Jefferies crossed the Irish Sea one last time to challenge the mountain course. Although she has never quite been able to put her finger on the reasons why, Louise Jefferies felt particularly anxious in the run-up to that year's TT. "It was really bizarre because I dreamed of Dave's funeral in minute detail the week before he went to the TT in 2003. I woke up and thought, 'Fucking hell. That was horrible,' but I never told anybody. The night before he left for the TT – 22 May – I went out for a beer with him at the Malt Shovel in Harden and that was the last time I ever saw him."

The uneasy feeling lingered through practice week as Louise remembers. "I always used to sleep with my phone on my pillow and on the Wednesday morning of practice week it rang at about 6am. The caller's name was displayed as 'Mum' and I didn't want to answer it cos I thought something was really wrong. When I did answer it, she just said, 'It's all right, he's only broken down.' That was all she said before putting the phone down."

Practice week did not start well as Hector Neill remembers. "We struggled with the bike in practice. They were all new models from Suzuki and we'd changed suspension companies as well which didn't help. It was like being on a beginner's course again. At one point I was wishing I'd brought the 2002 bikes along. A water hose came adrift on the F1 bike, the 600 threw a rod, and things just didn't really click until the Thursday afternoon practice session. You always get these teething problems with new bikes and new components, especially at the TT – it's a hard place to set a bike up for. There are so many different cambers and bumps, and leaps and jumps – to get it dead right for the Isle of Man is very, very difficult. You actually need more than a week's practice."

Following the first practice session on Saturday, 24 May, Jefferies reported that, "Wet and damp conditions on the first evening practice made the bike decision easy as I had a 600 Supersport bike to run-in. So why not have a couple of steady laps on the 600 just to familiarise myself with the circuit? It always takes a little time to adjust to the high speeds. After two laps I swapped to the Production bike. Once again conditions were a bit dodgy and that's the easiest bike to ride. Unfortunately a water pipe blew off on the way to Ballacraine so I had to sit that one out. Not a lot to report so far. Practice starts proper on Monday."

Following the early morning Monday session, Jefferies updated his website:

'Still wet and damp around the circuit. I was first off this morning at 5am on the Production bike. That seemed to go okay in spite of the major overheating it got on Saturday night. I did a 20-minute lap, which was a bit steady, but no point in chancing anything this early. It was quite alarming being first on the road on a production bike with a full silencer. I caught a few people completely unawares, including people on the track. It doesn't surprise me, as you can tell the marshals and spectators just can't hear you coming. It really is a big mistake using silencers.

'Things did not go so well on the 600 which I went out on next. Unfortunately I had a blow-up at Appledene, about five miles out, so not much achieved in that session. It looks like I'll miss out using the 600 in tonight's practice as we will not have a rebuilt engine in time, but the weather is damp and foggy so it will be two steady laps on the Formula 1 bike and one more on the Production in the last of this evening's session if all goes to plan.'

Jefferies's next entry on his online diary, posted on 26 May, would be his last. It read:

'Had to sit out the 600 practice as we have not been able to repair the engine from this morning's little mishap, but the conditions were not so good so I did not miss much. I went out on the Formula 1 bike intending to do two laps but came in after one lap as it started to rain and I was on slicks. Even though it was the first lap on the big bike, with the gearing found to be not quite right and some suspension adjustments to do, it was 19 minutes, 18 seconds. I then went out for a lap on the Production 1000 bike and did another low 19 minute lap with a bit of rain and mist. So again, not quite going to plan but there is time yet.'

But there wouldn't be time. Three days after posting this entry, David Jefferies was dead.

Chapter 14

RISK

"I'm not going there with a false sense of security – I know what could happen and I'm willing to accept it."
David Jefferies

The village of Crosby lies about four miles into the TT circuit. It is preceded by Ballagarey corner (the super-fast nature of which led DJ to christen it Balla-scarey) and the flat-out run through Glen Vine. In ideal conditions, and with a well set-up bike, the left-hander that leads into Crosby village would be taken flat-out, but Jefferies himself admitted that it took a full week of riding to build up to doing that.

Thursday, 26 May, was only a practice session, not a race, so Jefferies would perhaps have rolled slightly off the throttle on the approach to the corner just to be safe. That said, he had also just posted a 125mph lap on his previous circuit – the fastest of practice week – so he wasn't hanging around either. He would have been approaching the corner at over 170mph.

Precisely 3min 12sec before Jefferies tipped into the left-hander, Daniel Janson's Suzuki GSX-R1000 had blown up, spraying oil over the circuit on the approach to the corner. Travelling at the speed he was, David Jefferies didn't stand a chance. His bike reportedly hit the oil and slammed into the garden wall of number 29 Woodlea Villas, demolishing the wall, before both bike and rider were hurled back across the road, taking heaps of rubble with them. Jefferies was killed instantly. As it was thrown back across the road, his bike brought down a telegraph pole, leaving its wires hanging dangerously across the path of oncoming riders. It was one of the most devastating crashes in TT history – and there was no shortage to choose from. John McGuinness described the aftermath of the impact as looking 'like a war zone.'

Some of the residents of Woodlea Villas had watched the horror unfold. One found various pieces of Jefferies's bike in his garden, including brake discs, the remains of the front forks, and various bits of metal. A wheel had also ended up on the roof of his house. Another resident, Eric Lyall, was working on his garage roof when he heard 'metal grinding on tarmac' and turned to see the drama unfold. He told *MCN* 'The next thing I saw was the telegraph pole had snapped. It looked like the engine or the back of the bike had hit it. There were three bikes parked up at the side of the road and one of the riders took his helmet off and began running to the marshals to try and get hold of a flag because they were obviously desperate to make sure nobody else was involved.'

Someone else *was* about to be involved. In the confusion which followed, approaching riders did not see any red flags being held up to stop the session and, while some slowed and stopped in time, Jefferies's former team-mate Jim Moodie did not. He approached the scene still travelling at speed and caught the telegraph wires on his neck. At this point, Lyall took cover. "I could see what was going to happen," he said, "and I just ducked behind a wall."

For one horrific moment it looked as if Moodie would be killed. John McGuinness, who had managed to stop his bike and was sitting stunned by the side of the road, could only watch in horror. "I honestly thought Jim was going to be decapitated," he said. "He must have been doing 50–60mph when the cable got caught around his neck. I turned away. How he's still alive is a miracle."

Mercifully, the telegraph wires snapped. Moodie suffered a deep gash to his neck but was extremely fortunate to escape with his life. "Everything happened in a split second," he said shortly afterwards, "but I still had time to think 'This is it.' I saw four cables across the road – slightly below the level of my screen. The bike snapped three of them but one went over the screen and caught me across my neck. I got to the point where my right hand had lost grip, but just then the cable snapped. If the cable hadn't snapped then I was on the verge of blacking out. I'm just amazed that I'm still in one piece. It's a miracle. My time obviously wasn't up and that's it."

There was a growing sense of doom in the paddock as word started drifting back of a serious accident out on the course. Ian Lougher remembers being one of the first to hear the dreadful news. "I'd pulled into the pits at the end of the first lap of practice but David went straight through. Soon afterwards the session was stopped.

"Riders have very mixed emotions when a tragedy like that happens. We all know the consequences of what can happen and it's difficult knowing you have to carry on racing. It's also hard on those around you because they worry that it's going to happen to you."

Speaking just moments after the event, John McGuinness was clearly still in shock. When asked how he felt about it, he replied, "Eh, well, utter shock really. One of my closest friends in racing has paid the ultimate price there. I was the first man on the scene. I can't really comment on what's happened obviously, but in true DJ style he's been flat-out through the Crosby section and I was the next man behind. There was a marshal on the road with a yellow flag. I presumed the worst and slowed right down to maybe 30mph. I came round and it's been one of the most horrendous scenes I've ever seen in my life. There was a telegraph pole down, wires, you know…horrendous."

Tony and Louise Jefferies were at a BMW conference in London when they learned of David's death. "That was on the Thursday afternoon and we were due to fly out from Liverpool in the evening to go to the Isle of Man," Louise explains.

"After the meeting was over, I was moaning at my dad that we had to get moving but he was more interested in enjoying his free lunch. So I was stood outside having a fag and talking to some other BMW dealers and noticed my dad was on the phone. I said 'Would you look at him – he's always on the bloody phone.' Then I saw tears running down his face. I walked towards him and heard him say to my mum – who was obviously on the other end – 'I've got to go. I've got to tell Louise now.'

"I knew straight away, but as he told me I just started screaming. I was hysterical. It was the most hideous feeling I ever had in my life. Ever. My dad said, 'Shut up you – we do not behave like that in public! Sit down and be quiet. Someone give her a cigarette.' That pulled me round a bit. It might sound harsh but he did the right thing because I was hysterical.

"By this point there were all sorts of helicopters and what-not on standby to get us over to the Isle of Man. We ended up being whisked across to London City Airport to get on a normal flight that had been held for us. And it was very obvious that two people had gotten off the plane to allow us to get on.

"I remember, on the plane, the feeling was just shock – just hideous. There are absolutely no words that can describe it. But I'll never forget my dad looking at me, taking hold of my hand and saying, 'Promise me something. Promise me you won't waste your life wanting for something you cannot change.' I'll never forget that. Here was a man who had been in a wheelchair since he was 25; who had just lost his only son, and he was *still* an absolute rock. I knew then that I had to get a grip. My dad is phenomenally strong. He knew we couldn't change it and from that moment on, reality sank in and we just had to deal with it."

Tony took some comfort in the fact that his son had clearly been enjoying himself before tragedy struck and that he wouldn't have known anything about the crash, such was the speed he was travelling at. "Knowing the way David operates he'd have been thinking – 'Right, we've got it right now, we've got the bike in the ball park', because you can't do a 125mph lap on a bike that isn't working, you just can't. So he'd have been on it, he'd have been concentrating hard, fully on it. Some say he'd have had a big smile on his face.

"Well, I don't know if he would have had a big smile on his face but he'd have been quite content about the way it was going and I'm pretty sure he'd have been pretty happy with what was happening. And that's something we've got to be thankful for, because he wouldn't have known anything about the crash. It was such a speed, so fast, it would have been instant and I know that he's gone out doing what he wanted to do. And without a shadow of a doubt he's done, in his 30 years of life, more than just about any of us."

Nick Jefferies is another who will never forget that fateful day. "I was visiting a fellow bike dealer and he received a call from someone at Allan Jefferies. When I heard him saying, 'Yes, Nick's here with me now' I knew it was bad. I thought 'That's David.' And it was."

The TT organisers released an official statement later in the day. It read:

It is with regret that the organisers of the Isle of Man TT Races, the Auto-Cycle Union, announce that David Jefferies, of Baildon in West Yorkshire, who crashed on the second lap of this afternoon's practice session, received injuries, which proved fatal. Thirty-year-old Jefferies was involved in an incident at Crosby. The red flag was displayed at the Grandstand and all riders finishing their first laps were brought back into the paddock. Those who had already embarked on their second lap were halted at Glen Vine. Jefferies was the outright lap record holder at the TT and had lapped at 125mph on his first lap today riding his 1000cc Temple Auto Salvage GSX-R Suzuki. The organisers have instituted an immediate enquiry into the details of the incident.

The inquiry would be a highly controversial affair with organisers insisting that marshals had carried out their duties correctly. Riders contested this, saying they were not shown enough flags to warn them of the seriousness of the incident.

But that was still some time away and, however incredible it may seem, practice had to continue. The afternoon's solo session was cancelled but the Sidecar crews were allowed out later in the day. For the solo riders, including those like Moodie and McGuinness who had been involved in the tragedy, the next practice session was the following day. One can only imagine the courage it took to ride past the scene of Jefferies's death with the throttle pinned to the stop.

McGuinness ultimately decided, after much soul searching, that it was all part of his job. "I wanted to go home, I didn't know what to do really," he says now. "I was just shocked and I didn't know how to deal with it. I went back to the pits and the strongest person in the whole paddock was Pauline Jefferies. Everyone was crying and everyone was upset but Pauline was saying, 'You can't stop – you can't stop riding. You have got to race, you have got to ride – DJ would have wanted you to ride. Try and go out and win for Dave.' What can you do about that? You know you have got to ride. I was there to ride, that's what I do, it's my job – that's what it's all about."

There was still the mental block of riding past the accident spot to overcome. McGuinness decided there was only one approach. "I just went through it flat-out," he says. "I thought, 'I've got to go through just flat-out as normal.'"

Losing Jefferies was particularly hard for McGuinness as the two had become very close in the last few years of David's life. As well as a fearsome racer, McGuinness also knew Jefferies as a big man with a soft heart who had agreed to be godfather to his first son, Ewan – a promise that would now never be fulfilled. "What brought us together was my little lad being born," he says. "When Ewan was born, I remember phoning Dave to tell him and he said 'Where are you?' I told him I was in Lancaster infirmary and he just put the phone down and was there within 45 minutes.

"It was unbelievable – really nice of him. He was in his Mitsubishi and must have rallied it all the way across the moors from Baildon. He must have been flat out to get there so fast.

"He spent a lot of time with Ewan at the races. Whenever he got parked up, little Ewan would ask for him and he would take him for a walk round the pits on his shoulders.

"We asked Dave to be Ewan's godfather. That was mega that – it really took him back because he was a softie at heart. After the accident, Ewan kept asking for Dave. But he wasn't there, and that was quite tough you know?"

Adrian Archibald remembers the subdued field heading back out for the first practice session the day after Jefferies's death. "The first time we all went back out again for practice was on the Friday evening. It took me a few laps just to settle in again, but once the race got going on the Saturday I was back to full race mode and concentrating 100%.

"I'd lost a few racing friends but it was a different scenario when it was my own team-mate. Obviously I thought about whether I wanted to continue racing that week or not, but ultimately it was a decision for David's family and the team to make. There were discussions between the team and the family and the Jefferies said that under no circumstances was the team to pull out on their behalf.

"They wanted to know if I was happy to race and asked how I was taking the whole thing. They said that if I wanted to race then I should go ahead and win a race in memory of David. And, luckily enough, that's what I did. For me, it wasn't a case of what *I* wanted to do, but what the family and the team wanted.

"In the end I decided that racing was my job and I had to get on with it. I went into Douglas with the team that night. We had a few beers to try and take things easy and get to grips with everything. There was never any pressure on me to race; Hector Neil said if I didn't want to race then he would just pull out of the TT and that would be it."

Archibald proceeded to turn the TAS Suzuki team's fortnight into an emotional rollercoaster. Having never won a TT before, he took the brave decision to carry on racing and won the Formula 1 race in honour of his fallen team-mate. He backed it up by winning the Senior for good measure, though not before a confrontation with the race organisers, as he explains. "I was number Three for the Formula 1 race but at that time the numbers for the Senior were allocated depending on who was fastest in qualifying. David should have been number One, I would have been Two, and I think John McGuinness would have started at number Three.

"When the starting numbers came out for the Senior, the organisers had just wiped David off the board and wanted me to start at number One. There was a bit of an argument between the team and the organisers because we thought it was disrespectful for me to ride with the number that David had earned. In the end we managed to start the race with the number '0' plate as a mark of respect, which must be the only time anyone's been given the number zero at the TT."

Archibald still wonders how successful he might have been that week had his team-mate been there to challenge him. "It would have been interesting to see how close David and I would have been during race week if he'd been there," he says. "Philip Neill said to me he thought David's experience would tell in the F1, but the Senior at the end of the week would have been one hell of a race. He said it would have been hard to know who would have come out on top in that one. But David's parents called to congratulate me on my wins and everyone was really pleased that we'd managed to do it for David."

With the racing over, everyone breathed a sigh of relief to get away from the Isle of Man. It was the first time in the event's history that the current fastest rider and biggest star had been killed, and the message was hammered home that if it could happen to someone as experienced and safe as Jefferies, it could happen to anyone.

Only when the racing was over did the real controversy over DJ's death begin. An inquest into the death was opened and adjourned on Thursday, 5 June. High Bailiff Michael Moyle, Coroner of Inquests for the Isle of Man, read out a statement from Pauline Jefferies in which she formally identified the body. Moyle said that a post mortem report by Dr Christopher Clague, consultant pathologist at Noble's Hospital on the Island, revealed that Jefferies died of multiple injuries as a result of his crash at Crosby on 29 May. The report said that there were at least ten injuries that could have caused death and confirmed that a routine screening for unlawful substances had proved negative.

Moyle also explained that the court had access to two videos from the scene of the crash, but pointed out that neither showed the point at which Jefferies lost control of his machine – they only showed the aftermath. Peter Saunders, representing the TAS Suzuki team, requested an adjournment, explaining that he had only been asked to represent the team that morning and needed time to interview witnesses, including other riders. After the adjournment Philip Neill said, "All we're looking to do is establish the cause of the accident and we have the full backing of David's family to pursue this."

Following the adjournment, all parties left the courtroom to begin the biggest investigation ever held into a fatality at the TT. The findings would shake the event to its very core and herald an unprecedented revamp of safety measures.

But for the Jefferies family, and countless thousands of others, the most important thing at that time was to give DJ a fitting send-off. His funeral was held on Friday, 13 June, at St Peter's Church in Shipley. Thousands of bikers brought Shipley and Baildon to a standstill as they turned up to pay their last respects to their hero. Chris Moss, who had made his TT debut alongside DJ in 1996, was among them. "It was a massive funeral," he says. "It was very upsetting – there were a lot of people in tears – but it was good that he got such a good send-off. I stood outside the church deliberately because I didn't want to go in. It was just horrible. It's horrible just thinking about it now. We went back to the reception afterwards and absolutely everyone from the bike industry was there. His popularity was so underlined by the turnout. He was such a lovely, decent chap, who was ridiculously modest. I don't think I ever heard him make a single claim to anything."

Tony Jefferies was astonished at the reception his son received. He described it in detail shortly afterwards. "The funeral was an amazing experience," he said. "Shipley and Baildon seemed to come to a stop as we followed the hearse to the church. The police provided a five-rider escort so the route was clear to the church, but how did so many people know he was on his way?

"People stood at the bottom of their gardens, shopkeepers stood in their doorways, and traffic came to a complete standstill as we made our way through the town. And then, at the church, there were two mounted police on beautiful horses, and hundreds of fans and bikes lining the pavements and the sides of the road. It was very moving.

"The church held 500 people and was absolutely full. And thanks to some friends at Universal in Bradford, outside speakers had been set up for all the people outside. The service was simple with one hymn picked by each of us. Pauline chose the 23rd Psalm, one of her favourite hymns, played by DJ's cousin, Robert, on the church organ. Louise chose 'Morning Has Broken' for its youthfulness (and, as she pointed out, it was about the only hymn that DJ really knew), and I chose 'Jerusalem' so that we could sing loud and powerfully amongst our 'dark satanic mills.'

"The eulogy was given by race commentator Fred Clark, who did a magnificent job. He had known Dave throughout his career and had become a real friend – who else better to describe the life and achievements of 'DJ from Yorkshire way'. The Rev. John Rainer made a fitting tribute to David's closeness to his family – something which he had very carefully thought about.

"Leaving the church was unbelievably emotional. We were able to spot faces of friends who we knew had travelled so far to pay their respects, and to see the hundreds outside who had been listening to the service from the loudspeakers.

"Again the police escorted us to the crematorium with our family for a short service. On the way back to the hotel for refreshments, DJ would have been laughing his socks off. Even the police could not break through the traffic to the hotel. Shipley had become gridlocked and it is the only time we have ever had a police escort to the pub!

"At the hotel we were amazed by the number of David's friends that had come so far. His all time hero Colin McRae, who never ceased to amaze DJ with his driving capabilities, was there; as was Geoff Duke – an all-time legend in motorcycle racing. Schoolmates who he hadn't seen for years, and girlfriends whose hearts he had deeply touched, were also there. There were also fans who had never actually spoken to him, but made the effort to be there and to just say 'sorry' to one of the family."

Soon after the funeral, Tony experienced another touching moment. David's gold dog tag had been ripped off and lost at the scene of the accident and despite extensive searches, had never been found. Just after the funeral, Isle of Man travelling marshal, Alan 'Kipper' Killip, contacted Tony. "He called me to say that they had found David's gold dog tag which had become detached from his chain in the accident. We had asked the marshals and people around Crosby to look for it, and after three weeks they found it. I can't believe they were still looking, but they were, because they loved the guy just like we all did."

The inquest into Jefferies's death was held in August, and while Coroner Michael Moyle recorded a verdict of misadventure, the procedure led to the biggest shake-up of safety considerations the TT had ever witnessed. It was clear that the standard of marshalling had been poor and that Jefferies's death could possibly have been avoided by more prompt action, particularly regarding the showing of flags to stop the session. Tony Jefferies wrote a lengthy comment on the whole scenario, in the hope that the TT organisers would learn from his son's death and avoid a similar tragedy in the future. It read as follows:

'I have noted with obvious interest many of the emails regarding DJ's accident and the subsequent emails from various marshals on the www.iomtt.com website. I have read all the statements and watched the video of the bike blowing up before David and Adrian

Archibald came round to Crosby. I believe that I am now in a position to make fair and constructive comments about the accident. I also believe that my experience as a rider and three-times TT winner allows me to have an objective view from which the authorities should seriously take note.

'There are certain facts that are not in dispute, in that the bike leaking oil, three minutes and 12 seconds prior to DJ coming round the corner at Crosby, had a major blow-up and that the video evidence showing the complete blanket of blue smoke left behind by that bike indicates a massive amount of oil being spread across the track. The video shows that the blow-up took place just prior to the entry to the corner. In my opinion there should have been no doubt that an oil flag should have been put out. The still pictures of the blown bike smothered in oil parked at Crosby crossroads, exhibited in court, were taken directly after the accident. The state of the bike alone parked alongside the sector's chief marshalling point should have indicated there would have been oil on the track and the rider was also reported to be covered in oil, but no official took any action.

'The video also shows the marshal, carrying a yellow flag which was rolled up, going to the spot where the bike blew up. He was ambling along on the outside of the track, on the pavement, completely unprotected, where bikes were taking a corner at 170mph. Not only without protection, he was smoking a cigarette and chatting to spectators who were behind a wall or in gateways. In any other race circuit in the world, with the exception of the Isle of Man, his presence alone on the side of the track would be enough to bring out a yellow warning flag. You simply cannot have marshals walking up and down the track in one of the fastest parts of the circuit without warning. The lack of urgency of the marshal shown on video indicates a complete lack of understanding of the situation. The video evidence of the blow-up by the Number 39 bike is alone enough evidence to put marshals on a major alert, something which seems to have been completely disregarded by the officials at the scene and who carried out the investigation.

'My opinion, and I may add the opinion of other riders and organisers from race meetings on the mainland, is that a warning flag should have been shown as a result of the oil cloud alone. It is always correct to put out a flag if unsure rather than not show one and have an accident (especially in a practice period).

'I will no doubt be chastised by the marshals for making these comments, but please let them understand that my main reasons are to try to prevent another avoidable accident and that I feel the problem lies with the organisers who do not give the marshals enough training and experience of racing. In my opinion there are an inadequate number of marshals. I believe that the previous marshal before Crosby was just after Glen Vine, approximately half a mile away. It would therefore be impossible for a marshal to be near the actual place where the bike blew up. However if that marshal had been looking in the right direction (i.e. where the competitors are *going* and not as stated in the *Island Racer* Magazine article called 'Marshalling the Forces' where it states marshals should be looking where bikes are coming from), and seen the oil smoke cloud, he should have put out a warning flag.

'It should also be noted that when the sector marshal left his post to walk back along the circuit, there was only one marshal, his daughter, left at the Crosby marshal post. She was the only marshal available to contact race control should there be an incident, but did not have the authority to contact race control if there was an incident, which is exactly what happened. No wonder the following riders did not know what was going on and had to take the matter into their own hands. She did her very best under the circumstances, but also had to cope with contacting race control by telephone, so who could have held the flag out? And on top of that, race control gave pathetic responses to vital information from her on the marshal's telephone, by asking, 'Who are you? How old are you? Where is the sector marshal?' She had been put into an intolerable position, as the aftermath of the accident was horrendous. She had no way of communicating with other marshals, as they have no radio link.

'From emails posted on the www.iomtt.com message board it is apparent that the marshals themselves are not happy about many of the situations they are being put into. They are also concerned about the lack of numbers.

'I, along with other experienced race colleagues, never anticipated systems which are so far removed from what we now experience in safety measures on the mainland. I was very close to David and we often discussed the dangers of riding at the TT. But talk was about riding within his capabilities, not pushing the envelope to extremes, not rising to the pressure of the press anticipating more lap records. We were aware of the problems that could arise through rider error. We were both aware of the stone walls and no run-off like on short circuits. David, more than anyone, was very conscious of responding to yellow flags. He had not had a crash of any kind through his TT race career and should there have been a warning that there could have been oil on the track through one of the fastest corners on the whole of the TT circuit, he would have slowed and anticipated danger. But the more I have looked into the matter, the more statements I have read, the more discussions I have had with current riders, the more I am convinced that the current competitors and team managers have no idea how undermanned and basic the Isle of Man's marshal system is.

'I realise that there are a lot of marshals who do put their time and effort into the TT, but the question that I have to ask is just because someone has been a marshal at the TT for a good number of years – of which there are many – are they experienced enough in modern racing and up to date with the modern techniques? Most only do the job once or twice a year. There is a document called 'Incident Management', prepared by Dr Stephens, which I believe is a requirement to be read by all marshals. I know that not all have read it, and the sector marshal at the inquest did state that he did not know what to do in the case of a fatal accident, even though the procedure is fully described in the document.

'At the inquest, the sector marshal at Crosby said that, should a similar incident take place again, he would show a warning flag. It has taken a life to bring that statement out. But is that the fault of the marshal or the organisers that should have trained him? I do not think that the TT organisers fully appreciate the speeds and power of the modern Superbike in the hands of the top riders. That is why there can be no doubt about pointing out dangers, such as slippery conditions on corners where riders are travelling at 180mph. The commitment that the fast riders have to make into the high speed corners is intense and they cannot be riding on the basis that should there be an incident that changes the track or the surface in any way, there would be no warning. Take NASCAR and Indy racing in the states. On oval tracks where the speeds are really high with good visibility, it only takes a small blow-up and a suspicion of fluid on the track or a small piece of debris to bring out a full yellow lap caution.

'The Coroner, in summing up, stated that he "was not there to determine if there was oil on the road, although evidence suggests that there well might have been oil on the road, and that David may well have lost control as a result thereof." Bear in mind that this was a delayed inquest to bring out the truth of what really happened, unlike the first part of the inquest, which was almost cut and dried without many of the key witness statements. The Coroner also stated that it was not up to him to decide if the police should be involved in investigations, but if they were it may well be the death knell of the TT. The Coroner then indicated "That may be a price that should be paid". That statement alone does sum up the inadequacies of the current organisers' capabilities to investigate the death of a rider under unclear circumstances.

'The Coroner was quite critical of the organisers (the ACU/Tourist Board), on how they conducted their own inquiry into the accident. That all the evidence should be swept away for the sake of another practice (Sidecars) was mentioned as a critical point.

'It came as quite a surprise to the Coroner at the inquest that both David's family and the TAS team were represented by solicitors. Although this has been a costly exercise I believe that we have avoided the investigation being swept under the carpet and have brought into the open questions that the organisers should answer. There is no doubt that improvements in the appointing, recruiting, equipping and training of marshals is necessary, along with the systems they adopt.

'The conclusion of this statement is that it is totally unacceptable for there not to be an oil flag on the corner at Crosby, or at any point on the circuit. It is totally unacceptable to leave one lady in charge of one of the most devastating crashes in the TT, where a 180mph stretch of circuit was destroyed by the remains of a rider, a smashed up bike, half a ton of rubble, a telegraph pole felled with wires across the track, and only one yellow flag being intermittently waved on the actual corner. It was in fact a spectator waving a red jacket that stopped some of the riders. The speeds of the modern Superbikes are making new corners that are still being marshalled as though they are straights. The organisers are just not prepared to understand advice about the high speeds now being attained and must listen to professionals about the dramatic increase in speed.

'Myself and David argued strongly from last November about the issue of silencers on Production bikes. I wrote to the Tourist Board, the ACU, and even flew to the Isle of Man to put my case to the Tourist Board. David also had a serious argument with the Clerk of the Course, Neil Hanson, during the TT practice on the same issue when he proved the dangerous aspect of quiet bikes with approaching speeds of 175mph, especially when first on the road. During an early morning practice he encountered marshals not in position and spectators on the track. But what was so annoying from my point of view was the attitude of the Tourist Board in that they just would not take my argument seriously. My letters were read and discussed by the ACU Race Committee but it was dismissed as a done deal by the Tourist Board. The press have indicated that it would seem that 1000cc production bikes will be in the 200mph mark next year; perhaps it is time they started to listen. Perhaps they will also include the rule that the lower half of the fairing must act as an oil catch-tank, as every other major race organisation does throughout the world. The stupidity of excluding that rule at the TT is beyond belief and is another indication of how safety issues at the TT must be improved.

'I have been advised by my advocate that I do have a case for negligence against the organisers of the TT. It would be unlikely that I ever pursue a claim in that David does not have any dependants, but I do hope this statement will make the people responsible look at the issues I have mentioned, and make the necessary changes to prevent anything like David's accident ever happening again. If I asked the question today, 'Does the TT have a marshalling system in place to the standards expected in 2004?' the answer would be no. That has to change."

Tony himself has since stated that, "The true cause of the accident will never be known, and whether it could have been prevented or not will always be open for debate. But it is beyond doubt that DJ died doing what he enjoyed most – racing around the TT circuit at a level which is unlikely to be surpassed."

Following the inquest into David's death, a multitude of changes were brought in to try and improve safety at the TT. Marshals were given better training and a recruitment drive continues to this day in a bid to attract higher numbers of marshals. A line-of-sight rule was instigated so that every marshal could see the following marshal all the way round the 37.74-mile course. Marshals are now equipped with TETRA radios to improve communication and early morning practice sessions have now been abandoned. New riders are given guided laps before being set loose on the circuit; miles of state-of-the-art safety fencing has been introduced; and a whole host of other measures have been, and will continue to be, introduced to improve safety.

But in 2005, it seemed that all the effort had been in vain when a marshal wandered over the course during the Senior race, causing her own death and that of experienced racing journalist Gus Scott. Scott had been a good friend of DJ's and his tragic death bore some uncanny resemblances to David's. Yet again, marshals failed to display sufficient warning flags despite there being a person on the circuit at one of the fastest parts of the course. Ryan Farquhar perhaps best summed up the feelings of fellow riders over the chaotic handling of the incident. "The flags should have been at Douglas Road Corner [on the entry to Kirk Michael village where the accident occurred], not when you're right on the incident. It's a fucking disgrace."

Coroner Michael Moyle, who had also carried out the inquest into Jefferies's death, stated that, had the marshal, April Bolster, survived the incident, she may have faced charges of committing an unlawful death.

In 2007, another tragedy occurred during the Centennial Senior race when Marc Ramsbotham lost control of his machine at the 26th

Milestone and was killed. The crash also cost the lives of two spectators. It was the first time in the TT's 100-year history, that spectators had perished and the implications for the future of the event were obvious and ominous. Once again, marshalling standards were questioned when it emerged that 'restricted area' signs had not been in place where they should have been.

Since then, even more safety procedures have been introduced, including many more restricted areas from where spectators cannot watch the races, but there is only so much the organisers can do. The TT, or any other pure road race meeting, can never be made 100% safe. Craig Jones's tragic death at Brands Hatch in 2008 proved that even relatively 'safe' World Championship-level short circuits can prove lethal. But deaths on purpose-built circuits are much rarer than on public roads.

Louise Jefferies continues to support the sport that claimed the life of her only brother. "Would I change 29 May 2003? Of course I would," she says. "Would I have changed Dave racing at the TT? Absolutely not. He absolutely loved riding there and he just wouldn't have been Dave if he'd been a postman."

Tony Jefferies doesn't want to see motorcycle racing banned either. He simply wants, like most people involved in it, to see it made as safe as humanly possible. Ultimately, in the current climate of health and safety concerns, pure road racing may be forced out of existence because of public insurance issues, and that's something that no fan of the sport, including David Jefferies, would want to happen. As he himself said, "At the end of the day, I'd rather go out doing something I enjoy doing than get run over by a bus. I enjoy the TT and I'm willing to accept the consequences that could happen to me. I'm not going there with a false sense of security – I know what could happen and I'm willing to accept it."

Following David Jefferies's cremation, a headstone was erected in Charlestown Cemetery in Baildon, just half a mile from the Jefferies's family home. Carved on the stone, alongside a hand-painted picture of David on the TAS Suzuki, are some lines from a poem by an unknown author:

'Those who risk nothing, do nothing, achieve nothing, become nothing.'

The poem has been attributed to various writers including William Arthur Ward and Janet Rand, and the work has even been reproduced under various titles including *'Risk'*, *'To Risk'* and *'Only a Person who Risks is Free.'* Ultimately, it matters not who wrote the words – what matters is their meaning. This is the poem in full:

RISK
by Author Unknown

To laugh is to risk appearing the fool.
To weep is to risk appearing sentimental.
To reach for another is to risk involvement.
To expose your ideas, your dreams,
before a crowd is to risk their loss.
To love is to risk not being loved in return.
To live is to risk dying.
To believe is to risk despair.
To try is to risk failure.
But risks must be taken, because the
greatest hazard in life is to risk nothing.
The people who risk nothing, do nothing,
have nothing, are nothing.
They may avoid suffering and sorrow,
but they cannot learn, feel, change,
grow, love, live.
Chained by their attitudes they are slaves;
they have forfeited their freedom.
Only a person who risks is free.

Chapter 15

LEGACY

"That was a funeral that broke her heart. I don't think she ever really recovered from that time."
Tony Jefferies

As the last motorcycles pulled away from the TT start line on Glencrutchery Road, the leaders of the memorial lap were cruising up the Mountain Mile, some 30 miles away. Between the vanguard – headed by John McGuinness and Pauline and Louise Jefferies – and the rear were 5,000 bikes of every make and denomination. Bikes from all over the world: Japanese, British, Italian, German, American. Their riders had travelled from even more destinations to pay tribute to their fallen hero. Countless thousands more lined the 37.74-mile TT course, waving, clapping, cheering or just quietly contemplating the magnificent spectacle and taking in its true significance.

The David Jefferies Memorial Lap held at the 2004 TT was just the first of many tributes that proved he would not be forgotten. There were many more. From a memorial race meeting held at DJ's beloved Oliver's Mount circuit – where part of the course was also named 'Jefferies' Jump' – to a replica of his famous V&M racer which was auctioned for charity in 2007, DJ's name has been kept alive in many different ways. But the most important legacy is undoubtedly the David Jefferies Memorial Fund which was set up by his father on the first anniversary of David's death. "The fund will be a registered charity," said Tony when it was launched in 2004, "whose aims are to regularly provide income to other charities which are connected to motorcycle sport and to children. Motorcycle sport was David's life, and his affinity and natural manner with children was a joy to experience."

In November 2007, the inaugural David Jefferies Memorial Dinner was held in Bradford as a means not only of raising more money for the fund (an astonishing £60,000 was raised on that one night alone), but to present cheques and awards to the worthy causes it was set up to help. Hosted by television presenter Vernon Kay, the evening was attended by 410 leading figures from the motorcycling world including World Superbike Champions James Toseland and Neil Hodgson and TT hero John McGuinness. Several presentations were made including a £10,000 cheque to Tommy's, the baby charity, and the handing over of a 17-seater minibus to David's old school, Salt Grammar.

Tony Jefferies also used the evening to announce the new David Jefferies Award Scheme which offers financial rewards to up-and-coming young bike racers. In its first year, the scheme awarded cash prizes of £500 to the best under-16 rider in the 125cc British Championship class, and to the best under-18 in the Junior Superstock class, at each of the 12 rounds of the 2008 British Superbike Championships. The winner of both junior championships received an additional £1,500 for their efforts. The total prize fund for the year amounted to £15,000 – money which was all raised in memory of David Jefferies. Eleven young riders benefited from the scheme in 2008 but it will be expanded to offer cash prizes to the top three finishers at each round in 2009 and beyond so that even more youngsters can benefit. To date, the fund has raised over £200,000.

On 30 May 2008, just one day after the fifth anniversary of David's death, Tony Jefferies was to receive another devastating blow when his wife passed away after suffering an embolism. He believed that Pauline Jefferies never truly recovered from the loss of her only son. As part of a eulogy to Pauline which was read out at her funeral, Tony wrote: "It was just five years ago that we were here in this church for the funeral of our son David. That was a funeral that broke her heart. I don't think she ever really recovered from that time. David was quite simply everything to Pauline. Yes, she got on with life to a point. She made our garden beautiful with more plants and pots than Kew Gardens. She supported me as only a true Yorkshire wife could. But her heart had been broken. There was nothing left – or was there?

'Once again we were in this church for Louise's marriage to James. Louise then became pregnant and just over six months ago our first granddaughter, Megan, was born. The most beautiful granddaughter in the world you must understand. This was a new lease of life for Pauline. She absolutely adored her and had her reason to live again. The last six months have been very special for her and it is a tragedy for her, for Megan, and for Louise, that she will not be able to see Megan grow up."

As always, Tony Jefferies's thoughts were only for the suffering of others. He himself has lived through the unimaginable pain of losing his son and wife and has to cope with the everyday trials of being in a wheelchair. Yet his love of life cannot be extinguished. As well as driving souped-up and specially adapted BMWs at speeds he should be ashamed of at his age, he has also gained his private pilot's licence and now has the complete freedom of the skies at his command as well as the open roads. He continues to campaign tirelessly to raise money in his son's memory and dotes on Megan. His courage in the face of adversity and what, for others, would be overwhelming grief, is an inspiration.

Five years after David's death his closest friends still meet up on every second Thursday at Tony Jefferies's house, where David also lived. They crack open a few beers, sit round the kitchen table and reminisce about their lost friend. There are no tears and there's no morose atmosphere. These are the people who miss David the most yet they don't remember him with sorrow, they remember him with laughter. How could they not? Their tales of crashing cars, falling off bikes, helping DJ in the pits at the TT and chasing girls could fill several books, despite half their tales being unprintable. Tony still roars with laughter as he discovers yet more mischief he didn't know his son had got up to. This is how DJ is remembered by those who loved him best – as a fun-loving, daft-as-a-brush young man who squeezed three lifetimes into his 30 years on earth.

His close friend John McGuinness shared more of those laughs with DJ than most and there is no-one David would have wanted more to succeed him as the TT's new top rider. The flame that Jefferies passed on is in safe hands: McGuinness is now the second most successful TT rider in history and has lapped the circuit at more than 130mph. He is undeniably the event's biggest star and ranks as one of the all-time greats alongside Mike Hailwood, Joey Dunlop and Jefferies himself. Yet he has only achieved that success with a little help from his old friend. "Every time I go through Crosby now I always ask him to look after me," McGuinness says. "Even now, five years down the line, every lap – practice lap, race lap – I just say 'Look after me Dave.' I just say it to myself…"

DAVID JEFFERIES

MAJOR CAREER RESULTS

Key to abbreviations

400cc = Supersport 400 class
600cc = Supersport 600 class
Prod 600 = Production 600cc class
Prod 1000 = Production 1000cc class
Prod Powerbike = Production Powerbike
Open = no capacity limit
Triumph Challenge = Triumph Speed Triple Challenge
Aprilia Challenge = Aprilia RS250 Challenge
BSB = British Superbikes Championship
WSB = World Superbikes Championship
500cc GP = 500cc Grand Prix World Championship

1990

Circuit/Event	Class	Position
Mallory Park	600cc	6th
Mallory Park	600cc	3rd/2nd
	Open	2nd/3rd
Cadwell Park	600cc	6th/4th/5th
Snetterton	600cc	9th/5th/7th
	Open	7th/8th
Mallory Park	600cc	4th
Mallory Park	600cc	4th
Cadwell Park	600cc	2nd/3rd/1st/2nd
	Open	4th/2nd/1st

Cadwell Park	600cc	5th/1st
	Open	3rd/2nd/4th
Elvington	600cc	1st/1st/2nd/1st
	Open	2nd/2nd/2nd
Cadwell Park	600cc	4th/6th/2nd
	Open	5th
Mallory Park	600cc	1st/1st/1st
	Open	6th/3rd/4th
Cadwell Park	600cc	2nd/1st/1st/1st
	Open	3rd/4th/1st/1st
Cadwell Park	600cc	1st
	Open	1st/1st
Snetterton	600cc	1st/1st/1st/2nd/2nd/1st
Cadwell Park	600cc	10th
Mallory Park	600cc	23rd
Cadwell Park	600cc	1st/3rd/1st
	Open	1st/4th
Cadwell Park	600cc	11th
Donington Park	600cc	23rd
Cadwell Park	600cc	3rd
	Open	5th

1991

Circuit/Event	Class	Position
Mallory Park	600cc	12th/4th
Snetterton	400cc	6th
	600cc	13th
Brands Hatch	600cc	13th
Scarborough	400cc	1st
	600cc	2nd
	Open	6th
Donington Park	400cc	7th
	600cc	18th
Brands Hatch	400cc	4th
Cadwell Park	400cc	11th
	600cc	20th
Oliver's Mount	400cc	1st
	600cc	3rd
Snetterton	Superteens	4th
	600cc	11th
Mallory Park	Superteens	6th
Oulton Park	400cc	9th
	600cc	14th
Cadwell Park	Superteens	4th
	600cc	10th
Mallory Park	400cc	10th
Oulton Park	Superteens	5th
Cadwell Park	400cc	10th
	600cc	6th
Donington Park	Superteens	4th
	600cc	1st
Knockhill	Superteens	5th
	400cc	11th/2nd
Brands Hatch	Superteens	3rd

British 400cc Championship: 3rd
MCN Superteens Championship: 5th
British 600cc Championship: 6th

1992

Circuit/Event	Class	Position
Thruxton	BSB	8th/11th
Snetterton	BSB	7th/5th
Donington Park	750cc	12th
Brands Hatch	750cc	14th
Donington Park	750cc	6th/7th
Castle Combe	BSB	6th
Mallory Park	750cc	8th/9th
Knockhill	750cc	9th/7th
Snetterton	750cc	7th/10th
Mallory Park	BSB	7th
Cadwell Park	750cc	7th
Donington Park	BSB	10th/10th
Cadwell Park	BSB	7th/8th
Oulton Park	750cc	7th/8th
Oliver's Mount	750cc	2nd/2nd*
Brands Hatch	750cc	9th
Mallory Park	BSB	8th
Darley Moor	750cc	5th/5th
Brands Hatch	BSB	13th/10th
Donington	750cc	3rd

British Supercup 750cc Championship: 7th
MCN Superbikes Championship: 8th
* Scarborough International Gold Cup winner

1993

Circuit/Event	Class	Position
Brands Hatch	WSB	9th/14th
Silverstone	750cc	5th/3rd
Knockhill	BSB	12th/1st
Oliver's Mount	750cc	2d/2nd
Mallory Park	BSB	4th/5th
Donington Park	500cc	8th/8th
Brands Hatch	750cc	6th/5th
San Marino GP	500cc GP	17th
Cadwell Park	750cc	5th/10th
British GP	500cc GP	20th
Cadwell Park	750cc	8th
Czech GP	500cc GP	19th
Oulton Park	BSB	6th
Italian GP	500cc GP	22nd
USA GP	500cc GP	16th
Mallory Park	750cc	6th
F.I.M. GP	500cc GP	18th
Brands Hatch	BSB	8th/10th
Sentul, Indonesia	750cc	15th

British Supercup Championship: 9th

1994

Circuit/Event	Class	Position
Oulton Park	750cc	6th
Donington	BSB	13th/10th
Brands Hatch	750cc	4th/5th
Mallory Park	BSB	8th
Oliver's Mount	750cc	1st
Donington Park	BSB	7th
Mallory Park	750cc	3rd
Knockhill	BSB	9th
Donington Park	BSB	4th
	Triumph Challenge	5th
Pembrey	BSB	5th/4th
Cadwell Park	BSB	4th/6th
Brands Hatch	BSB	13th/4th
Oulton Park	BSB	4th/4th
Oliver's Mount	750cc	1st/1st*
Brands Hatch	BSB	11th/8th
Donington Park	WSB	21st
Brands Hatch	750cc	6th/7th
Darley Moor	750cc	3rd/3rd

British Supercup Championship: 7th
* Scarborough International Gold Cup winner

1995

Circuit/Event	Class	Position
Mallory Park	750cc	5th
Oulton Park	750cc	3rd
Donington Park	750cc	6th/8th
Hockenheim	WSB	25th/22nd
Misano	WSB	20th/26th
Donington Park	WSB	19th/19th
Monza	WSB	13th
Salzburgring	WSB	18th
Laguna Seca	WSB	16th
Brands Hatch	WSB	14th/15th
Sugo	WSB	19th/20th

British 750cc Superbikes Championship: 9th

1996

Circuit/Event	Class	Position
Donington Park	BSB	DNF/8th
Thruxton	BSB	10th/9th
Mallory Park	Triumph Challenge	8th
Cadwell Park	Triumph Challenge	1st
Donington Park	WSB	17th/17th
Oulton Park	BSB	5th/6th
North West 200	Superbikes	5th/7th
Donington Park	Triumph Challenge	9th
Isle of Man TT	Junior	16th
	Production	10th
	Senior	16th
Brands Hatch	BSB	9th/DNF
Oliver's Mount	Superbikes	2nd/1st/2nd
Donington Park	Triumph Challenge	1st/3rd
Brands Hatch	TT Prod Challenge	3rd
Knockhill	BSB	8th/7th
Cadwell Park	BSB	4th/DNF
Oulton Park	TT Prod Challenge	1st/2nd
	Triumph Challenge	4th
Mallory Park	BSB	4th/7th
Silverstone	Triumph Challenge	1st
Brands Hatch	BSB	7th/2nd
Donington Park	Triumph Challenge	10th
Silverstone	TT Prod Challenge	2nd/1st

British Superbikes Championship: 9th
British Powerbike TT Production Challenge champion
Triumph Speed Triple Mobil 1 champion

1997

Circuit/Event	Class	Position
Thruxton	Prod Powerbike	16th/15th
Donington Park	Prod Powerbike	15th/11th
	Triumph Challenge	4th
Castle Combe	Triumph Challenge	2nd
Le Mans 24 Hour	Superbikes	27th
Oulton Park	Triumph Challenge	1st
Mallory Park	Triumph Challenge	6th
Brands Hatch	Prod Powerbike	11th
Knockhill	BSB	7th/10th
Donington Park	Triumph Challenge	8th/13th
	Prod Powerbike	9th/12th
Cadwell Park	BSB	DNF/6th
Brands Hatch	BSB	13th/11th
	Triumph Challenge	6th
Oliver's Mount	Superbikes	1st, 1st, 2nd*
Donington Park	Triumph Challenge	10th

* Scarborough International Gold Cup winner
Triumph Speed Triple Mobil 1 Championship: 4th

1998

Circuit/Event	Class	Position
Donington Park	Prod Powerbike	1st
Snetterton	Prod Powerbike	1st
North West 200	Prod Powerbike	2nd
Isle of Man TT	F1	8th
	Junior	8th
	Production	4th
	Senior	4th
Donington Park	Prod Powerbike	DNF*

* A broken pelvis sustained at Donington in July brought a premature end to the season

1999

Circuit/Event	Class	Position
Cadwell Park	Aprilia Challenge	1st
Mallory Park	Aprilia Challenge	6th
Donington Park	Superstocks	1st
	Prod Powerbike	1st/5th
Snetterton	Aprilia Challenge	10th
North West 200	600cc	1st
	Superbikes	1st/1st
Donington Park	Aprilia Challenge	9th
Isle of Man TT	Formula 1	1st
	Junior	2nd
	Production 1000	1st
	Senior	1st
Mondello	Aprilia Challenge	2nd
	Prod Powerbike	2nd/2nd
Silverstone	Prod Powerbike	2nd
Donington Park	Prod Powerbike	1st
Oliver's Mount	1000cc	1st/1st/1st
	600cc	1st/1st
Oulton Park	Aprilia Challenge	5th
Brands Hatch	Superstocks	1st
Ulster GP	1000cc	1st/2nd
	600cc	2nd
Assen	Superstocks	2nd
Oliver's Mount	1000cc	1st/1st/2nd*
	600cc	1st/1st
Brands Hatch	600cc	DNF
Donington Park	600cc	4th
Kirkstown	Superbikes	2nd, 3rd
Macau GP	1000cc	1st

2000

Circuit/Event	Class	Position
Brands Hatch	Superstocks	3rd
Donington Park	Superstocks	2nd
Thruxton	Superstocks	4th
North West 200	600cc	3rd
	Superbikes 1000	2nd/2nd
Oulton Park	Superstocks	1st
Isle of Man TT	Formula 1	DNF
	Junior	1st
	Production	1st
	Senior	1st
Snetterton	Superstocks	5th
Silverstone	Superstocks	3rd
Oulton Park	Superstocks	1st
Knockhill	Superstocks	4th
Ulster GP	Superbikes	1st/1st
	600cc	4th
Oliver's Mount	Superbikes	1st, 1st*
Mallory Park	Superbikes	7th/11th
	Superstocks	1st
Brands Hatch	Superbikes	7th/DNF
	Superstocks	2nd
Macau Grand Prix	Superbikes	2nd

British Superstocks Champion
* *Scarborough International Gold Cup winner*

2001

Isle of Man TT cancelled due to foot and mouth outbreak

Circuit/Event	Class	Position
Donington Park	Superstocks	4th
Silverstone	Superstocks	7th
Snetterton	Superstocks	12th
Oulton Park	Superstocks	2nd
Brands Hatch	Superstocks	6th
Oulton Park	Superstocks	1st
Knockhill	Superstocks	5th
Ulster Grand Prix	Superbikes	2nd, 2nd
	600cc	2nd
Cadwell Park	Superstocks	1st
Brands Hatch	Superstocks	5th
Mallory Park	Superstocks	3rd
Rockingham	Superstocks	6th
Oliver's Mount	Superbikes	1st, 1st, 1st*
Donington Park	Superstocks	7th
Macau Grand Prix	Superbikes	3rd

British Superstocks Championship: 2nd

* *Scarborough International Gold Cup winner (record-equalling 5th win)*

2002

Circuit/Event	Class	Position
Mallory	Superbikes	2nd
Silverstone	Superstocks	2nd
Brands Hatch	BSB	13th, 11th
	Superstocks	DNF
Donington Park	Superstocks	2nd
Oulton Park	Superstocks	1st
North West 200	Production	2nd
	600cc	5th
	Superbikes	1st, DNF
Silverstone	Superstocks	1st
Isle of Man TT	Formula 1	1st
	Prod 1000	1st
	Prod 600	7th
	Junior	DNF
	Senior	1st
Brands Hatch	Superstocks	1st
Rockingham	Superstocks	1st
	BSB	9th/8th
Ulster Grand Prix	Production 1000	1st
Cadwell Park	Superstocks	3rd
Oulton Park	Superstocks	1st
Mallory Park	Superstocks	DNF
Donington Park	Superstocks	3rd

British Superstocks Champion

2003

Circuit/Event	Class	Position
Silverstone	Superstocks	2nd
Snetterton	Superstocks	4th
Thruxton	Superstocks	1st
Oulton Park	Superstocks	1st
North West 200	600cc	8th
	Production 1000	3rd
	Superbikes	5th
Knockhill	Superstocks	5th

INDEX